CONTENTS

PART SIX: GETTING STARTED ON
HEALING A MEMORY

APPENDIX

HEALING LIFE'S HURTS:
Healing Memories
through
Five Stages of Forgiveness

by

Matthew Linn, S.J.

and

Dennis Linn

Revised Edition

PAULIST PRESS
New York, N.Y./Mahwah, N.J.

ACKNOWLEDGMENTS

This book could not have been written without the expertise of the following who read the manuscript and offered helpful suggestions: Rev. William Connolly, S.J.; Abbot David Geraets, O.S.B.; Rev. James Gill, S.J., M.D.; Morton Kelsey, Ph.D.; Bernard Klamecki, M.D.; Elisabeth Kubler-Ross, M.D.; Rev. William Kurz, S.J.; Sister Mary Jane Linn, C.S.J.; Martin Lynch, Ph.D.; Rev. Francis MacNutt, O.P.; Susan and Robin Mitchell, Ph.D.; Larry Samuels, M.D.; Margaret Schlientz and Barbara Shlemon, psychiatric nurses; Rev. William Sneck, S.J.; Ms. Marie Towley, and our parents who have given life not just to us but to this book by their typing and constant encouragement.

IMPRIMI POTEST
Bruce F. Biever, S.J.
Provincial, Wisconsin Province
Society of Jesus
August 12, 1977

Library of Congress
Catalog Card Number: 77-14794

ISBN: 0-8091-2059-3

Published by Paulist Press
997 Macarthur Blvd.
Mahwah, N.J. 07430

Printed and bound in the
United States of America

Dedicated
in gratitude
to Sr. Mary Jane Linn, C.S.J.
whose life of prayer
gives life to us

Introduction
to the
Revised Edition

During the fifteen years that have elapsed since Paulist Press first published *Healing Life's Hurts* in 1978, its basic thesis has received universal acceptance. With hundreds of thousands of copies sold in English alone, it has also appeared in nearly a dozen foreign languages. We have given hundreds of *Healing Life's Hurts* conferences accredited by professional organizations such as the American Medical Association and by various universities. We have also given them to jail inmates and peasants with no formal education. After giving these conferences in every continent and in almost forty countries, we have found that the same process of forgiveness which worked for a client at Wohl Psychiatric Clinic in St. Louis also works for a Guatemalan, African, Australian or Korean. The process of forgiveness is universal.

When we (Dennis and Matt) started writing *Healing Life's Hurts* in 1975, we were writing mainly for our clients at Wohl Psychiatric Clinic as well as for a local prayer group we attended. The problem at the psychiatric clinic and in the prayer group was the same. Often people knew they would be a lot healthier if only they could forgive those who had hurt them. But they seemed stuck in their inability to forgive and didn't know what to do. Somehow they thought that since we were Jesuit religious and worked at a psychiatric clinic, we could help them out.

What we noticed as we gave thirty-day retreats following the *Spiritual Exercises* of St. Ignatius to prayer group members, and as we worked with our psychiatric clients, is that the steps in forgiving someone who hurt us generally follow a certain predictable process. We realized that hurts are like small deaths. We discovered that the stages of forgiving someone who hurt us are the same five stages that Dr. Elisabeth Kubler-Ross found to be experienced by a dying person. As our clients and retreatants entered

vii

into this process of the five stages of forgiveness, they became unstuck and experienced healing of their hurt. So we wrote *Healing Life's Hurts* to share this discovery.

In the past fifteen years people from many cultures and backgrounds have taught all three of us two things: first, the five stages as described in this book are indeed an innate process of healing that works, and second, there are always new ways of entering more deeply into each of these stages. The updated notes, the epilogue, and this introduction will share some of these new ways.

Some of our new understanding of the five stages has come through Christian feminism, opened to us by Sheila, who joined our team in 1981. For example, I (Dennis) remember praying together with Sheila for a woman named Linda who had been sexually abused. Linda felt guilty because she could not forgive her abuser. But the more I tried to help her forgive, the angrier Linda became. Finally, Sheila told Linda:

> I sense that Jesus' first concern is not that you forgive but rather that you feel his outrage at what happened to you. Jesus is more angry about the desecration of the temple of your body than he was about the desecration of God's temple (Jn 2:13–17) when he drove out the money changers. The anger you feel is God's anger over the abuse that you experienced.

At this, Linda, then in her fourteenth year of psychotherapy, began to cry for the first time. When we asked her why she was crying, she said:

> That Jesus would get so angry for me . . . that he would love me so much. He just wants to share all of me. If I am angry, he is angry. If I am crying, he will cry.

In this prayer, Jesus gave Linda what she needed most: to know she was loved in the midst of her hurt and anger, and even to know that her anger was Jesus' anger.

That experience with Sheila and Linda taught me two things. First, my emphasis had always been to change and fix things, in this case Linda's anger, so that she could forgive. What I missed was the dimension of being with things just as they are, in this case, helping Linda to be with her anger and to know that God's life was there, too. The miracle is that once Sheila allowed Linda to be with her anger, without trying to change or fix it, she automatically moved through the process of forgiveness.

Second, Sheila and Linda taught me the value of receiving affirmation not just from God but also from human beings. When we first met Linda, she seemed stuck in early childhood, the very time in her life when she experienced the most severe sexual abuse. For example, when Linda first came to us, she always wore slacks and had short, straight hair like a tomboy's. She often curled up silently in a corner, looking like a frightened child. Linda asked Sheila to provide an affirming environment in which her missed developmental growth could take place. Thus Sheila encouraged Linda as she explored new hairstyles and clothing, and helped Linda make healthy choices in how she related to men. Now Linda has developed a healthy sense of femininity and makes relationship choices on her own.

In summary, Linda and Sheila invited me to a more feminine way of being. As we will explain in more detail in the epilogue, the masculine mode emphasizes the transcendent dimension of God. God is "out there," always calling us to change and grow (e.g. calling Linda to forgive the one who abused her). In contrast, the feminine mode emphasizes the immanent dimension of God, a God who meets us in whatever we are experiencing (e.g. within Linda's anger). A second contrast is that the masculine emphasizes autonomy while the feminine emphasizes connectedness. Thus we now notice how much this book speaks of choosing God alone and often discounts our need for affirmation from other human beings. It is true that we can become overly dependent on what others think of us. Yet the feminine balance reminds us that the normal way to God for most people is, as Linda experienced with Sheila, through the love we see in the eyes of another human being.

Thus, if the three of us were to write this book together today, we would include the feminine mode. Because it wasn't written that way originally, you will catch not only sexist language but also clericalism which idealizes celibacy and the vows, and narrows the idea of "vocation" as if it applied to religious only.

When we first thought about updating this book, we planned to include here not just the few ideas mentioned above, but all that each of us has learned over the past fifteen years and how we would write this book differently now. But we thought it best not to do that and rather have you first discover on your own what you think we should change. We have two reasons for doing this. First, what you discover on your own is more likely to become a part of you. Second, as authors we know that every day we grow and that by the time any of our books are finally published, in a sense they are already "out of date." We always wish we had said some things differently. This has made us aware that in reading any book or document (even the Bible), we must remember that it was written for a certain time and a certain culture. The important question then becomes: "How does what I am reading match with my life experience today?"

At the end of the book we have added the "Epilogue: Fifteen Years Later." (Don't cheat and read the epilogue first.) We hope that by then you will have come up with some changes that even we missed. If so, send your suggestions to us at Paulist Press. Updating is an everyday process. We need your help to keep growing and changing.

Matthew, Sheila and Dennis Linn
January, 1993

Healing Harvest

O memory of a painful time,
are you seed or stone?
A dark and deadly tomb,
Or seed with life to bloom?
Only if I say "I want you,"
Will I really know.

O sprouting seed, are you angry
At the dark and choking dirt?
What grates your tender shoot
And blocks your chosen route?
Only if I say "I forgive you,"
Will I really know.

O tender shoot, are you bargaining,
Demanding sun before you grow?
Or would you rather as the sun
Pour warm love on everyone?
Only if I say "I forgive you first,"
Will I really know.

O roots, do you wander depressed
Searching in drought for tears?
Or do you need more sun
To dry the tears that run?
Only if I say "Forgive me,"
Will I really know.

O golden wheat, can you accept
The gifts of pulsing seed?
Are you wheat or golden bread?
Are you bread or Christ instead?
Only if I say "Thank you,"
Will I really know.

Unless a grain of wheat
Falls into the earth and dies,
It remains alone:
But if it dies,
It bears much fruit. (John 12:24)

Part One:
What Happens
in Healing a Memory

Picture the grade school you attended. Now in your mind's eye walk up the steps, open the heavy door and walk down the long dark corridor to the classroom you least liked. Walk in and sit down where you squirmed during long, hot days. Look around and see the bulletin boards with your papers, the spitballs on the floor, the blackboard smelling of chalk dust, and the smirking kid who always teased you. Look inside the desk at the books—arithmetic, history, geography, spelling, reading, science, English—and take out the one you least liked.

Now look up and see the teacher calling on you. You give the wrong answer and your classmates snicker. Look at their faces: the frowning teacher, the best student smiling and ready to recite, and the teasing kid whispering something to make others giggle. How do you feel?

Experiences like these crippled us all. They made it harder for us to recite the next time, crippled our self-image, prodded us to be sick or play hooky on test days, and made us hate certain subjects we may still dislike today. Maybe today we still get stage fright when speaking before a group because our memory hasn't forgotten the snickers and jeers from our peers.

Such painful memories can be healed to gift rather than cripple us (Chapter 1). They can just as easily drive us to be better teachers, never to cripple another by laughing at him rather than with him, to reach out to those unsure of themselves, to be better prepared so we aren't mocked, and to seek our support more from God and less from people who can hurt us.

How heal a memory to obtain these gifts? Christ heals our memories from hurts much as a mother teaches a child not to fear the dark. When my three-year-old cousin, Paul, hears strange

1

noises in his room at night, he ends up sleeping in his parents' bed. Later his mother, in the bright morning sunlight, takes Paul by the hand back into his "haunted" bedroom. Together they look at all the fearful places, under the bed and in the closet. Then she reads him a story and plays with his toys until the room again seems peaceful. In the afternoon, she repeats the same thing and again in the evening making a game out of hiding a Hershey bar under the bed and in the closet. Because Paul has spent pleasant moments in his bedroom, he no longer objects to being left alone there.

In healing a memory we do the same with the Lord. We take him by the hand and go back to a hurt we don't want to see. This time we see it in the bright sunlight of his view, looking for the good he sees just as Paul looked for the Hershey bars. Healing a memory drains out our old fears and feelings and pours in Christ's feelings when we take his hand.

We know that we have taken Christ's hand to heal a memory not when we can say, "That's O.K." but when we go through the struggle to forgive those who hurt us. This is the same struggle with feelings of denial, anger, bargaining, and depression that the dying experience in forgiving God, others, and themselves for their declining life (Chapter 2). We are healed when we can say not "That's O.K." but "I forgive you for hurting me because it brought so much growth that I'm *grateful* it happened." If that sounded like a mouthful, this is a book not to be tasted but to be chewed and digested.

1
WHAT IS HEALING A MEMORY?

3:00 A.M. Who can be calling at this hour? They probably have the wrong number.

"Father, I can't face another day. What happens if I kill myself?"

While the lump in my throat swelled, Cecilia said that she lived alone in a gray one room flat. She hated her lonely existence as much as she hated the drudgery of teaching. She had no friends and her whole life centered around the school where she taught. At school she was overwhelmed by parents constantly phoning to challenge her authority and question why their children, so well behaved at home, returned from school with ripped clothes and missing teeth. She worked late hours and frequently stayed after school with another teacher to plan the next day's lesson. Then she would trudge home alone to finish class preparations.

Life had always been hard for Cecilia. As a child she often had to stay home from school to help with the farm chores, and was kidded for being stupid. Her mother died when Cecilia was four or five, and she spent the next fifteen years trying to eke out an existence with her stormy, alcoholic father. She had little chance to play with her peers, never dated, and never had anyone who cared specially for her.

As we talked on the phone at 3 A.M., I assured her that I cared and would like to meet her immediately or in the morning. When she decided that she was too exhausted to talk then, I breathed a sigh of relief because I was drained and had no idea how to help her.

After a short night's sleep, I still had no answer when Cecilia arrived at my home looking exhausted, her shoulders slumped and tension in her pinched face. As we talked about her hardships, I felt more and more like I could commit suicide if I were Cecilia. That feeling prompted me to ask her what one thing kept her going all these years. When she said she didn't know, I asked her to pray and think about what moment she appreciated most in the last few years. I then went to make a few phone calls.

Before returning to Cecilia, not only did I make some phone calls, but I also prayed and prayed. I even bet the Lord that Cecilia would stump him. But I lost my bet. When I returned, Cecilia told me she especially appreciated the moments she spent with three different people who asked her to stay with them as they each faced death.

It made sense to me that Cecilia could appreciate the dying because she experienced all their fears and interior suffering. The dying sometimes feel angry and ask, "Why me God?" They have difficulty with forgiveness, both forgiving themselves for not savoring life more and forgiving others who have disappointed them or abandoned them; and they frequently feel out of control, and need to depend on others like nurses or ministers. Cecilia had experienced all of the above. She had spent most of her life feeling angry and wondering, "Why me, God?" She had struggled all her life both to forgive herself for being so down on life and to forgive others such as her alcoholic father or nagging school parents; and she knew what it was like to feel out of control and have to depend on others like myself or another school teacher. Cecilia's depression gradually disappeared as she began to discover during the next few months just how her painful past blessed her with sensitivities to be with struggling people.

Today, Cecilia finds herself not only free from suicidal depression but also able to direct a hospital unit which trains people to work with terminal patients. For six years now Cecilia has appreciated how her death-giving moments of the past have sensitized her to the struggles of hundreds of terminal patients. Healing of memories happens when we, like Cecilia, discover that a painful moment of our past need no longer cripple us but can bless us. In coming to appreciate how every moment can gift us, we discover for ourselves what spirituality and psychology has recognized as key to the healing process.

Any Moment Can Be a Gift

Psychiatrists like Rollo May recognize that any moment may be taken in two ways: a blessing for growth or a curse that cripples.[1] Rollo May's conclusion that any event can bless or cripple became evident to me when I was working at Wohl Psychiatric

Hospital in St. Louis, and when giving retreats. At Wohl, I remember treating three people for depression. The first complained that she lost a sizable amount of money in the stock market; the second, that she lost her fourth boy friend and faced the fear of being single the rest of her life; and the third, that he hated the boring slavery of his assembly line job. These situations led the first one to contemplate suicide, the second to run away from home, and the third to quit his job, thus leaving his family without any financial support.

One weekend I gave a retreat where three other people described situations similar to those that had brought my three patients to Wohl. However, the retreatants found that instead of bringing on psychological depression, their turbulent situations brought new life.

The oldest woman on the retreat spoke about how the 1929 depression gifted her family, despite losing a sizable amount in the stock market. She and two brothers, who hadn't talked to each other in years, pulled together as they put in long hours to keep a faltering family business going. Not only were they able to keep the business alive, but they eventually pooled their money to put another brother through college and to build herself a home.

A second woman felt most blessed when sixteen years ago she accepted not being married and opened her home to the disabled. Through the disabled, she became aware of how much she took for granted. For instance, now, as she takes two blind men for walks and helps them cook meals, she becomes more alive as she tunes into their world of smell, touch, and sound.

Finally, the third retreatant said that he was grateful that he lost his job as a corporation salesman and had to take a tedious job on a road crew. When he joined the road crew, he could no longer expect his old friends or his old job to give him his worth. Feeling so rootless, he began to take prayer seriously. Without Christ he could see no reason for his tedious day-to-day existence. For sixteen years he worked on road crews. In doing it optimistically he made himself and other workers question: what makes life worth living?

The same three moments that crippled my patients at Wohl and yet blessed my retreatants, also crippled many in the Old

Testament yet blessed Christians taking vows. The vows of poverty and obedience as well as the promise of celibacy bless what both my Wohl patients and many in the Old Testament considered the three greatest curses: to be without possessions, to be a slave, and to be without children. When Israelites like Job found themselves without land, animals, and possessions, they felt cursed just as did my Wohl patient who lost her possessions through the stock market crisis. And just as my patient felt cursed when working like a slave on an assembly line, so did the Israelites feel cursed when working as slaves in Egypt or Babylon. And finally, since Israelites lived on chiefly through their children, they considered barrenness a tremendous curse (Gn. 30:1, Is. 4:1, Lk. 1:25), just as did my patient who lost her fourth boy friend and faced the fear of being single the rest of her life. But Christians living the spirit of the vows witness that those events, instead of cursing us, can bless us. Missionaries who vow poverty leave their possessions behind to go to a foreign land, witness the blessings of living without possessions. Many priests and sisters who vow obedience and commit themselves to serve one another and to serve the poor, witness the blessings of being a servant. Finally, men and women who promise celibacy and offer to give up having their own families with the hope of belonging to all families, witness the blessings of being childless. In challenging us to bless events that crippled my Wohl patients and many in the Old Testament, the vows challenge us to heal memories.

God the Father knew how Israelites feared being without land, children, and freedom. Thus in his love covenants with Israel, he promises them land (Gn. 12:15; Jer. 31:17); children (2 Sm. 7:12; Gn. 12:16), and freedom from slavery (Ez. 34:27; 2 Sm. 7:11). The Father also knew the blessing of being without land, without children, and without freedom. When he sent his Son to us he gave him no place to lay his head so that he might belong to all nations (Mt. 8:20), no children that he might belong to every family (Jn. 17:21), and a slave's existence that he might love by laying down his life (Phil. 2:7; Rom. 5:7). What the Father declares by treating his covenant people one way and his Son in yet another is that any moment can be life-giving. Nothing can separate us from the Father's love (Rom. 8:31).

Our Life: Any Moment Can Be a Gift

As the Scripture writers recount Israel's struggle when childless, landless or in slavery, they recount their faith history. Scripture writers keep going back to five memories as the core of their faith history: Abraham's call, slavery in Egypt, wandering in a desert, Mount Sinai's law, and the promised land (Ps. 105; Dt. 26:1). Some of the memories, such as the promised land, they counted as gift immediately.[2]

In writing our faith history, we too have some memories like the promised land, such as the day we graduated from school or the day we spent with a friend we hadn't seen in years. At these times our feeling of "let's stay here forever" perhaps matched Israel's jubilant feeling of finally settling on the banks of the promised land (Jos. 4:14). But for Israelites not all memories were promised lands. The other four memories they didn't appreciate right away but only in time.

We too have many memories that we didn't appreciate right away. Perhaps when we took a job in a new town or went away to serve our country, we felt the chaos of seventy-five-year-old Abraham cutting off earthly ties and leaving his familiar land with his childless wife (Gn. 12:14). In studying while others had fun, or in working a monotonous job, or in experiencing financial hardship, we may have felt penned up like the slaves in Egypt. At times we may have resented being called on the carpet like the Israelites at Mount Sinai (Ex. 32:19). Perhaps we felt rootless like the Israelites wandering in the desert when we started classes at a strange school, left home for scout camp, or moved away from our closest friend.

Many of our memories that once seemed painful—such as the constant pressure to make ends meet or the separation from a close friend—we now appreciate realizing that the financial crisis gave us an appreciation of goods and people or that the separation made us expand our friendships. Perhaps those five moments of the Israelite nation brought back to us faces of people we once disliked but now treasure. These are a few of our healed memories where we, like Cecilia, my retreatants, and the people of Israel took what at first seemed only a curse and began seeing it from the Father's viewpoint as a blessing.

2

HEALING A MEMORY IS LIKE DYING

Why do some people heal a memory only to come back later with the same memory bothering them? Why don't some people get well with one prayer? While serving as a hospital chaplain and observing both physical wounds heal and how the terminally ill face death, I found a partial answer to these questions.

Jim arrived at the hospital very upset about his youngest daughter Karen. She had turned down a first class college education, had disgraced the family by running away and becoming pregnant, and now had the nerve to ask if she could return home with her boy friend and new born child. After venting his anger regarding unappreciative children, Jim asked if I would pray with him so that he could forgive his daughter. Later in the week when Jim's daughter returned home, he felt like the father who welcomed home the prodigal son. Just as that father gave thanks that he could be closer to his prodigal son than ever before, Jim found himself giving thanks that he could now be closer to Karen because he forgave her much.

But this feeling of gratitude lasted only about a month. Jim came back again complaining with the same memory bothering him. But this time Jim was not angry with his daughter. Rather, Jim was angry with himself. As a workaholic father, he hadn't taken much time to love Karen. Thus Jim could understand why she had run away to find love. Before Jim could fully heal the memory of his daughter running away, he needed to forgive himself, just as one month before he had forgiven his daughter.

Healing this kind of painful memory is a process much like that of healing a physical wound. We all know that when we get cut, the wound doesn't heal all at once. Rather platelets form, fibers make the blood clot, skin cells grow under the protective scab, and finally the scab falls off. In healing memories we deal with emotional wounds that heal in stages much like physical wounds.

Perhaps we feel most emotionally wounded and the stages of healing are most evident when we are faced with the prospect of our own death. Elisabeth Kubler-Ross concludes that dying people in dealing with that emotional wound usually go through five stages: denial, anger, bargaining, depression and acceptance.[1] She sees these five stages as the normal way of healing any deep hurt.[2] We find that in healing memories, people usually go through those same five stages. Though a memory can be healed with one quick prayer, just as death can be immediately accepted, the normal way of dealing with memories and death is working through the five stages over a period of time. Thus Jim didn't "lose his healing," but rather in a month's time he struggled through the anger stage where he was blaming his daughter, to the depression stage where he was blaming himself.

Another friend, Margaret, struggled through the five stages both when facing death from terminal cancer and when healing a memory regarding India. When Margaret was refused readmittance to India, where she taught for three years and wanted to spend the rest of her life, she became anxious and depressed. For months she anxiously paced the halls at night. Yet, during the day she felt too depressed to eat or talk with others, thus she spent the days alone in her room. After one year of anxiety and depression, six different doctors diagnosed cancer and gave her tired, worn body only a short time to live. For two years the doctors tried every kind of treatment with no success. Then, because medication could no longer help, she became bedridden for two years during which time she began healing memories especially concerning India. This chapter will describe how Margaret experienced the five stages both in facing her death, and in healing the memory about India.

Five Stages of Dying

After Margaret spent two years confined to a hospital bed, I asked her if she looked forward to dying. Margaret said she felt like a recent swimmer who set out to swim the English Channel. Suddenly one of the men aboard her lifeboat suffered a heart attack. In the midst of taking care of him, the crew lost track of the swimmer. Only when the swimmer was within one-half mile of shore did the boat crew spot her. When the crew asked how she was doing, the swimmer responded that she felt fine now and wanted to finish the swim, but that if the boat crew had spotted her earlier, she would have quit the swim because she had suffered severe cramps.

Margaret said that she too wanted to finish her swim and reach the shore of death. But both of us remembered how many times she wanted nothing to do with death. Many times, if it had been possible, she would have climbed back into the boat. Only after working through denial, anger, bargaining and depression could Margaret stop focusing so much on getting back into the lifeboat. Working through those stages gave her a new acceptance of death which allowed her to focus all her energies toward reaching death's shore.

Usually when we are told we are going to die, we initially deny it. We say, "Maybe he will die, but not I." Second, we become angry and blame others for letting death hurt and destroy us. Third, we tend to bargain by setting up conditions to be fulfilled before we will be ready to die. Fourth, we go through depression (different from anger where we blame others), when we blame ourselves for letting death destroy us. And, finally, we frequently go through the fifth stage of acceptance, saying, "Yes, I am looking forward to dying."

During her journey to death, Margaret could remember days of denial, days when she would refuse to visit a friend dying of brain cancer because she couldn't face that she too might die that way. She remembered too her days of anger—blaming the nurse for restricting visitors, the doctor for not discovering the cancer sooner, and her own friends for being healthy enough to go places during the summer. Her "only if" bargains also would change from day to day. She would be ready to die only if they allowed her to die in India, or only if the two current nurses were fired and two others hired who could comfort her in those final hours. During days of depression she blamed herself for not savoring life more, or for letting her disappointment about India eat away at her until it made her sick. During her two bedridden years she could recall moments of denial, anger, bargaining, and depression when she wanted to quit swimming and climb back in the lifeboat. But now looking forward to death, she found herself in the stage of acceptance, much as the channel swimmer yearned for the shore.

FIVE STAGES

STAGES	IN DYING	IN HEALING A MEMORY
Denial	I don't ever admit I will die.	I don't admit I was ever hurt.
Anger	I blame others for letting death hurt and destroy me.	I blame others for hurting and destroying me.
Bargaining	I set up conditions to be fulfilled before I'm ready to die.	I set up conditions to be fulfilled before I'm ready to forgive.
Depression	I blame myself for letting death destroy me.	I blame myself for letting hurt destroy me.
Acceptance	I look forward to dying.	I look forward to growth from hurt.

Five Stages of Healing a Memory

Margaret began another journey through those five stages the day she received word that she could not go back to India. She never felt so shattered in her life as that day. Her whole life had found its meaning in preparing to go to India, and after being there for three years she desired to devote the rest of her life to those people. Then for reasons of jealousy and in-fighting among her supervisors, Margaret was refused readmittance.

When we are suffering the ultimate hurt of death, not going to India, or some other hurt, we usually go through the same five stages of dying. We first of all tend to deny it by saying that this hurt really didn't happen or at least doesn't bother us at all. Second, we begin to get angry and blame others for hurting and destroying us. Third, we tend to bargain and set up conditions to be fulfilled before we'll forgive the one who hurt us. Fourth, we go through depression as we begin to blame ourselves for letting the hurt destroy us. And, finally, we frequently go through the fifth stage of acceptance as we say, ''I'm looking forward to the growth that will come from this hurt.''

Before describing how Margaret went through the five stages in healing her memory about India, we need to give special attention to the second and fourth stages. For Kubler-Ross, the biggest difference between the anger stage and the depression stage is that in the anger stage most of the anger is focused outward, and in the depression stage most of the anger is focused inward. While in the anger stage people are still blaming doctors and nurses, in the depression stage they are blaming themselves as they look back and see all the opportunities they missed or things they wish they didn't do. Thus, in this book when we talk about *depression*, we refer to feelings of guilt, or anger turned inward. On the other hand, when we talk about *anger*, we limit the word to refer to the anger stage, or anger turned outward. In modern usage ''they feel depressed'' or ''they feel angry'' are ambiguous phrases since the people could either be in the anger stage or in the depression stage, or in both stages at once. They are in the anger stage to the extent they are blaming another; they are in the depression stage to the extent they are blaming themselves.

As Margaret considered the first stage of denial, she remembered how when she packed her bags in India to come back to the United States for a vacation, she was encouraged to pack everything. Deep down she felt that she probably wasn't wanted back, but she denied those feelings and thus ignored confronting the situation. The hurt she felt when she finally got a letter refusing her readmittance to India was the same hurt she could have felt and dealt with a month earlier before leaving India.

Margaret remembers the second stage of anger that boiled up when she read the words, "Because we fear you may get malaria, you will not be allowed back in the country." Since she had just received a clean bill of health from the best doctors, she felt angered by words which skirted the real issues. She imagined the face of the person responsible for this letter speaking the words that the letter should have said, "Because you're a young whippersnapper trying to take the place of the top boss, we don't want you." Margaret recalled how she thought about the lay catechist program and all the good that would come to an end because of this jealous person. The same words came to her mind then that came to her mind after she was told she had cancer, "Why me, why me?"

In the third stage of bargaining, Margaret considered that she would forgive those responsible only *if*—if they would change their minds, if they saw the destruction they had done, if they never did it again. But the people never changed their minds, never saw the destruction they had done, and continued to shatter other people through similar maneuvers.

In the fourth stage of depression, Margaret became aware that rather than the hurt, her reaction to the hurt had crippled her. She began to see that if she had acted differently before, during or after the hurt, the hurt would not have disabled her. Why had she tried to base all her worth on what she did in India rather than on being loved by the Father wherever she was? Why hadn't she communicated better before she left the country? But what made her most depressed was realizing that she was acting in the same way as those who hurt her. After being turned down for India she was given the job as mission director and found herself jealously searching for legalistic reasons to say "no" to mission volunteers.

During the healing of that India memory, Margaret once again felt like the channel swimmer. Some days when praying through the stages of denial, anger, bargaining and depression, she felt uprooted like the cramped-up swimmer looking for her boat crew. But just as the channel swimmer reaching shore could finally see the hidden gift in her boat crew losing her and not being able to pick her up, Margaret began to see hidden gifts that being turned down for India could give her. In the fifth stage of acceptance she experienced how the hurt opened her to a deeper relationship with God and others than she had ever experienced.

She found that the hurt put her in touch with the fact that she could no longer get her worth only from what she did or what people thought of her, but now only from God. She recalls that when this realization struck her, she tried everywhere to find a priest to hear her confession. She simply confessed, "I'm sorry for being away so long, heavenly Father." With that began an unforgettable experience, the feeling of being able to love her heavenly Father much because she was forgiven much. Even though the priest hearing her confession spoke broken English and didn't understand what Margaret said, she felt a "quiet and stillness" that has endured.

The hurt deepened her relationship not only with God, but also with people. She found herself more sensitive to her own jealousy, especially catching herself jealously saying "no" to mission volunteers. But perhaps her greatest gift was a sensitivity toward those who felt uprooted. A few months ago she even found herself embracing a woman who was also upset for being turned down for readmittance to India. Margaret felt a deep compassion for her, but what was very special is that this was the same woman who had refused to allow Margaret to return to India!

Healing memories blessed Margaret not only with new relationships, but also with new health. Because no more therapy could be used, Margaret spent two bedridden years, helped only by what came from being unconditionally loved by friends as she healed memories. Now, after much love and healing of memories, Margaret has just finished her first year of work, despite the consensus of six cancer specialists that she should have died years ago. Margaret works an eight hour day as counselor to cancer patients.

Though Margaret is not totally healed, she continues to improve each day. If she lives, she will continue to reach out to cancer patients who, faced with an uncertain future, feel uprooted in many of the same ways Margaret felt uprooted from India. If Margaret dies from cancer, she will die with less fear because she walked through the five stages of dying in both her struggle to face death with cancer and in her struggle to heal a memory of India. Now she knows how both death and being uprooted from India can be a gift.

Though Margaret found how both facing death and being uprooted from India could be a gift, many in similar situations get immobilized and never get to the acceptance stage. Dr. Kubler-Ross and her associates find that, those able to express and have their feelings accepted by a person significant to them will reach more quickly the acceptance of death.[3] The next section describes how Margaret, in facing death and healing memories, found it important to share her feelings with friends and with Christ on a daily basis.

Sharing Feelings with A Friend

Margaret's anxiety and depression as well as the severity of her cancer remained almost unchanged until one day Larry re-marked, "You're angry." That simple comment allowed her to pour out two years of fear and anger. In fact, so much poured out that Margaret spent the next weeks and months speaking her fears and angers into a tape recorder. She would send Larry the tapes, then call him long distance a few days later. Larry also encouraged her to keep a diary and to write poetry. Finally, Larry also invited his friends to visit Margaret; that is how I got to meet her.

For the next two years I saw Margaret's emotional and physi-cal condition improve as she shared her feelings with friends. If Larry had said, "Think how blessed you are that the Lord has called you to suffer this way," instead of, "You look angry," Margaret might still be in the stage of denial, if indeed she were living at all. Instead, Margaret moved very naturally from one stage to the next as she shared her present feelings. Finally as she reached the acceptance stage, she began speaking about her death with her friends. Among other things, she read a burial service she had written. Above all, she wanted the occasion to be a joyous celebration, bringing together all those who had died and risen with her.

Sharing Feelings with Christ

Just as it was important for Margaret to share her feelings with Larry and friends, it became important to share them with Christ. Christ became someone steady in her life, providing her with stability, especially in later years as friends like Larry moved on. Just as Margaret didn't immediately tell Larry, "I am ready to die now," so too she didn't immediately say to Christ, "I am ready to forgive my India supervisor now." As Larry got Margaret in touch with her anger, she began to also express it to Christ. She told Christ that she couldn't ever forgive her supervisor, "that envious so and so." If Margaret had said immediately, "I forgive you," without having a chance to work through her feelings about that "envious so and so" she probably would have ended up feeling the buried anger toward her supervisor. But instead, Margaret felt like embracing her supervisor and giving her the same love Margaret felt from Christ who unconditionally accepted her, even with all those "negative" feelings.

Seeing Margaret become emotionally healthy, as she shared her feelings with Christ, made me more grateful for whatever I felt. I used to be disappointed when all I had to share were "negative" feelings such as anger and depression. But Margaret has shown me there are no "negative" feelings; it can be just as healthy to feel anger or depression as it is to feel acceptance or gratitude.

The most healthy stage, or the most healthy feeling, is whatever one the Spirit brings to our consciousness. For example, Margaret's physical and emotional health almost always improved when prayer put her in touch with blazing anger. The more angrily she complained to Christ about the coldness and indifference of the nurses, the more she mobilized herself to get out of the infirmary. And the angrier she boiled about the non-communication, the more she felt Christ's call to get out of bed and begin setting up channels of communication, especially with cancer patients.

Not only anger, but each stage is crucial in Margaret's healing, just as each stage is important in healing a physical wound. If we rush the process by picking the scab before it's ready to fall off, we need to repeat the whole process. So too, Christ and other friends, by not rushing us, can allow us to share our feelings and move naturally from one stage to another until our emotional wounds become healed memories.

Healing Memories Every Day
by Sharing with Christ and Friends

Memories, like deep wounds, usually take weeks or even months to heal. By daily sharing memories with Christ and other friends, Margaret had time not only to move from one stage to the next, but also to enter into a given stage at a greater depth. For example, for the last three years Margaret has entered into the acceptance stage at greater depths. Initially, she accepted death as a way of escaping from the whole India situation and other unfortunate circumstances. But later, especially after being present at the peaceful death of two friends, Margaret began to accept death not as running away from something but rather as running toward something.

Margaret found herself not only moving into greater depth in each of the stages when facing death from cancer, but also in each of the stages when healing the memory regarding India. For instance, Margaret moved back and forth between the depression stage and the stages of anger and bargaining. But each time she returned to the depression stage, she found herself at a deeper level. For example, the first time she was in the depression stage, she felt guilty because her reactions made her look bad. Later in the depression stage she felt guilty because her reactions had hurt others; at still a later time she felt guilty because her reaction had hurt her relationship with God. By healing memories every day, we will find ourselves not only moving from stage to stage but also penetrating each stage at greater depth until we begin seeing the moment as God does.

Uses of the Five Stages in Prayer

Though the five stages can heal hurts by allowing us to begin to see a moment as God does, we don't want to make the stages a rigid way of praying. Two extremes would be to have nothing to do with the stages or to follow everything stage by stage. The five stages simply point out the normal way the Spirit heals our hurts, but the creativity of the Spirit sometimes takes short-cuts too. Just as a person can skip some of the stages by immediately accepting his death, the Spirit can also help us skip stages in accepting our hurts. We suggest the five stage model of psychiatrist Dr. Elisabeth Kubler-Ross because, as Vatican II pointed out, psychological insights help us live more maturely.

> In pastoral care, appropriate use must be made not only of theological principles, but also of the findings of secular sciences, especially of psychology and sociology. Thus the faithful can be brought to live the life in a more thorough and mature way.[4]

Kubler-Ross' psychological findings allow us to live more maturely by describing an age old process. For instance, most Scripture passages involving in-depth forgiveness also involve facing those wounds in a healing way through the five stages. Thus later chapters describe the prodigal son's journey through the five stages, as he discovers that his running away need not wound him, but can give him a closer relationship with his father. Even the father describes his son's memory healing journey as a struggle through the five stages of dying. "This son of mine was dead and has come back to life" (Lk. 15:24; Lk. 15:32). Traditional prayers such as the "Our Father," prayer experiences such as the Spiritual Exercises, and celebrations such as the Eucharist are based on the five stages.[5] All these deal with healing of hurts through healing memories and can take us through the five stages.

How can we get started on the five stages and heal memories? The remaining five sections of the book deal with how we can experience what Margaret did. Part two that follows opens us to the possibilities for emotional and physical health that Margaret found as her increased physical strength kept adding extra years to a body that was no longer anxious and depressed. But Margaret couldn't mobilize herself or make any headway through the five stages until she began daily sharing her feelings. Through part three, by encountering God as a lover with whom we wish to share our feelings, we can predispose ourselves for healing. Part four helps us to recognize and move through the stages of healing; parts five and six suggest practical ways of doing healing of memories on a daily basis.

Part Two:
Emotional and Physical Healing

I don't know how my mother knew I gave my brother's red ball away to the Salvation Army. Both were away taking swimming lessons when I chased down a Salvation Army truck and surrendered my brother's most valuable possession to the truck driver. When my brother returned, it didn't take him long to find the ball missing; it took me even less time to assure my mother that I didn't know what happened to it.

Even though my mother didn't have a lie detector, she declared me guilty. She probably read the anxiety in the goose flesh forming on my arms, or the fear as sweat formed on my forehead. If she waited a few moments longer, she could certainly read the anger on my red face as I was sent to find that truck driver. For a long time we have known that anxiety, fear, anger, and guilt trigger physiological changes that can be read by perceptive mothers as well as by lie detectors.

Now doctors are also reading these physiological changes and finding that those four emotions can trigger everything from an upset stomach to even cancer and heart attacks. These four emotions, besides triggering physical illness, tend to find themselves at the core of the ten major neuroses described by the American Psychiatric Association, as well as at the core of most emotional instability in our life.

We have nearly 3,500 accounts from people relating emotional and physical healing, especially as they have worked through the four emotions of anxiety, fear, anger and guilt by healing memories. Chapter 3 focuses on how healing of memories brings emotional health, and chapter 4 on how it brings physical health especially by working through those four emotions. Chapter 4 has three sections on how healing of memories has brought physical health: first, in Christian tradition; second, in medical science; third, in my own life. In reading these chapters we can have the same experience as Margaret who found her anxiety and depression decrease and her physical health increase as she healed memories.

3
EMOTIONAL HEALING THROUGH
HEALING MEMORIES

Margaret learned that a hurt such as being refused readmittance to India could either send her anxiously pacing the hallways at night, or fill her with compassion for others, such as cancer patients who also face an uncertain future. We have nearly 3,500 written accounts from people like Margaret revealing how healing of memories brought them emotional health. Some wrote that their marriages were saved, others that they were freed from alcoholism, or irrational fears and compulsions. A few are mentioned in later chapters, such as Phil, who was freed from a twenty-three year phobia of dentists, or Annette, who despite eleven years of therapy, still awakened as many as nine times a night to check the lock, the stove, and the closet.[1] What is it about healing of memories that encourages so much emotional healing?

Key to Emotional Health: Healing Anxiety, Fear, Anger, Guilt Behind Hurts

Psychologically speaking, healing of memories brings emotional health to Margaret, Phil, Annette and countless others by treating the same hurts that models of psychology have treated for years. For instance, Freudian therapy tends to treat past hurts, reality therapy present hurts, and rational emotive therapy even future hurts. Different schools take different sets of hurts. Freud, for example, focuses more on psychosexual hurts; whereas Adler focuses more on hurts involving power struggles, such as the infighting involved in Margaret being refused readmittance to India.[2]

Psychologists know that responding inappropriately to hurts causes emotional instability such as Margaret's depression and anxiety, as well as Phil's phobic neurosis, or Annette's obsessive compulsive neurosis. Many psychologists agree, after studying men like Adler and Freud, that four emotions tend to be not only at the core of the ten major kinds of neuroses outlined by the American Psychiatric Association, but also at the core of most emotional instability in our lives. Whether we suffer from a neurosis, or from common fears such as a fear of people, or a fear of our feelings, we can begin to heal that area by working through the four emotions of anxiety, fear, anger and guilt.[3] Like other emotions, these feelings are neither good nor bad in themselves. These four emotions if buried lead to emotional instability but if worked through lead to health. As Margaret found out, those emotions when buried led to suicidal depression, but when worked with gave her strength to reach out to others.

Working Through Anxiety, Fear, Anger and Guilt by the Five Stages

Some sleepless nights as Margaret paced the hallways, she could not identify what made her anxious. In the denial stage, anxiety works like pain. Just as a cramp's shooting pain warns us that our muscles are overworked, anxiety warns us of an emotional overload. Thus Margaret's anxiety warned her that she was emotionally overloaded, especially with fear, anger and guilt. As she worked through the denial stage, she began to identify what made her anxious. She found herself pacing the halls especially when anxious about starting over with a new job, new friends, and a new way of life. Having been uprooted from India, she felt anxious about her future.

But anxiously pacing the halls at night became less frequent when friends sat down with Margaret and helped her get in touch with three of crippling anxiety's components: fear, anger, and guilt. Anxiety is a feeling of emotional distress without an object. But as friends helped Margaret pinpoint the object of her emotional distress through such questions as "What about your job makes you anxious?" or, "What about your future makes you anxious?" her anxiety decreased as her fears were identified. Many fears formed the object of Margaret's emotional distress, such as the fear that other key decisions in her life would also be made on the basis of jealousy and infighting. But the main object of her distress was the fear that her life had lost meaning.

Once Margaret pinpointed her fears, her fears lessened as she worked through two of the core components of crippling fear:

anger and guilt. Fears are usually actual or potential sources of frustration and are often followed by anger if the frustration source is outside ourselves, or by guilt if the source of frustration is inside ourselves.[4] Insofar as Margaret's fear came from frustration outside herself, she needed to work through anger. Thus Margaret's fear lessened when in the anger stage she worked through the anger she felt toward her supervisor whose jealousy and infighting blocked Margaret from returning to the land and people who had given her life so much meaning. And insofar as Margaret's fear came from frustration with herself, she needed to work through the depression stage and work out her guilt. As Margaret worked through her guilt for not communicating before leaving the country, or for trying to get too much of her meaning from what she did in India, her fear continued to decrease. One indication of Margaret working through fear, anger and guilt was that in the bargaining stage she set fewer conditions for forgiveness. Thus she found herself forgiving her supervisor, even though her supervisor hadn't changed her mind regarding the India situation.

Healing of memories works through the anger and guilt until the fear and anxiety that crippled us begins in the acceptance stage to be a gift. Although all of Margaret's anxiety about the future and fear of a meaningless life didn't vanish, what remained no longer sent Margaret sleeplessly pacing the halls at night. Rather it gave her a new sensitivity towards those who also faced an unsure future such as her hospital patients or her supervisor who was also refused readmittance to India.

But in working through anger and guilt, we don't always see new sensitivites and feel we are making progress. Sometimes working through anger and guilt puts us in touch with new fears and anxieties. Thus the second time Margaret found herself in the depression stage, she came in touch with how often she jealously said ''no'' to other mission volunteers. She then became aware of a new feeling of anxiety when around mission volunteers, and aware of a new fear: I fear I have harmed these volunteers. As she worked through the anger and guilt, this new fear and new anxiety also gave Margaret new gifts. For instance, Margaret found that she gained many lifetime friends as she went to each of the volunteers and asked for forgiveness. Regardless of how many new fears and new anxieties are uncovered, we can become more open to experiencing and growing from all of them.

FIVE STAGES*	ANXIETY, FEAR, ANGER, AND GUILT
DENIAL STAGE	Anxiety decreases as fears gradually pinpointed.
ANGER STAGE	Fears coming from outside factors decrease as anger worked through.
BARGAINING STAGE	Fear and anger decrease as fewer conditions set for forgiveness.
DEPRESSION STAGE	Fears coming from factors within decrease as guilt worked through.
ACCEPTANCE STAGE	What made me fearful and anxious gradually becomes a gift. I am more open to growing from future anxiety, fear, anger and guilt.

*Any stage can also put us in touch with new fears and new anxieties which can also become a gift as anger and guilt are worked through.

By emphasizing anxiety, fear, anger and guilt, we are not overlooking, but rather treating all the other feelings we have when hurt. That is because these four feelings form the root of all the potentially crippling emotions, such as resentment, hatred and loneliness—which if worked through can also bring us health. For instance, at night when walking the halls, Margaret considered suicide, so intense was her loneliness. But the intensity of her loneliness depended on the intensity of those four emotions. Thus her loneliness intensified as her anxiety about a rootless future or her fear about life having no meaning intensified. Margaret's loneliness also became more suicidal as she angrily considered the supervisor who took her away from her India friends, or as Margaret felt guilty for not having prepared herself by developing interests other than India. In dealing with the four core emotions, Margaret does not guarantee that her future will be free from emotions such as loneliness, hatred, or resentment, but she does set the foundation for being able to grow from those feelings. Next time Margaret feels an emotion such as loneliness, rather than longing to commit suicide, she might long to be more sensitive to lonely patients or to develop new friends.

"Forgive Us as We Forgive Those"
Summarizes Healing Memories and Emotional Health

Not only through healing memories prayer, but also through prayerful meditation on the "Our Father," emotional health grows by dealing with four core emotions.[5] Both prayers ask us to get in touch with a moment that made us fearful or anxious, then to deal with the anger (forgive those) and guilt (forgive us) in that situation, until the fearful or anxious moment that crippled us begins to bless us (Kingdom comes). Thus both prayers ask Margaret to take the India situation that filled her with fears and anxieties about her future and deal with her anger by forgiving those involved in the infighting, and her guilt by forgiving herself. The kingdom promised in the "Our Father" and in the acceptance stage did come to Margaret as she forgave and became grateful for how her fear and anxiety of being rootless opened her to God and others.

In both prayers, forgiveness manifests itself by gratitude for what before only made us anxious or fearful. Thus as I work through the four crippling emotions by forgiving, I can never say "I am done healing," because I can always forgive at a deeper level by becoming more grateful. The key in dealing with the four core emotions behind most emotional neurosis is found in the twofold forgiveness of both the healing of memories and the "Our Father": forgive us (guilt), as we forgive those (anger).

Besides Margaret, many others have found relief from emotional neurosis and instability through the power of this twofold forgiveness. For example, after dropping out of school, Kate became anxious as she found herself unable to hold a job or form lasting friendships. She feared that because she couldn't settle down, she might never get married. Four years ago when all this led to depression and two suicide attempts, Kate began seeing a psychiatrist. These years of psychotherapy showed Kate that she was afraid to form close relationships because she feared these people might abandon her just as her grandfather once had. When Kate was only four, her grandfather died leaving her feeling very alone, because her grandfather was the person who cherished her the most. Instinctively Kate told herself: "Don't ever let yourself love someone, or they'll leave you too.

Though Kate had this psychological insight for several years, she still didn't have power to change her behavior. One day Kate found herself asking Jesus to be present with her grandfather and herself. Kate began praying, "I want to forgive you, grandfather, for having abandoned me and I ask forgiveness for not having cherished you more." Then she found herself walking with Jesus and her grandfather, until they came to the Father. She placed her grandfather's hand in the Father's, turned around and walked away. Two weeks after that prayer experience, Kate's psychiatrist gave her a clean bill of health. Kate has since formed close friendships, continues to hold the same job, and plans on getting married later this year. Kate becomes more and more healed as she becomes more grateful for even those anxious and fearful days when she feared forming a close friendship. As Kate moves toward marriage, she appreciates the gifts of cooking, decorating and homemaking that she developed when she stayed home, afraid to go out and form lasting friendships. Through healing memories Christ helped Kate get in touch with the power of twofold forgiveness that brings emotional health. As a psychiatrist told us: forgiveness is at least as important a discovery for treating emotional illness as penicillin is for treating physical illness.

Christ Heals Memories and Brings
Emotional Health through Twofold Forgiveness

Not just with Kate, but with others such as the men on the road to Emmaus, Christ uses the twofold forgiveness to bring emotional health (Lk. 24:13-35). Though the Emmaus disciples know that Christ's death fills them with anxiety about their future, and with a fear that life lost its meaning, the insight alone doesn't give them power to change their depression. Rather, power to change comes when they meet the unconditional forgiveness of Christ that helps them work through anger and guilt.

In walking at their pace, Jesus accepts the disciples angry feelings toward the chief priests and leaders for putting the Messiah to death, and toward the prophets for apparently misleading the disciples. No doubt, too, Christ knows they feel guilty and downcast about being foolish men (Lk. 24:25). They probably ask themselves, "Why didn't we listen when Christ warned us that he would die? Why didn't we stand by him? Why didn't we have the courage to stay with his fearful friends, hiding from the authorities in Jerusalem?" After Jesus explains the Scriptures to them, they can indeed plead guilty to being foolish men, but they need not be depressed about their foolishness, because it puts them in touch with a forgiving Christ.

In fact, they feel so at home with Christ's forgiveness, that they invite him into a home to eat with them. As he makes himself comfortable at their table, Jesus gives them the feeling of being loved, just as they are. As they feel Jesus accept them, regardless of how negative they may have felt or what they may have done, the disciples no longer have downcast faces, but forgiving hearts that burn within them. The disciples "return at once to Jerusalem" to be with people who put Christ to death, and to extend to them the unconditional love that Christ extended on the Emmaus road.

While returning, the disciples consider the memory of the Messiah's death, but it no longer makes them fearful or anxious. Instead they count it as a blessing which gives to Israel the hoped for Savior and to themselves an unconditional lover who makes forgiving hearts burn. With a healed memory they joyfully re-enter Jerusalem, the source of their previous anxiety and fear. By healing a memory through twofold forgiveness, Christ brings health as he helps us work through anxiety, fear, anger and guilt behind emotional neurosis and instability. The next chapter shows how Christ uses healing of memories' twofold forgiveness to heal not just emotionally but also physically.

4
PHYSICAL HEALING THROUGH HEALING A MEMORY

During a summer workshop, Agnes asked for prayers and anointing for her vision. Because of a degenerative retina, Agnes was legally blind in her right eye. At times I tend to forget that Jesus is a healer and wish I could pray for something easier like a back problem or arthritis rather than blindness. When I forget that Jesus is a healer, my prayers become very spiritual, asking God that in her darkness she become dependent on him for her light, her direction in life. And if I do get bold enough to pray for physical problems, I do it in a whisper so that people won't be able to see that God didn't answer my prayer for physical healing of her eyes.

After I prayed for Agnes, no change occurred in her vision. With her right eye she could only see a round, greyish-black spot at the point of focus. When her blindness struck fourteen years ago, she checked with eye specialists in both Oklahoma and Kansas. Both specialists told her that the right eye retina had degenerated, for which condition there existed no cure or treatment. For the past fourteen years she had continued going to the ophthamologist yearly, since she expected her left retina to also degenerate, the normal course for this condition. Each year the doctor confirmed that nothing could be done for the right eye, and that the vision in her left eye was also deteriorating.

Agnes' anointing happened at a week long workshop on healing of memories. During the three days following the anointing, people continued to pray with Agnes. As they prayed, Agnes experienced a healing of memories in regard to her father who had stopped communicating with her when she left home about forty-five years ago to become a nurse. Agnes always tried to bury this memory because thinking about it made her anxious about her own development. She feared that she hadn't developed properly, because she had lived a lonely, isolated existence without the encouragement and support of a loving father.

During the first day of prayer, Agnes told God how angry she felt at her father's abandonment, and then how guilty she felt because she had not tried to reach out to her father. On the second day, Agnes allowed the Father to embrace her in that lonely moment forty-five years ago when she so much needed a father's love. After Agnes felt the arms of the Father melt her feelings of loneliness and isolation, the Father took her by the hand and invited her to extend that same love to her own father who had died fifteen years ago. On the third day as Agnes continued to reach out with more love toward her father, she began to appreciate how even the pain of that moment forty-five years ago had gifted her. She appreciated how feeling isolated had given birth to a desire for a personal relationship with God in prayer, and to her desire to care for the abandoned and lonely as a nurse for thirty-eight years.

Furthermore, the more that painful memory was healed by seeing it from the Father's viewpoint, the more sight began to return to her right eye. It wasn't sudden. One day she would show everyone how she could distinguish color and form; another day she would be anxious to show workshop participants how she could pick out huge flowers or giant lettering on a banner.

On the final day of the workshop, Agnes, who had been legally blind in her right eye, used it alone to read to all of us the Biblical story in Mark 8:22 about the blind person whose sight was gradually restored. Then she explained to everyone how during the last three days she had found that the more the memory was healed of her father abandoning her, the more her sight returned. As she began to see this relationship in a new light, her vision began to return.

I don't remember what else Agnes said. I was still stunned that she could see. I expected that the Lord would heal her the first night, if he was to heal her. It took me most of the way through the Eucharist to finally concede that maybe the Lord had healed her in the workshop as an example to us of the importance of forgiveness and healing of memories in praying for physical healing. In recent months, the letters from this woman keep reminding me of how important the healing of memories aspect was for her.

True the healing of my eye is wonderful, but oh, the deep healing of memories I have had with my father is beyond any blessing I have ever experienced or expect to experience. I can now thank God for the blindness I had, for I realize through it I was inspired to make your retreat which has brought me true memory healing, true happiness and peace.

The sign of deep forgiveness and healing of memories is that the memory of Agnes' father, which before she tried to bury because it made her anxious and fearful, is now "beyond any blessing."

This chapter will treat how healing of memories by working through anger and guilt brings physical healing as in the case of Agnes. Many times we will refer to "working through anger and guilt" to describe the process of forgiving ourselves and others, until what before made us anxious or fearful begins to bless us. Thus "working through anger and guilt" involves all four of the core emotions. The three sections which follow treat the findings of Christian tradition, medical science, and my own life which indicate that "working through anger and guilt" can heal us physically, just as it did Agnes.

I
CHRISTIAN VIEW:
PHYSICAL HEALING THROUGH HEALING A MEMORY

Though I was surprised that vision returned to Agnes, the Church has taught for centuries that the dynamics behind healing a memory bring physical healing. From the earliest times when Christ healed a paralytic only after forgiving his sin (Mk. 2:1), even up to the latest teaching on the sacrament of the sick, the Church has always stressed the importance of forgiving others (anger) and being forgiven (guilt).

The latest teaching on the sacrament of the sick encourages us not to use the sacrament only to insure people a happy death, but also to use the sacrament to bring physical healing, as did the early Church. The context for the sacrament of the sick or anointing comes from James who speaks about physical health resulting from prayer and forgiveness:

Is there anyone sick among you? He should ask for the presbyters of the church. They in turn are to pray over him, anointing him with oil in the name of the Lord. This prayer uttered in faith will reclaim the one who is ill, and the Lord will restore him to health. If he has committed any sins, forgiveness will be his. Hence declare your sins to one another, and pray for one another that you may find healing (Jas. 5:14–17).

In recommending that people pray for one another and declare their sins to one another, James emphasizes the unconditional love of Christ that helps us work through anger and guilt with confidence that we will be forgiven. Thus the anointing rite uses the same dynamic that Agnes used in healing a memory to bring physical health.

Early Church writers emphatically state that prayerfully anointing people in this way was common and that it did bring physical health. Hippolytus (250) writes how the oil for anointing was offered along with bread and wine at the offertory.[1] People then took the oil home and blessed their sick after forgiving one another. St. John Chrysostom (410) complains that his lamps are always out of oil because the laity keep taking it for their sick.[2] The accounts of St. Irenaeus (150), St. Ephrem (350), St. Caesar (502), St. Bede (735) and many others testify how anointing physically healed when all else failed.[3]

Before the eighth century, all known documents explain the rite of anointing as preparing the sick for health and not for death.[4] The change from anointing to seek physical healing, to anointing in expectation only of a happy death had to do with the development in the understanding of "Declare your sins to one another" (Jas. 5:16).

In the first centuries, those wishing physical healing declared their sins to one another and anointed each other. The Church allowed for two kinds of anointing: a private one performed with blessed oil by the sick person himself or his relatives, and a liturgical anointing by a priest or a bishop. Up to the eighth century lay anointing was not only accepted, but also encouraged. After the eighth century, anointing became reserved to a priest.[5]

Anointing became reserved to a priest partially because "declaration of sins" began to mean formal confession of sins to a priest. But priests gave strict penances such as abstaining from meat or even from sexual intercourse. Since confessional penances lasted for the remainder of life, people waited until their deathbed before they declared their sins to a priest so that they could be anointed. After the eighth century physical healings through anointing with oil were infrequent, because by the time people had confessed their sins so they could be anointed, they no longer desired to live.

Vatican II called for a return to the traditional way of celebrating the sacrament of the sick, not just on a person's deathbed, but to bring physical healing.[6] Before praying for physical healing, the new rite continues the tradition of the Church by beginning with a penitential rite. The rite also uses the "Our Father" which stresses reciprocal forgiveness which manifests itself in the Kingdom coming, even into painful situations such as when Agnes felt abandoned by her father.

By including the forgiveness rite and the "Our Father" in the new rite of the sick, the Church emphasizes once again the connection between working through anger and guilt in healing memories and physical healing.[7] Both are usually connected as in the case of Agnes. When I first anointed Agnes, no physical healing was evident. She needed to experience first the depth of forgiveness through healing of memories, the very thing insisted on by the "Our Father," Scripture and the Fathers of the Church.

II
MEDICAL SCIENCE:
PHYSICAL HEALING THROUGH HEALING MEMORIES

Not only the Church but also medical science recognizes how healing of memories facilitates physical healing by dealing with anger and guilt. But to understand how doctors like Carl Simonton can arrest cancer and Meyer Friedman can restore health to a heart patient by working with anger and guilt, we need to understand what anger and guilt do to the body.

"Fight-Flight" Triggers Detrimental Physical Changes

In 1914 Dr. Walter Cannon began describing how the refusal to deal with anger and fear can trigger physical illness.[8] When Dr. Cannon measured the physical changes in a cat exposed to a barking dog, he opened the way for doctors to begin plotting the body's reaction to fear and anger. Dr. Cannon discovered that both the emotion of fear, which stimulates us to take flight and the emotion of anger, which stimulates us to fight, trigger the autonomic nervous system causing physical changes.[9] For instance, digestion, assimilation, and elimination halt as blood vessels to the stomach and intestines shut down.[10] Blood increases in the areas important in carrying out the decision to either fight or flee: the brain, heart, lungs, and external muscles. The heart and lungs pump faster, while the bronchial tubes relax so more oxygen can enter. A number of changes occur also in the blood. The spleen releases more white blood cells in case they are needed to combat infection in a wound. The number of platelets increase thus insuring a quicker blood clot if a wound is inflicted. More recently other doctors added to Cannon's list of physiological changes, such as Dr. Hans Selye who describes the changes set off in the pituitary-adrenal system.[11]

All these fight-flight physiological changes are a healthy body's way of readying itself to fight or flee. Thus our hands are readied to kill a mosquito, or our legs to flee a bee. Physical damage, however, happens when the fight-flight mechanism designed for short term emergencies becomes an on-going response.

In situations where we feel fear or anger, whether we are conscious of it or not, the fight-flight reaction happens. A lie detector, for example, works by picking up physical changes set off by the emotions from memories that may be conscious or even buried deep in our unconscious. Depending on how we feel about different situations, the fight-flight response might be going on inside of us when we eat breakfast with our husband, report to our boss at work, and ride home with a cigar smoker puffing down our throats. If at the end of a day we continually bury the fear and anger, the fight-flight mechanism designed for short term emergencies can trigger a breakdown. Depending on where the breakdown centers, we may suffer any illness from mild constipation (when digestion, elimination, and assimilation halt) to hypertension (steady increase in blood pressure).

Some of the damage from the excessive continuation of the physiological process involved in the fight-flight response goes on in twenty-three million Americans who suffer from chronic hyper-tension. Not only is hypertension the primary cause of 60,000 deaths each year but also a major underlying factor in another million or more deaths a year from strokes and cardiovascular disease.[12]

Anger and Guilt Trigger Most Physical Illness

Unresolved anger and guilt in emotionally stressful situations trigger the fight-flight response and many other physical reactions. When anger and guilt remain unchecked, they can trigger both hypertension and much physical illness.

In the past, we didn't think anger and guilt could trigger any physical illness besides an occasional headache or possibly an ulcer. Thus we always attributed the cause of heart disease primar-ily to the misuse of cholesterol, exercise, or cigarette smoking, and cancer to carcinogenic particles. Now due to researchers like Dr. Meyer Friedman on heart disease,[13] and Dr. Carl Simonton on cancer,[14] doctors realize that unresolved anger and guilt also play a role in triggering heart disease, cancer, and other illnesses.

Doctors now state that except in the case of trauma (physical damage from a car accident, house falling, radiation etc.) anger and guilt play a role in triggering most physical damage done to our body. The question raised by doctors now who realize that emo-tional stress is behind most physical illness is not so much "Does emotional stress have anything to do with the cause of this ill-ness?" but rather "How much does emotional stress have to do with causing this illness?" Harvard clinical psychiatrist Dr. Sil-verman, a specialist for twenty-five years in psychosomatic medicine, insists that he cannot conceive of anyone getting sick without a stress factor involved. For Silverman the most important stress predictor is unresolved negative emotions such as anger and guilt.[15]

Physical Illness: Anger, Guilt and Other Factors

But don't germs rather than feelings such as anger and guilt cause sickness? Not only germs but many other factors play a role in illness. Who can deny that genetic factors play an important role in hypertension or sickle cell anemia? Climatic factors are important considerations in asthma and rheumatoid arthritis. A bacteria such as tubercle bacilli is needed for TB, or streptococcus for strep throat. Atmospheric particles such as ragweed and pollen play an important role in allergies. Carcinogenic particles lead to cancer. A high fat diet makes one more susceptible to a coronary condition, while a high acid diet induces ulcers. Previous illnesses such as respiratory infections increase susceptibility to bronchitis or asthma.

These and other considerations such as exercise and rest play an important role in illness. No single factor, including anger and guilt, can by itself cause an illness. When doctors refer to illnesses triggered by emotional stress, they do not mean that the emotional is the only factor involved in that illness.[16]

Diet, climate, virus, bacteria and other factors are often just as necessary as is the stressful situation which triggers a fight-flight or similar physical reaction. Even such "objective" illnesses as viral or bacterial infections can be emotionally helped or stifled. Tensions and frustrations lower the immunization mechanism of the body, thus opening the door for bacteria and viruses to cause physical illness.

Doctors are discovering that with identical twins with the same genetic tendency toward a given illness, or two people with similar bacteria within them, or two people who breathe the same polluted air, one might get sick while the other will not. The one who gets sick is generally the one exposed to an emotionally stressful situation in which overwhelming feelings of anger, guilt or fear are ignored.

Studies about the common cold also show that health flourishes when there is an absence of overwhelming emotional stress. Many have tried to alter climatic, dietetic, rest or exercise conditions in a futile attempt to avoid the common cold. But the easiest way to avoid a cold is to go on a honeymoon. Studies find that the lowest incidence of colds occurs with couples on their honeymoon. You would think if anyone would catch another's germs and get sick, it would be newlyweds. But when people are feeling good about themselves and each other, they have a low level of crippling fear, anger and guilt and a high level of health.

Whether or not we agree with all the specifics of these findings, we can not reasonably deny that emotions play a major part in physical illness. The process of healing needs to take into account all factors. We can't work just with the anger that may be eating away at the tissue of a cancer patient and do nothing to combat carcinogenic pollution of the atmosphere. Neither can we afford to send asthmatics or those suffering with rheumatoid arthritis to a warmer climate without working through feelings of anger and guilt that might give them a sense of being tied down or choked. If anger and guilt are not dealt with, a doctor could do surgery and remove the peptic ulcer but find his patient a year later with stomach cancer or some other illness.

Because unresolved anger and guilt in emotional stress trigger physical illness, we could expect that people in emotionally stressful situations would get sick more often. Dr. Holmes and his colleagues confirm this hypothesis.

Emotionally Stressful Situations Trigger Physical Illness

What could cause you the most stress? Dr. Holmes categorized some forty events such as "fired at work," "sex difficulties," "personal illness" and other stressful situations in terms of life change units. Dr. Holmes found that the two situations people found most stressful were first, the death of a spouse, and second, divorce.[17]

Dr. Holmes then ranged these stressful events on a scale of impact—death of a spouse rated one hundred on the impact scale, divorce seventy-three, and minor stresses such as "minor violations of the law" rated eleven. Dr. Holmes found that persons exposed in recent months to more than three hundred stress units had a major illness rate of 80 percent in the next two years.

For example, Dr. Holmes found that ten times more widows and widowers get sick and die during the first year after the death of their husband or wife than do all others in their age group. Sickness also correlates with divorce. In the year following divorce, divorcees have an illness rate twelve times higher than that of married persons. Dr. Holmes categorized stress in terms of life-change units. Change evokes feelings. The most emotionally stressful situations will involve changes which evoke feelings of anxiety, fear, anger and guilt.

One measurement of emotional stress in a changing situation is the depth of anxiety, fear, anger and guilt. Stress in a changing situation increases the more we feel that the change is out of our control (anxiety), that there is nothing anyone can do about it (fear), that someone else could have changed the situation and didn't (anger), or that we could have changed the situation and didn't (guilt).[18]

Some situations such as divorce or the death of a spouse are potentially more emotionally stressful because of our personal investment. The more we have personally invested, the deeper we can experience all emotions including anxiety, fear, anger and guilt. But not all who experience deep emotional stress, such as a divorce or loss of a spouse, get sick. When we begin to resolve emotional stress by identifying and working through anxiety, fear, anger and guilt, we reduce the chances of becoming physically ill through fight-flight or other physical responses.

To better understand how unresolved emotional stress can trigger illness, the next section will confine itself to two specific illnesses: cancer and heart disease. More and more doctors question whether without an emotionally stressful situation such a factor as carcinogenic pollution could induce cancer, or whether such a factor as high fat diet or lack or exercise alone could induce a heart attack. Three such questioning doctors are Drs. Meyer Friedman and Ray Rosenman who usually find emotional stress an important factor in triggering heart disease, and Dr. Carl Simonton in triggering cancer.

Heart Disease: Triggered by Guilt and Anger in Emotionally Stressful Situations

More Americans die of heart disease than any other single cause. In 1960–61 Drs. Meyer Friedman and Ray Rosenman began a study with 3,500 healthy men to try and classify the causes of heart attacks.[19]

After ten years, 250 of the 3,500 healthy men have suffered heart attacks. In looking back over the records of these heart patients, the doctors found that neither factors like diet nor exercise patterns gave them clues in predicting who might suffer a heart attack. But what did give them clues was Type A Behavior. In the absence of Type A Behavior, coronary heart disease almost never occurs before the age of seventy. With Type A Behavior, coronary heart disease can easily erupt in one's thirties or forties.[20]

Since the Type A Behavior personality hurries to do more and more in less and less time, doctors refer to a coronary heart disease as "hurry sickness." Whether writing, eating, or sleeping, these people put themselves under continual time pressure. I find this behavior in myself when I begin feeling guilty right now that it has taken me two days to write four pages, so I try to squash the next five pages into a day. I always feel as though I'm falling behind and not meeting the deadlines of this writing, even though the deadlines are of my unreasonable making.

When Type A people like myself finally take a lunch break, we tend to walk fast, check our watch two or three times on the way, cross corners against red lights, and cut in front of old folks only to wait in line. As we edge our way ahead in the lunch line, we keep staring ahead to see who is taking so long to pick out his salad. Many of us can't stand the waiting and so go down the block to see if one of the other eating places couldn't serve us faster.

When we finally do sit down to eat, if we are having a 100 percent Type A day, we find ourselves trying to shift the conversation to our own interest, or if that doesn't work, we try to finish another's sentences or hurry him along by saying "yes." After having quickly fed our aggressive competitiveness, drive to achieve, and general hostility, we'll feel a great success at having finished our lunch so efficiently so that we can get back to work. When we get back to work, we can hardly wait for work to finish. Type A people enjoy finishing things but don't take pleasure in doing them.

Beneath Type A Behavior usually fester four intense feelings: anxiety, fear, anger and guilt. Unless worked through, the intensity of these feelings can drive us to Type A Behavior. As the intensity of the core feelings deepens, the greater probability of such behavior as running yellow lights or gulping down food. Intense anxiety about things getting out of hand, or fear that everything depends on us, could keep us gulping down food. Or an intense anger that someone could have changed the situation and didn't, or a guilt that I could have changed the situation and didn't, could keep us running yellow lights as our Type A Behavior makes up for lost time.

A Type A personality has its opposite, the healthy Type B personality. The Type A personality is an angry man in a minute by minute struggle against time, other people or both.[21] The Type B personality has little or no free floating anger and takes plenty of time to enjoy other people.[22] Unlike Type A, a Type B person can work without getting angry, and relax without feeling guilty. Those with Type A Behavior are prone to heart attacks, but those with Type B seldom suffer a heart attack.

Since one with Type A Behavior lives in constant emotional stress, we would expect the physical illness rate to be much higher than with Type B Behavior. In fact, ninety percent of patients under sixty years of age with heart attacks exemplify Type A Behavior. With only a few rare exceptions, Type B individuals appear to be immune to the early advent of coronary heart disease no matter how much cholesterol and fat their diet contains, how many cigarettes they smoke, what they weigh or whether one or both of their parents suffered coronary heart disease. As in other illnesses, evidence is leading doctors to look at not just diet or exercise, but at emotional stress as an important factor.[23]

Heart Disease: Healing and Prevention
by Treating Anger and Guilt

Since emotional stress frequently plays an important role in triggering heart disease, Drs. Friedman and Rosenman found that by treating anger and guilt they can take measures to speed up the healing process or even prevent a heart attack. Thus their treatment includes counteracting anger as you "seek out and assess the intensity of your free-floating hostilities."[24] They also recommend taking measures against guilt. They ask you "to examine critically your ethical and moral principles. How honest have I been in my life, how often and under what circumstances have I cheated, lied, and borne false witness against my neighbor?"[25]

In treating anger and guilt, Drs. Friedman and Rosenman recognize the importance of healing memories. They recommend using your reasoning powers to check your tendency to see every situation as designed to annoy you. The "crucial" element in removing emotional stress and Type A Behavior is a "stock of fulfilling memories" instead of annoying memories.[26] "Fulfilling memories" are your memories of the past that yield pleasure, and are much like healed memories of your past that yield pleasure when you consider them as gift.

Heart Disease: Triggered by Fight-Flight

As with other diseases, emotional stress is not the only factor. Drs. Friedman and Rosenman also work with other factors such as exercise, weight, and low cholesterol diets. They find that once a person has Type A Behavior, then these other factors become important. For example, high cholesterol, though not particularly dangerous for a Type B personality, can set off a heart attack in someone with a Type A personality; to cause artery damage cholesterol needs to combine with other elements of the fight-flight response such as the hormones epinephrine and norepinephrine constantly triggered by Type A Behavior.[27]

In saying that emotional stress is at least as important as diet, smoking, physical activity, and heredity in inciting heart disease, Drs. Friedman and Rosenman have departed from traditional ways of viewing heart illness, such as the view taken by the American Heart Association. But not only is the American Heart Association taking a second look. So too are many doctors such as Dr. Henry Russek, research professor of cardiovascular disease, who confirms Dr. Friedman's conclusions on Type A Behavior.

After twenty years of research Dr. Henry Russek found that at the time of a heart attack, ninety-one out of one hundred patients suffered stress from either holding down two or more jobs, working more than sixty hours per week, or experiencing unusual insecurity, discontent or frustration with employment. Though ninety-one out of one hundred with heart attacks experienced these stresses, only twenty out of one hundred of the general population experienced the same. Though Russek found major differences in the amount of stress experienced by heart patients compared to the general population, he found little difference in factors such as exercise, diet, and cigarette smoking.[28]

Dr. Russek also studied the physical damage incurred when the fight-flight mechanism designed for short-term emergency needs became a chronic on-going response. Dr. Russek like Dr. Friedman found high cholesterol, hypertension, diabetes, lack of exercise and other factors "exert their influence only secondarily" by exaggerating certain components of fight-flight.[29]

According to Drs. Russek and Friedman, any treatment of heart disease which simply treats factors such as diet, exercise or cigarette smoking to the exclusion of emotional stress remains an incomplete treatment. Many heart attack victims don't even have problems with such factors, but almost all heart patients have problems dealing with anger and guilt in stressful situations.

Both the study of Dr. Russek and the findings of Drs. Friedman and Rosenman emphasize that we can avoid heart attacks and treat the ones we have by dealing with anger and guilt. Through healing memories we work through anger and guilt and lessen the need for responding to emotional stress with Type A Behavior that sets off the flight-fight response in our bodies.

Cancer: Triggered by Anger and Guilt in Emotionally Stressful Situations

What Drs. Friedman and Rosenman find about the importance of dealing with anger and guilt for heart patients, Dr. Carl Simonton and Stephanie Matthew-Simonton find equally important for cancer patients. Dr. Carl Simonton, an oncologist in Fort Worth, and his wife Stephanie find cancer often develops six to eighteen months after an emotionally stressful situation such as divorce, retirement or death of a spouse.[30] Just as Type A Behavior characterizes a heart patient, Dr. Simonton finds four traits typical of one prone to cancer.

The first trait, "a great tendency to hold resentment and a marked inability to forgive," demarcates anger or an inability to forgive others. The second and third traits, "a tendency toward self-pity" and "a very poor self-image," deal with guilt's inability to forgive ourselves. If we fail to forgive others or ourself, we can't trust and so develop the fourth trait, "a poor ability to develop and maintain a meaningful long-term relationship."[31]

These four traits indicate that one prone to cancer has a tendency to prolong feelings of anger and guilt. Thus a situation that another might work through can easily become for the cancer-prone patient an emotionally stressful situation that sets off the fight-flight and other body reactions that can trigger cancer.

These four traits and the fight-flight syndrome manifested themselves in one of the Simontons' patients who developed breast cancer shortly after her children graduated from school and left home to be on their own. The father reacted to that emotionally stressful situation by burying himself in his work. The mother had no place to turn. Not receiving affection from others (anger), she found herself overcome with feelings of worthlessness (guilt). These feelings gradually began to eat away at her until finally her body picked up the signals and began to eat away at itself.

Cancer: Healing and Prevention by Treating Anger and Guilt

In treating patients such as this mother with breast cancer, Dr. Simonton combines conventional treatment such as chemotherapy or radiation therapy with psychotherapy. The Simontons insist on psychotherapy in order to deal with the anger and guilt involved in the emotionally stressful situation. From the very beginning even through the completion of psychotherapy, the Simontons use many of the steps we find helpful in healing of memories.

They begin their psychotherapy by helping the patient to go back and get in touch with any emotionally stressful hurt that may have occurred six to eighteen months before the cancer. Their cancer patients deal with anger and guilt in two ways. First, they are encouraged to change what they can change in the uncovered stressful situation. Second, they get a different perspective on those things they can't change.

For example, the mother with cancer would confront anger and guilt by changing whatever she could. Perhaps she feels angry at her workaholic husband for ignoring her needs, and guilty as homemaker for ignoring his needs. In psychotherapy the wife could discuss with her husband some of his workaholic patterns and ways in which he could cut down his work load. The husband might also tell his wife ways that she could make their home more inviting.

Besides changing what they can, the cancer patients can work through anger and guilt by getting a different perspective on emotionally stressful situations that they can't change. Perhaps the mother feels angry because after her last child left home, her rebellious children no longer communicate with her. The Simontons insist that even though the children might never again communicate with the mother, the mother can still remove the emotional part of the stress by responding differently with her anger. In therapy the Simontons help patients find creative outlets for their anger and guilt. For example, the mother feeling lonely and worthless since her last child left, could give those feelings a creative outlet by opening her home to a foster child or by doing volunteer work with children. Anger and guilt usually stop damaging the body when they are first recognized and then given a creative outlet.

When working through anger and guilt by changing what can be changed and viewing from a different perspective what can't be changed, the Simontons use the dynamics involved in healing a memory. According to the Simontons, the patients who do well are frequently the ones who, by working through anger and guilt, find "routes to combat events that caused life to lose meaning."[32] By healing memories as they work through anger and guilt, the Simontons' patients can frequently restore the normal process in their body for disposing of cancer cells.

Cancer: Triggered by Fight-Flight

Dr. Robert Good claims that cancer cells develop and are disposed of daily in our body. In a movie sponsored by the American Cancer Society we can watch this daily battle as white blood cells attack and destroy colonies of cancer cells on living tissue.[33] What slows down this process and allows cancer cells to dominate? Doctors claim that emotional stress which triggers the fight-flight response plays a key factor. Dr. George Solomon concludes that the production of "stress" hormones can slow down the formation of antibodies that fight cancer cells.[34] Dr. Carl Simonton focuses on the adrenalin stress hormone.

> When confronted with stress, an adrenalin response prepares an individual for a physical discharge; a fight or flight reaction. When the response is not neutralized through physical activity or emotional expression, tissue destruction results.[35]

Thus stress hormones triggered in emotionally tense situations play an important part in offsetting the body's normal process of disposing of cancer cells.

Many of Simontons' findings regarding the interrelationship of emotional stress and malignancy are substantiated by others including Dr. William Greene researching the question for fifteen years at the University of Rochester Medical Center, Dr. David Kissen of Scotland studying five hundred lung cancer patients, the doctors on the task force of health research of the American Psychological Association, and two hundred articles in medical literature.[36]

We Help Create Most Physical Illness

The Simontons insist that in illnesses ranging from cancer to the flu and upset stomach, we are not just victims of some outside agent acting on our bodies. Rather our mind and emotions and body act together and cannot be separated. They insist that when we get sick, we ask ourselves either why do we need this illness or what purpose does it serve. In taking responsibility for creating illness, we admit that we have emotional and physical participation in our disease such as is indicated in the fight-flight response where emotional stress can trigger everything from an upset stomach to cancer.[37]

In reading through the Simontons' study, I liked everything they said except that we help create physical illness whether it be an upset stomach or cancer. At first, that statement made me feel guilty. I felt that because I had a lot of unhealthy anger and guilt creating my upset stomachs, I must be bad.

The main drawback in the Simontons' treatment is that a patient is hesitant, just as I was, to take responsibility for his illness. Before they will accept a cancer patient, the patient must take responsibility for creating the illness.[38] The Simontons say that a patient doesn't like to admit responsibility because he feels as though someone is accusing him: "You have cancer; therefore, you must be bad."

The Simontons insist that cancer and other diseases don't point an accusing finger at the patient any more than they point the finger at all of us. When someone is sick, it usually means that he and others have failed to care for him, especially in emotionally stressful situations. Our unresolved emotional stress can trigger the body processes that can create the flu to avoid an exam, a cold to avoid a situation at work, a heart attack to help us catch up with ourselves, or even cancer to put an end to life. All of us have emotional needs, and when we don't take care of ourselves and of each other, we create the conditions for cancer and other illnesses to manifest themselves. But even knowing that I wasn't solely responsible for my upset stomach didn't seem to remove the feeling that I must be bad.

I could read the Simontons and in theory agree that I and others did create most of our illness. For example, I could see how through psychotherapy the Simontons had helped a mother discover what the body already knew: the reason she needed to create her particular illness. The mother saw how her feelings of worthlessness and loss of affection had eaten away at her until even her body started eating away at her. She could see more clearly how her body could have developed cancer either to get her workaholic husband to give her affectionate care, or even to put an end to what seemed a lonely and worthless existence. Cancer eats away at life itself and frequently grows out of a time that was so emotionally stressful that we question the value of our life.[39]

Theoretically I could see how not only the mother's but my own body had sometimes chosen to create physical illness rather than work through the anger and guilt in emotionally stressful situations. But even though I knew the statement that we do help create most physical illness to be true, it didn't make it any less repulsive to accept its truth.

Whether in the case of heart disease, cancer or other illnesses, medicine is discovering the need to deal with anger and guilt in emotional stress to restore physical health. This confirms both the tradition of the Church concerning the relationship of forgiveness to physical healing, as well as our discoveries regarding healing of memories with people like Agnes and her legal blindness. The following section deals with my struggle to accept in practice that I did indeed help create physical illness, and that I too could begin to heal most of my illness by working through anger and guilt by healing memories.[40] The key in this struggle was finding that just because I had a lot of unhealthy anger and guilt creating my physical illness, that didn't make me bad, just human and capable of being loved.

III

MY LIFE:

PHYSICAL HEALING THROUGH HEALING A MEMORY

It took me four years of putting up with an upset stomach every two or three weeks before I would admit that healing of memories could physically heal me. For four years the findings of men like Dr. Carl Simonton, that I create my own illness and therefore needed to deal with my unhealthy anger and guilt, seemed ridiculous to me. Instead of admitting that I created my own illness, I always blamed something else.

Since the upset stomachs started when I moved to South America, I blamed them on the diet or change in weather. When in Bolivia I blamed them on the strong red peppers called *aji*. The diet was just too strong. Then when I moved to Chile and started to eat a ton of beans and rice, I figured the diet was too bland. When I wasn't on the diet kick, I blamed the weather. After all, when I left the United States it was summer and when I arrived in Bolivia it was winter. It was the weather that threw off my body.

But then when I moved back to the United States, my stomach upsets still continued for three more years, so I got better at making excuses. Living in St. Louis, I had a bullet-proof excuse. I lived by a chemical plant and the polluted air smelled so foul that I figured it would explode if I lit a match on my front steps. Of course, I was swallowing all that pollution and that was giving me an upset stomach. When the wind shifted and the pollution left, I blamed something else. If I visited the hospital, then hospital germs got blamed. Even my dad's side of the family got blamed. Since they all have stomach problems, I must have inherited an upset stomach. Finally, I could always blame the stomach upsets on not getting enough rest, or if I was getting enough rest, I blamed them on not getting enough exercise. Since my many excuses convinced me that I didn't create the sickness, I felt I would be a victim to stomach upsets the rest of my life.

Three years ago I saw in the space of a few moments how I had deceived myself with my excuses. It was during the second day of an eight day retreat when I was thanking God for the health I was enjoying at that retreat day. While giving thanks, it occurred to me that in those four years I had never been sick while making my yearly eight day retreat, and almost as quickly it occurred to me that I had never been sick during those four years when on vacation. In fact, during those years stomach upsets came only on days when first of all, I found myself with sixteen hundred and twelve things to do, and, secondly, when I had to spend a good deal of time that day waiting. Many days I could finish writing a chapter of a book, make pecan pies for dinner, answer fifteen pink phone messages, and still not get an upset stomach. But if I had to wait for someone to return the magazine article I needed to read before I could write a chapter, if the pecan pies didn't get done on time, or if I got a busy signal every time I made a phone call, watch out!

Having to wait upset me because it upset my worth. On days when I decided my worth came from what I produced, I survived with perfect health if I produced many things. But as soon as waiting upset my ability to produce, my self-worth became upset. Feeling angry about the person who made me wait, and guilty that I hadn't produced, my stomach would physically "pick up" how upset I was. On the other hand, when during my retreat or on a vacation I deeply experienced that my worth didn't depend on what I produced but on just *being*, I didn't get stomach upsets. I knew the answer was to find my worth in being loved by Jesus, not in doing.

During the rest of the retreat, I gave Jesus many memories when I felt worthless because I failed in doing something. So, for example, I gave the time when I felt worthless when a "D" appeared on my report card in junior year of high school. I gave the Lord all the anger rising from that situation—after all wasn't it the teacher's fault? Twenty-eight other students received a "D" that time too.

Besides working through anger as I saw the teacher's failures, I also worked through guilt as I saw my own failures. After all, I sat through all those confusing trigonometry classes without asking questions and I allowed that "D" to cripple me. I then let the Lord also tell me how that whole situation gifted me. For example, I suspect that getting a "D" and at times feeling worthless has something to do with my ability to empathize with less gifted students who perhaps feel inferior to others because they aren't as smart. Besides the "D" on my report card, I gave Jesus all the times I felt worthless because I failed in doing something. I gave Jesus the anger and guilt I felt and let him show me the gifts that came from it. I felt by the end of the retreat that I would be gifted whether I did things well or not. In the future, my worth would depend much less on what I did and much more on just being.

During the past three years since making that retreat, I have tried to get my worth not from doing sixteen hundred and twelve things, but from being loved by God. During those years, I have had an upset stomach only once or twice. I have spent part of those past three years in St. Louis and in foreign countries, and I have encountered many of the same factors as before (climate, diet, pollution, hospital germs), but with no detrimental effect. My experience confirms what Carl Simonton and many doctors find. Perhaps the most important factor in creating illness is a stressful situation filled with unhealthy anger and guilt.

First Misconception: I Am Responsible
for My Illness; Therefore I Am Bad

Why did it take me four years to say I was responsible for my illness? What made me blame a bland diet, a Bolivian winter, a chemical plant's pollution, a hospital's germs, or my dad's side of the family rather than myself? I should have known better. I had prayed with many so that they could change their life style and be healed of asthma, ulcers, or arthritis. I saw how those prayers helped many change their life style and become physically healed. I even gave workshops on the connection between emotions and illness. Yet I kept denying that a simple upset stomach of mine could have anything to do with what I saw in others and talked about everyday. The main reason I didn't want to take responsibility for my illness was because I felt I must be bad, because my physical illness must mean I had more unhealthy anger and guilt than other people who were physically well.

Looking at my unhealthy anger and guilt seemed less threatening after I joined a prayer community and found myself loved regardless of what I did. After dinner our community would have someone share for two or three hours his life story. In listening to these stories, I found two things. First, I found that almost everyone has unhealthy anger and guilt. Sometimes these manifested themselves in physical illness such as my upset stomach. Other times these manifested themselves in a father's irrational fear of being alone, in a daughter's compulsiveness to keep everything overly tidy and clean, or in a wife's daily spending spree that topped the defense budget. Second, I found that as people shared their brokenness, I felt greater love for them. Discovering these two things helped me face and share with them my own brokenness. When I finished sharing my life story and the community gathered around to pray with me, I felt what sinners felt with Jesus: sin and mistakes did not make me bad, but only very human and very capable of being loved (Lk. 7:50).

Because my community loved me in the midst of my mistakes, I found it easy during my eight day retreat to experience that Christ also loves me much in my brokenness. Thus with Christ I could face in a matter of moments what I had put off facing for years— just how my unhealthy anger and guilt were triggering my upset stomach. Now when I get sick, I try and get in touch with unhealthy anger and guilt knowing that these do not make me bad, but only very human and capable of being loved much.

Second Misconception: God Is Responsible
So I "Offer Up" My Illness

For four years I also looked at my upset stomach as something I could "offer up." I did not take responsibility for my upset stomach because, after all, wasn't it God's will? I could certainly "offer up" a few days of discomfort, especially after all the discomfort Christ went through in dying for me. So I prayed "his will be done" and thought during those four years that his will must be for me to keep gritting my teeth and "offering up" my upset stomach.

God Isn't Responsible for Illness, Only Health

I don't know how much I actually believed that God was responsible for my illness and that he willed me to be sick. If I really believed God was responsible, then theoretically I shouldn't have sought out doctors or used medicine to try and make myself well. One of the missions of Jesus (Ieschouah) which in Hebrew means "salvation" or "healing of Yahweh" was to correct my concept and the Old Testament concept that Yahweh wills sickness, and instead to proclaim that Yahweh wills healing, not sickness. The long tradition of Christian hospitals and even religious orders set up to combat illness testifies to the scriptural belief that God doesn't will sickness, but only health. Sickness like injustice is evil. God doesn't send sickness any more than he sends injustice. When Jesus tells me to do the same things that he does (Jn. 14:12), Jesus is telling me to be a healer like him and to wage war on sickness. When I passively "offered up" my upset stomach, I was not doing God's will or being a healer like Christ.

My Illness Was Not Redemptive Or To Be "Offered Up"

The problem with "offering it up" is that, as far as we know, Jesus never told anyone who came to him for physical healing to "offer it up." "Offering up" bodily illness became stressed only after the third century when Christians no longer faced martyrdom, and wanted a new way of "offering up" their bodies. But even though Jesus and his early followers didn't stress "offering up" physical illness, they did stress redemptive suffering.

But redemptive suffering meant not enduring illness but enduring all the suffering that came from living as Jesus did. But my upset stomach and most people's illnesses I called redemptive were not, because these kept us from living like Jesus did. For example, when I suffered my upset stomach, because I did sixteen hundred things and proved my worth by what I did, my suffering was not redemptive because I wasn't living like Christ and getting my worth from being loved by the Father.

As I got over my upset stomach, I found myself living more like Christ. For example, in needing to get less of my worth from producing, I found myself drawn to spend time with the unwanted.

Thus I invited to dinner an alcoholic man who for sixteen years hadn't set foot in another's home. Also in counseling and spiritual direction, I found myself more at home with workaholics that others had given up on. In being with an unwanted alcoholic or workaholic who might never change, I felt some of the suffering that made Christ sad even to the point of wanting to die (Mk. 14:35). At times when I wanted so much for my new friends, yet felt they wanted so little, I felt a little of the sadness of Jesus in the garden, or how Jesus felt when he wanted me to have a new life style, and for four years I said to him, "No, wait, I would rather have an upset stomach."

Now, not only waiting with friends who might never change, but even waiting for a magazine to return, puts me in touch with not only how Jesus waits but also how people wait. Now when I wait, I still get angry. But once I recognize the anger, it no longer gives me an upset stomach but rather it helps me feel how my boarding house friend feels as he waits for an invitation, or how the hospital patients I visit feel as they wait weeks to get well. In health, not sickness, I find myself redemptively suffering as I discover experiences that before turned me in on myself with an upset stomach now open me to how God and others feel.

Usually I Am Responsible for My Illness and It Is Not Redemptive

After working through these two misconceptions, I no longer thought that God caused my "redemptive" illness, nor did I think I was bad for triggering my upset stomach. In accepting these two things, I was saying that my illness wasn't much different than anyone else's. Having treated healing of memories in the usual case where I am responsible and the illness is not redemptive, we will now treat healing of memories in unusual cases either where I am not responsible for my illness or where my illness brings redemptive suffering.

Sometimes I Am Not Responsible for My Illness

Now in trying to accept responsibility for my illness, I ask Dr. Simonton's question, "Why do I need this illness?" If no answer comes, it could either be because I am overlooking something, or because I am not responsible for my illness. In the Gospel story of the blindman, for instance, Jesus indicated that the blind man was not responsible for his illness.

> As he went along, Jesus saw a man who had been blind from birth. His disciples asked him, "Rabbi, who sinned, this man or his parents for him to be born blind?" "Neither he nor his parents sinned," Jesus replied (Jn. 9:1–3).

Though I may not be responsible for blindness caused by physical trauma in the womb or by physical trauma when some foreign object injures my eye, I can be responsible for blindness caused by hypertension. Whether or not I am responsible for my blindness, healing of memories can bring healing to even permanently damaged areas as happened with the blindness of Agnes.

Some Illness Brings Redemptive Suffering To Be "Offered Up"

While my upset stomach and most illness I called redemptive suffering was not redemptive but rather a settling for mediocrity in prayer and action, I know some whose illness brings redemptive suffering because they use it to pray and act like Christ. One such person is my friend Larry whose blindness has not crippled him but rather made him like Jesus.

Many people come to Larry from all over the country for spiritual direction. When I was trying to work through getting less of my worth from doing and more from just being loved by the Father, I traveled five hundred miles so he could give me a retreat. Larry's blindness attunes him to help me walk blindly—to not be so busy running that I don't listen for what step the Lord might ask me to take next.

Larry's blindness has taught him to see with his heart. Sometimes he will tell me things I wasn't immediately aware of, such as "You're depressed" or "You're nervous." By listening to my lingering footsteps or my shifting back and forth in the chair, Larry picks up things my eyes miss. Larry also claims I am the only man who can sit on a curb while dangling his feet. I have not figured out yet how he can tell I'm so short; I thought my high-pitched laugh could fool him.

What I and others find in Larry is an ability to reach the poor, the lonely, and those who feel abandoned, because his blindness puts him in touch with what it is to feel powerless. When I celebrate the Eucharist with Larry, I have a sense of offering it with a man who long ago has given everything to Christ. When I watch him hold up the chalice, I have a sense of how much he counts on others, especially on God, for his existence. Larry suffers his blindness redemptively because he uses it to pray and act like Christ: as one totally dependent on the Father, yet reaching out to the poor and the lonely because he knows what powerlessness is.

When the messengers of John the Baptist ask Jesus who he is, he defines himself as a healer who lets the blind see, the lame walk and the deaf hear (Mt. 11:4). John and others also define Jesus as the light (Jn. 9:29), the way (Jn. 14:6), and the word (Jn. 1:1). He heals blindness so people can see his light, the lame so they can walk his way, and the deaf so they can hear his word. In healing us of blindness, lameness, and deafness, he is saying that he wants to heal us of anything that keeps us from knowing him intimately.

After Agnes through prayer received her sight, she experienced God and others in a new way. During the previous sixty-five years she had always prayed, but she found prayer to be a job, like going to work. She also found changes in the way she could relate to others. When she lost her sight, she had to retire after thirty-eight years of nursing. Now she finds herself once again with new power to heal as she visits the elderly and shut-ins or occasionally helps us with a workshop. Since the healing of her sight, she has found that for the first time she can relate with God as a lover.

I have never prayed with Larry for sight as I did with Agnes. Nor have I felt drawn to pray with him. Perhaps if I did, the Lord would heal Larry just as he did Agnes. On the other hand, since Larry's illness is redemptive now, God may continue to work through his blindness. It may be that Larry is to continue to get to know others and God intimately through his blindness just as Agnes has discovered others and God more intimately through her healing. They both sing ''Amazing Grace'' and give thanks for ''I was blind and now I see.''

How To Pray

Whether illness is redemptive or not, whether I am responsible or not, how do I pray with healing of memories to fight physical illness? Some people get a "word of knowledge" where the Lord tells them just how to pray and exactly what's going to happen. I seldom get a word of knowledge.

But when I do ask the Lord for guidance about how I should pray, whether it be for my upset stomach or for the blindness of Agnes, I find that he usually tells me to do two things. First, he tells me to pray for the physical healing, and, second, to pray that the illness which lingers becomes as redemptive as possible. The only exceptions seem to be when I strongly feel the Lord is calling a person home through death, or when I feel the Lord is calling a person to redemptive suffering as in the case of Larry. But I find that even with people like Larry, the Lord frequently wants to heal them physically.

In praying for physical healing and in praying that the illness will become more redemptive until that physical healing arrives, I am following the two suggestions St. Ignatius gives for fighting desolation. Ignatius describes desolation as a feeling of being cut off from God and others. Then I feel "slothful, tepid, sad, and separated."[41] Most physical illness brings desolation, some more than others. Yet, I expect that Larry with his blindness experiences less desolation than I did with my upset stomach.

The more sickness turns me in on myself and leaves me feeling desolate, the more it is *not* to be offered up but rather fought against. I fight against sickness with the same zeal that I fight against anything that closes me to God or others such as temptation or desolation. The following are the two suggestions that Ignatius found helpful for fighting desolation and that I find helpful in fighting physical illness with healing of memories.

First, St. Ignatius says that when the first sign of desolation strikes, we intensify our activity against desolation. "We can insist upon more prayer, upon meditation, and on much examination of ourself."[42] It helps during times of illness which leave me feeling desolate to examine my life style to see what changes I ought to make and intensify my prayer for physical healing.

Second, Ignatius suggests that while I struggle with desolation, I also try to find the gifts present even during the desolation. Ignatius suggests several gifts from desolation such as the gift of not taking happiness for granted, the gift of showing me how dependent I am on God, or the gift of showing me how I can grow by changing something in my life style. Frequently while I follow the first suggestion of Ignatius and intensify my prayer for physical healing, I also follow his second suggestion and pray that until I am physically healed I can grow more and more from my illness just as Larry grows from his.

What Do I Expect When I Pray?

Although before I start praying I don't know everything that will happen, I do know that one thing will happen. I know that Christ will heal in his most loving way. Christ heals in his most loving way, first, by healing the physical illness, and, second, by beginning to remove blocks that keep me from reaching out to God and others. Though the first does not always happen, the second always does. Sometimes it takes just one prayer, but frequently it takes continuous prayer.

First, Christ heals in his most loving way when he heals physically, as in the case of Agnes' blindness or my upset stomach. During prayers for healing of memories, people are healed of many physical illnesses ranging from acute cases of leukemia and hypoglycemia, to common colds and stomach upsets. Sometimes in workshops when I am limited for time, I do not pray a specific prayer for physical healing, but just pray for healing of memories and expect the Lord to also heal physically. The power of healing in such prayer can either speed up the natural process, as in the case of my upset stomach, or heal where permanent damage seemed to be involved, as with the degenerated retina of Agnes.

Second, Christ heals in his most loving way when through prayer he removes blocks that keep one from reaching out to God and others. Whether physical healing happens or not, Christ's love always shows itself in this way when I pray with the sick. Such was the case of a sixty-eight-year-old heart patient even though he died a week after I prayed with him. After the prayer Alex found himself no longer running away from a depressing world but looking forward to the next life. If physical illness continues after healing memories, I would expect the illness to become more and more redemptive, as in the case of Larry's blindness.

God Heals in His Most Loving Way
Through Soaking Prayer

Sometimes God's love manifests itself clearly in these two ways with just one prayer. At other times, the improvement comes gradually and requires more than just one prayer, as with Agnes and her sight which took three days of prayer. Such continuous prayer is called "soaking prayer."[43] Usually the more I soak memories with prayer, the more two things happen: first, more and more physical healing manifests itself, and, second, the physical healing becomes less temporary and more permanent.

First, as in the case of Agnes' blindness, soaking memories in prayer brings increased physical healing. Just as I saw gradual improvement in her sight as Agnes healed painful memories over a period of three days, so I have seen gradual improvement in many illnesses. For example, I recall how after healing of memory prayer Thomas at first found himself without his usual gnawing cancerous pains. Several weeks later after continued prayer, he discovered that the cancer stopped spreading. Still later he discovered that the cancer had disappeared. Though the doctors had only given Thomas a few months to live, he continues to live in good health two years later. As memories soak in Christ's love, the physical healing usually deepens.

Second, in prayerfully soaking painful memories the physical healing becomes less temporary and more permanent. Many people prayed for my upset stomach, but the healing only lasted a few weeks or at most for a month. Finally, when I started healing memories on an everyday basis, the healing became permanent. When I combine healing of memories with the use of doctors, medicine, diet, exercise, and change in life style, the healing usually becomes permanent because I am treating the whole person. Soaking prayer heals permanently by getting at stressful roots provoking the illness.

Soaking prayer is frequently the opposite of "claim your healing." I have heard many people say that after you have prayed with someone about their broken leg, they should immediately "claim their healing" by walking on it, regardless of how their leg feels. Others say that in healing memories you should "claim your healing" and mean they will pray once about the hurt caused by your father abandoning you and then you can forget about it and get back to normal.

Sometimes the Lord does heal a leg or a memory with just one prayer. Sometimes the person praying does have a gift of knowing if the healing has happened and can ask you to "claim your healing." But frequently "claiming your healing" leaves people with compound broken legs or with a broken heart. In healing something physically serious like cancer, we use long-term X-ray treatment. In healing a deep hurt like the loss of a loved one we may take many days to mourn. So, too, when praying with a physical illness like cancer or when praying with difficult memories, it may take not just one prayer but soaking prayer.

The only healing I claim is what the Lord has done. Usually the person with the illness is the best judge of that. When I am praying with Agnes about her sight, she and not I can best judge the extent of healing. Rather than to falsely claim healing immediately and stop praying, it is wiser for Agnes to claim only what the Lord had done and pray for Christ's healing to continue his way at his pace. Some feel that when Agnes doesn't claim an immediate healing she lacks faith. But it may take more faith to keep praying and trusting that the Lord's pace and way are better than the immediate healing she desires. By "claiming healing" that hasn't occurred, Agnes could short-circuit what the Lord wants to give through soaking prayer, such as an experience of being unconditionally loved by people who continue to pray with her and a deep experience of forgiveness through healing memories.

By Agnes continuing for three days to heal memories, she follows the wisdom of Christian tradition. Both the early Church and modern teaching insist on repeating the dynamics behind healing a memory to initiate physical healing. As mentioned earlier, the rite of the sick contains many of the dynamics for healing a memory. In the early Church this rite was usually not just celebrated once but rather repeated on seven successive days.[44] The repetition of soaking prayer is also present in the new rite which recommends that the rite be repeated whether a person gets better or worse.

Whether with my upset stomach or with Agnes' blindness, the prayer of healing of memories does what medical science and Christian tradition say it should do. Frequently it restores physical health. Always it opens me to God and others. As medical science discovers more and more how I am responsible for my illness and recovery, the Lord has given me a way of being co-responsible with him for regaining my wholeness. Through healing of memories, I work through anger and guilt with him to bring health of mind and body.

Part Three:
Predispositions for Five Stages
of Dying and Forgiveness

As was noted in the last chapter, Dr. Kubler-Ross and her associates found two dispositions in patients who move through the five stages. Patients move with greater ease through the stages of dying when first, they are loved enough by a significant person to accept themselves, and second, when they share their feelings with this person. The dying person wants someone to hold his hand and his heart down the dark, lonely road to death.

To be loved enough by a significant person so that all feelings can be shared is necessary before and after death. Dr. Kubler-Ross found that those who have "died" and been resuscitated often speak of meeting a Being of Light who loves them so totally that together they can review all their painful memories and heal them. After this love experience they even return to life with no fear of dying again. Whether this "life after life" experience is a trick of the mind or a real journey to meet Christ, it heals man's greatest fear—dying.

Whether facing the painful memory of death, the future review of life to heal life's painful memories with the Being of Light, or the present review of a painful memory with Christ to forgive and heal it, we can succeed only if we experience two predispositions. First, I must trust some significant person loves me enough so that I can accept myself. Chapter 5 reveals God as that lover. Chapter 6 deals with the second predisposition—sharing my feelings with God.

5

FIRST PREDISPOSITION:
GOD LOVES ME UNCONDITIONALLY

Have you ever wondered what happens after the acceptance stage of death? What is it like after the doctor says, "He is dead"? Dr. Raymond Moody, like Dr. Kubler-Ross, interviewed more than 100 subjects who have experienced "clinical death" and have been resuscitated.[1] Both find that those who have "died" and returned to life have had a similar "life after life" experience despite different cultural and religious backgrounds.[2]

During a "life after life" experience, a dying man may hear his doctor pronounce him dead while feeling himself sucked rapidly through a long, dark tunnel. He then finds himself outside his own physical body looking down on the doctors still trying to resuscitate him. This spiritual body is very different—like a floating amorphous cloud that communicates by thought. Relatives and friends who have already died come to meet him and bring him to a "Being of Light" who accepts and loves him more than he has ever experienced. Like a magnet drawn to iron, he is drawn to the personal compassion and acceptance of this dazzling Being of Light.

Shortly after appearing the Being of Light asks the question, "What have you done with your life to show me?" The question isn't accusing or threatening but pervaded with a deep total love and acceptance no matter what the answer. The Being answers the question by presenting a panoramic review like a film of the individual's whole life to provoke reflection. The Being seems to know all and is displaying the review of life so that the deceased can understand two things: how he loved others and how he learned through his experience and mistakes. Only when a person learns how he has loved, and how he can deepen his love, does the Being ask him if he would like to return or stay. Although many would like to stay, some elect to return to fulfill a mission such as raising their young children. One man felt he returned to show others the total acceptance that the Being of Light radiated to him.

Those returning from "death" to life speak of the Being of Light in the way that Scripture speaks of God. Jesus calls himself the light of the world (Jn. 8:12) and compares his Father with the sun's light, calling us to love even our enemies:

> But I say to you, love your enemies and pray for those who persecute you, so you may be sons of your Father who is in heaven; for he makes his sun rise on the evil and on the good, and sends rain on the just and on the unjust (Mt. 5:44–45).

Even more than in Matthew's Gospel, the first chapter of John's Gospel links up light, life, truth, love, and eternity as if he sees an eternal light endowing men with life, truth and love.

When John says that God is love, he says that God is agape itself. God doesn't love us as a man loves a woman (*eros*), nor as a friend loves a friend (*philia*), nor even as a mother loves a child (*storge*). God's love for us is *agape*—the unconditional, unearned gift love that sent Jesus into the world to die for us. *Agape* is God's creative love breathing life into us not because we are good but because we need His love to be good.

Even if life after life experiences would prove to be solely within one's mind rather than an entrance to another world, they are still a healing time. If this review of life with the Being of Light sends people back with new power to love themselves and others and to accept death, couldn't we tap into that power of Christ's love before death? All of us have met people who, after suddenly discovering that Christ loves them, have a personality transformation through a retreat, the baptism of the Spirit, being born again, or simply a friend who made Christ's love real. I have seen teenagers trapped by drugs and alcohol make a retreat, discover that God loved them, and turn their lives over to serving others. This happens daily at Teen Challenge. Why doesn't it happen more often?

Finding the True Image of God—Unconditional Love

Two things seem to block this process of learning to love: our view of God and our view of ourself. How did the accepting Christ become in our minds the harsh judge keeping track of our sins so that we would suffer? We continue to view God through the eyes of our culture. In Semitic times a judge was not neutral like a modern judge, but defended the accused like our defense attorney. In medieval times the Church was the judicial branch, and even confessors were (until recently) judges. Now we are beginning to realize that we judge ourselves much as a smiling, nonjudgmental Mother Teresa of Calcutta awakens us to our injustice in neglecting the destitute and dying.

But, you may ask, isn't Christ a judge? I don't think on Judgment Day that Christ will search out every scrap of evidence that condemns us, but rather he will love us so much that we will feel the agony and guilt of all the ways we failed to respond to so much love. I will judge myself as I did when carelessly denting my father's car while parking. He didn't have to say judgmentally, "You should have been more careful parking," because just a look into his loving eyes made me kick myself for carelessly denting his car. The more dad accepted the dent, the more I hung my head for not returning his love by greater care of his car. God is love, and his love judges us.

Our false images of God come also from our parents. If God is a Father and our father was an alcoholic, what chance does God have to be a real Father? When I was teaching religion on the reservation to Sioux from homes broken by alcoholic fathers, I never spoke of God as a Father but rather as a Grandfather. Even the Sioux word for God, *tunkasila*, was *grandfather* because he cared and kept the family together.

Even our parents who cared didn't love us unconditionally just as much if we got A's or C's, were beautiful or ugly, made first string or sat on the bench. All parental love is human love, giving more when more is returned. We get loved more if we are quiet, clean up, eat all our food, and help around the house. Because we expect to be loved not for who we are but for what we do, we begin to feel that we must also "merit" God's love. It's too much to believe that God's love is so different—an unmerited, unconditional gift giving power to love.

Our image of God should mature as we grow but too often remains the same one we had when seven years old. Who was God then? Was God a policeman, an unconcerned old man with a beard, a meek and mild milquetoast, a teacher wanting perfection, the spoilsport sending suffering so that we could earn heaven, or the apathetic God who let us down when we really needed him?[3] Usually when someone doesn't believe in God, I find that he means his childhood God, who is the same God I don't believe in.

It's as hard to discover the true God as it is to discover a true friend. When I meet a possible friend, I react to him out of my history of being hurt by other friends, how he resembles another person, and how I see myself. If I have been hurt by silences, I will be hurt by his silences until I begin to trust him. This takes time and sharing of all facets of life—recreation, meals together, tears when a parent dies, and the deepest feelings until we have no secrets but have another self. To know and love God is the same process as knowing and loving a friend, because God is someone, not something.

Why all this bother about having the right image of God? If God is not seen as the Being of Light, then our view of life will not be a healing experience deepening our power to love and face death daily. We will remain crippled if we allow our culture, parents, and childhood concepts to distort our image of God, making it impossible to give and receive enough trust and love. Just as culture and experience made medieval man believe that the earth was not round, so, too, our loveless culture and experience make contemporary man believe that God is not love. Relying on our limited experience to know God is as foolish as asking a mosquito what it is like to be a man. God says that he is love and that he died for us.

Finding the True Self-Image—I Am Loved

Besides the wrong image of God, the second block to experiencing God's love is the wrong image of ourselves. God made man to his image and likeness. Since that day, man has returned the compliment and made God to his image and likeness. Just as when I am angry at getting a ticket for speeding, I am more apt to think that the next patrolman is angry and out to get me, I may also project my anger onto God. Very often the things I don't like about God are the things I don't like about myself, and thus I project them on my image of God. When I am feeling guilty and down on myself, I seek a God who is a judge and down on me. Fortunately, projection can work in reverse. If I see God as a loving provider, then I quit clinging to things and see myself as a loving provider. My image of God often tells me more about my image of myself than it does about God. To the degree that I love or hate myself, I will love and hate God and vice versa.

The real problem is not that we dislike God or our neighbor but that we don't love ourselves. Due to the conditional love offered by parents and friends, we cannot love our limitations and weaknesses. They program us to love ourselves more when we work hard, get A's, do our best, and succeed in the ways that make them proud of us. We keep straining for A's, a bigger bank account, a nicer car, a promotion, the feeling of being useful and helpful, or the right circle of friends who will approve of us and make us more secure. Our self-image gets propped up on what we have and can do rather than who we are—a unique person loved by God.

What are the symptons of not loving myself enough? Take thirty seconds to count up what you like about yourself and another thirty seconds to count up what you don't like about yourself. Do it. It only takes a minute and may be one of the best minutes you ever invested. If you don't want to do it, is it because you subconsciously fear what you may discover?

Which was easier? Most people find three times as many weaknesses as strengths, and very few get beyond five strengths in thirty seconds. When listing our good points, did it feel like hollow bragging rather than true strengths due to God's work? When we can't love ourselves enough, we feel that compliments aren't given as sincerely as criticism. I still find myself at times deflecting a compliment with a silent "You wouldn't be saying that if you really knew me." Chances are at such times that my friend sees more than I see in myself and I ought to thank him, acknowledge my gift, and also give God the credit. I especially find this debunking reaction with comments like "You are a good person" rather than "You are a good typist" or "You have on a nice shirt." Such struggles show that my self-image is seen in the mirror of what I can do or have rather than who I am.

We pay a high price for not loving ourselves as much as God does. Dr. William Glasser, the author of *Reality Therapy*, believes that *all* psychological problems, from a slight neurotic fear of heights to the deepest psychotic schizophrenia, are symptoms whose depth and duration indicate the depth and duration of our self dislike.[4] He seems to echo the great psychiatrist Carl Jung writing *Modern Man in Search of a Soul:*

> . . . the acceptance of self is the essence of the moral problem and the epitome of a whole outlook upon life. That I feed the hungry, that I forgive an insult, that I love my enemy in the name of Christ—all these are undoubtedly great virtues, What I do unto the least of my brethren, that I do unto Christ. But what if I should discover that the least amongst them all, the poorest of all the beggars, the most impudent of all the offenders, the very enemy himself—that these are within me, and that I myself stand in need of the alms of my own kindness—that I myself am the enemy who must be loved—what then? . . . Neurosis is an inner cleavage—the state of being at war with oneself. Everything that accentuates this cleavage makes the patient worse, and everything that mitigates it tends to heal the patient.[5]

All Americans suffer some emotional instability. Some psychologists say that seventeen out of twenty of us are neurotic and one in five will be treated for mental illness because Jung is right. Even illness which seems to be organic, as illlness that is hereditary or due to an imbalance of endocrine secretions, is often triggered and prolonged by a lack of self-love.

Unfortunately, when we don't love ourselves, we behave in a way that makes it harder to love ourselves. We cover our insecurity by broadcasting our success, criticizing whoever isn't present, renting a dark corner for our shyness, becoming overextended and unable to say "no," criticizing ourselves to get sympathy, taking no risks that might fail, and agreeing with those who like the weather and those who don't. It's a vicious circle in which we become less lovable the less we love ourselves.

Lack of self-love is the root of all sin. I get proud and stand on my soapbox when I am frowning at myself inside. When I am angry at myself, I jump down another's throat. Lust attacks when I need intimacy to assure myself that I am lovable. Sloth anchors me when I feel I have little to give. The graph of when I loved myself most and least in my life matches the graph of when I sinned most and least. When I most need to experience God's acceptance, I feel he is most distant because of my sin.

The True Self Image: God Loves Me Unconditionally

How can I break this vicious circle of self-hatred that programs me to fail and pushes away God and others who try to love me? I must find someone who can keep loving me unconditionally even when there is no return.

When I am at my worst I am like the heiress, Patty Hearst, needing the unconditional love of a Randolph Hearst. Patty had everything—beauty, wealth, a boyfriend, a loving home, popularity and a golden future ahead. But like the prodigal son, she didn't appreciate her gifts (a sign of self-hatred) and turned her back to join the Symbionese Liberation Army. With this band of guerillas she robbed a bank and wounded two bystanders, sent home a tape cursing her parents as facist pigs, rejected the name "Patty" for "Tania," demanded from her father a million dollars of food for the poor, and fled the police for nineteen months. What more could she do to hurt her parents?

Randolph Hearst, like the father of the prodigal, continued daily to return unconditional love no matter how Patty hurt him. He rejoiced that she was alive rather than dead, pleaded with the captors to return her unharmed at any price, immediately distributed the million dollars of food, and daily answered the phone with hope that it might bring news of Patty's return. Even when the tapes and bank robbery made it evident that Patty willingly remained with the SLA, Randolph never lost hope that if he continued to love her unconditionally, Patty would begin to love a deeper part of herself and quit lashing out at those who cared.

Patty made little response. Even after her SLA friends died in a house fire and their revolutionary dreams went up in smoke, she still eluded the FBI and clung to Richard and Emily Harris who felt Patty was committed enough to leave her alone and go out and jog on the day of her arrest. Even after her capture by the FBI, she refused at times to talk with her parents. Yet they continued to love the deeper part of her that she couldn't love, and even hired a top lawyer, F. Lee Bailey and then put up bail of $1,500,000. Nothing was spared for their daughter.

We know the outcome. Through their total, immediate, constant and unconditional love and forgiveness, Patty became herself again. She changed only because they didn't demand change before they cared; instead they responded to deeper hostility with deeper care and forgiveness. Randolph poured out *agape*—the unconditional, unearned gift love that created worth in Patty as she saw her true self in her father's eyes. Patty found in the depth of her parents' love her own worth only because she was loved unconditionally at her worst. She saw that she was loved for who she was and not for what she had or could do.

We all need a Randolph Hearst to help us discover our own worth when we are at our worst, In the story of the prodigal son Jesus told us that we have such a Father. We have even a better Father. Would Randolph Hearst do as much if Patty should run away again? Our Father would keep reaching out for us and forgiving us as many times as we run away, and share with us all he has forever. Would Randolph keep loving if he had a son who went to Patty's hideout and was slain by her? Our Father did.

If Patty were not his daughter and she killed his son, would Randolph adopt her and care for her? Our Father did (Rom. 8:23; Gal. 4:5). Would Patty still be adopted if after killing his son she were shot by the FBI and ended up paralyzed and unable to do anything without constant care? Our Father adopted us even though we can't move our little finger without his constant care moving each heartbeat and bringing each thought. If Randolph Hearst could care at all, it was only because his Father shared his power to care. Everything we can do or have is a gift from a Father who loves us not for what we can do or have, but simply for being his son or daughter.

Our Father loves us not just like a son or daughter but like Christ. The Father is love, and he can only love with 100 percent of his infinite love and with the same act of love he has for Christ. We may be one millionth the son Christ was, but we are loved just as much. What wouldn't the Father do for Christ?

Maybe God does love us infinitely, but can his vague, heavenly love make the difference that the concrete, real love of

Randolph Hearst made for Patty's life? Do we just have to believe in the power of God's love and never see it? We see the infinite power of God's love when someone desperate who has tried everything but final suicide turns to God. No amount of wisdom, money or effort can give a person the power to break free from alcoholism as can the higher power of AA. Toward the end of his term, Governor Ronald Reagan wanted to shunt California funds to Christian drug programs because they offered much more power to change than did the most sophisticated rehabilitation programs. Find someone who hit the bottom and found God and you will see the creative power of our Father's love.

God Loves Me Unconditionally Even in Tragedies

I have watched the power of God's love melt the icy grip of self-hatred not only in the lines of alcoholics and retreatants but also in my own life. When I was six years old, my three-year-old brother John became ill with bronchitis. I can still picture myself standing at the foot of John's bed and telling my mother not to worry because John just had a cold and would get better. After four days of this, my mother called a nurse next door who came and immediately called an ambulance. They left with the sirens screaming and tears flowing down my face. A half hour later the phone rang. John had died on his way to the hospital.

Tears and blame flowed from my broken heart. I blamed the ambulance driver for not going faster. Then my anger lashed out at God who could have given John a few more minutes so I would still have a brother. I was told that John was a saint, but I wanted a brother to play with, not a saint. Then finally I blamed myself for telling my mother not to get help. In my six-year-old mind this unconsciously translated into: "I killed John." I became hospitalized for bronchitis, missing John's funeral and the chance to work out my anger through grieving. I swallowed all the tears and loneliness while we prayed the family rosary and asked John to help our family.

The self-hatred for killing my brother was buried in my unconscious where it could wreak havoc. I quit making friends because deep down I was afraid that I might lose a friend the way I lost John, and that was too painful to risk. Furthermore, why would anyone want to be my friend when I killed my brother? How many times had I fought with John who was so good to me? I lost all self-confidence, stumbling over easy words when reading in class, playing only with younger children, and warding off love and compliments.

This continued all through high school. I tried everything to accept myself. Maybe I would like myself if I could overcome my shyness and learn to speak on my feet. I became an excellent debater but still didn't like who I was. I tried saving money so I could feel secure, and I had more money than any kid of my age I knew, but less self-respect. I studied hard to gain academic applause, graduated in the upper two percent of my class, and could tell you everything except why I disliked myself. On the outside I was smiling but inside I had an inverted smile.

After high school I joined the Jesuits to become a priest. Unconsciously I was probably thinking that if I gave my life totally to the Lord, I could begin to accept myself and finally have peace. Jesuit life began with thirty days of prayer to bring my life to Christ and receive his. I entered the retreat with a list of forty ways I wanted to change, since I didn't want to waste thirty days.

God's love slowly penetrated my cold heart the way that the warm sunshine melts an icicle, leaving behind a pool of tears. I discovered that all of creation was given to me by my loving Father who was as generous as the maple tree that scatters thousands of seeds to make one tree. If I was really made to his image, and was the temple of his Spirit, I had to be someone special. God doesn't make junk. I began to see all the ways he had especially cared for me: keeping my bronchitis from being terminal, saving my eyesight when a friend's golf club split my eyebrow, parents who would do anything for me. All the people and events showed that someone cared.

At this time I received a letter saying that my grandmother was paralyzed in her hands and slowly dying. I wanted to write what I feared would be my final letter to her and prayed over what to say. I angrily demanded to know why God would allow such a good woman who had gone daily to Mass now to be paralyzed and unable to even feed herself. Didn't he love her as much as I did? Slowly I began to see that just as I loved my paralyzed grandmother more than I loved someone who could do more things for me, so God also loved her in her helplessness. How much we are loved doesn't depend on how much we can do, but on who we are. Like a flash flood rolling me off my feet, I felt God's love sweeping me up to a new level of self-love. I could love my grandmother and myself not because we did great things, but simply because we were who we were.

But the Father wasn't through. During the retreat we were to bring all our past sinfulness, dumping it into the Father's lap so that we could have all the past forgiven in a general confession. As I asked Christ what to confess, he brought to mind a little boy standing by John's bed and saying, "Don't worry, John will be all right. He just has a cold." As I looked at myself at the age of six trying to keep my mother from worrying and trying to calm my own fear, I felt Jesus' great love for a frightened child. More amazingly I could look at my pile of sins, even the times I maliciously lied and hurt others, and still feel his love and acceptance. Just like a mother who cares more for a sick child by staying up nights and going without meals, the more I showed Jesus my sin, the more he cared for me. He smiled because he could forgive me five hundred times rather than just fifty. Suddenly his smile was within me, and, forgiving myself, I felt as though a huge concrete shell had burst open, giving me new freedom to leap like my real self.

This review of the best and worse in my life through the eyes of Jesus, the Being of Light, brought not just an emotional experience but a deep change. I threw away my list of forty ways to change and replaced it with forty reasons I knew I was loved. I began to make friends even though I knew many would leave the novitiate and bring the pain of separation that I felt at John's death. Previously I had clung to clothes and whatever made me feel secure. After the retreat I emptied my room and wanted only to rely on my Father. Even grades became unimportant, and I went through school never looking at the grades that before had measured my success. After competing with everyone for grades and recognition, I began to be grateful when others achieved the good grades and insights.

Seeing John's death through the eyes of Christ, the Being of Light, continues to give me a new perspective, replacing the pain of separation with gratitude for growth through the separation. I don't think we would have adopted my fine sister unless, in the loneliness following John's death, we knew that we needed a little girl to love. I have grown closer also to my brother, Dennis, until today we write and give retreats together sharing every breath of life. This closeness grew because, following John's death, we knew we couldn't afford to take each other for granted. I didn't want Dennis to die with fights unpatched or deep feelings unshared.

John's death also gifted my priesthood. As a hospital chaplain I could be with parents who had lost a child because I knew what they felt and wanted to be sure they didn't continue feeling guilty. As a confessor, I was eager to lift the penitent's burden of guilt because I knew the agony of feeling, "I'm no good." My suffering from events like John's death has moved me to pray for physical and inner healing when others are crippled. Perhaps my prayer for inner healing utilizes this book's five stages of dying because John's death illuminated the gift of life given through death.

I want to use well the gift of life that John had for only three years. I want my priesthood to be an extension of his care, his laughter, his tears. I want with John's help to live more for my Father and less for the praise of men who disappear. I want to help Christ heal memories as others review their lives through his eyes and experience new freedom.

Meeting the Unconditional Love of the Being of Light

What happened to me can happen to anyone who reviews his life with the eyes of the Being of Light. When I find that I am suffering again from a negative image of God or myself (maybe I can't accept compliments again), I have a "Review of Life" with Christ. I sit down with a blank piece of paper, and with as much light as possible flooding me to remind me that I am sitting in the presence of Christ. Then I look at that blank paper as if it were a TV screen for recording the parts of my life that Christ wants to show me. As events come to mind, I put a picture or word on that screen. Finally I spend a few minutes thanking Christ for whatever event of the screen spoke most of his love. After that prayer, Jesus says my name, "Matt," with more love than anyone has ever said "Matt."

Usually if I'm discouraged, my television doesn't work so well and I get no picture from Christ. Then I hear Jesus ask me one of the following questions to get me in touch with the ways he has loved me through others or others through me.

REVIEW OF LIFE WITH JESUS, THE BEING OF LIGHT

Loved

1. Who are the persons (family, friends, teachers) who loved me most? (I walk through the front door and through each room of the places where I lived until I find those who love me. Then I focus on one person and share with Christ, the Being of Light, how I am grateful.)
2. What events (challenges, prayer times, successes) made me grow most? (Walk through classrooms, jobs, happiest times and rest in the most growthful one.)
3. When did I most experience God's forgiveness for me (as Patty did from Randolph)? (Watch the times I said "I'm sorry" and really meant it.)

Loving

4. What are my gifts that God uses (my skills, what I enjoy doing, best times)? (Focus on each part of my body until I can thank God for its gifts.)
5. Who are better off because they met God in me? (Watch for pictures of those I listened to, prayed for, helped, laughed with.)
6. When did I most reach out for someone who hurt me and really forgive him (as Randolph did for Patty Hearst)? (Watch the times others didn't listen, weren't grateful, etc., and yet found me smiling.)

Hurting

7. Randolph Hearst, like the father of the prodigal son, loved Patty even at her worst. What is the worst thing I ever did in my life? How were Jesus and the Father loving me even then? (Watch those who love me most because I can hurt them most.)

Hurt

8. When was I hurt the most (e.g., John's death)? What growth came then? (Watch those who love me most because they can also hurt me most.)

The last several questions are harder to answer, but they also reveal deeper depths of God's love. That's because it is easier in good times for me to see that God loves me than it is in the bad times when I am hurt or hurt others. But I don't know the depth of God's love until I know how he loves the worst in me that even turns away my friends. Who but Randolph could love a Patty Hearst? Usually I have to keep soaking in God's love in the first six questions before I can try questions 7 and 8.

The rest of the book is about questions 7 and 8. Reading it will be a waste of time and energy unless questions 1 through 6 have been prayerfully answered, so that I know in my heart that Christ, the Being of Light, really loves me.

6

SECOND PREDISPOSITION: WITH A LOVING GOD I CAN SHARE ALL MY FEELINGS

I get irritated by people who smile piously and say, "Just pray and you will experience God's love." On days when even stamps don't stick, the healing Christ seems as far away as Emmaus or a life after life experience with the Being of Light. Prayerfully conversing with Christ over Scripture becomes as dry as conversing over *Webster's Dictionary.*

Many times prayer seems to make little difference, just as conversations often leave me feeling the same emptiness. When has a conversation really made a difference to my life? Deep conversations happen when I get past the clichés (the nice weather), the focus on others (Harry's problem), the talk about things (the best car for the money), what I am doing (giving retreats), and finally share my insides—what I am feeling. When, like the disciples at Emmaus, I can share that I am tired of the rat race for security, lonely because a friend died, scared by a future full of question marks, angry at a recent failure, and discouraged that a friend no longer responds, then the conversation becomes a transforming time to remember.

When I find that my prayer doesn't make much difference to my life, I am not praying like Teresa of Avila sharing her struggles but am hiding my real feeling from Christ. St. Teresa of Avila, the great teacher on prayer, would share her hurt of loneliness at being unable to pray and then would be healed as she watched Christ deal with loneliness.[1] But I speak in clichés (rattling off formal prayers), focus on others (stop wars and hunger), talk about ideas (why do you allow suffering), ask for help in what I am doing (planning a homily) and tell him all the things I would like to do for him. I sidestep how I feel—tired, scared, angry, blah, lonely, confused, or anxious. If I touch feelings, it is usually thanking him for positive feelings (joy, peace, patience, etc.), or telling him how I would like to feel. Too often I come to Christ, the Being of Light, wearing the same smiling mask I wear for anyone I can't trust with the feelings I want to hide. I keep unconsciously thinking, "Maybe if he really knows me, he won't like me."

The real problem is that I feel Christ won't like me because I don't like myself. When I feel angry, fearful, depressed, frustrated, etc., I project onto others what I am feeling toward myself. I am like my five-year-old cousin screaming at himself for breaking the vase and saying, in order to calm his father, "Don't scream at me, Daddy. I'm already screaming at myself." So when I say: "Maybe if he really knows me, he won't like me," I'm really saying: "I don't like myself, so Jesus won't like me either." If I can't accept my own anger, fear and depression, I will be facing a Judge, not the Being of Light, and seeing my edited rerun and not his review of all my life. How can I accept my feelings so that I can pray and be healed?

The Problem—Accepting Feelings
To Share with the Being of Light

After rewriting this paragraph three times, I am feeling very frustrated (my nice term for angry) in my cold room. I may have no control over feeling cold or frustrated, but just as I can decide whether to turn up the heat or remain cold, I can decide whether to keep feeling my frustration or do something about it. Cold rooms and feelings become dangerous only when ignored or pampered. If I ignore the cold room and my angry frustration, I may end up with a cold and more frustration. I can also err by pampering my feelings. Just as I don't let a cold room dictate to me to stop writing, so I don't let my feelings dictate how I should live. Always to follow feelings by doing and saying what I feel is not freedom but slavery to feelings. Freedom means welcoming whatever I am feeling, whether it be coldness, fear, loneliness, frustration, anger or joy, and then deciding how to react.

I was taught that some feelings like joy were good while others such as fear, anger, and frustration were bad. But feelings are like the fire in the furnace I just turned on. In a furnace the fire warms me and protects me against the cold. Like fire, feelings are neither good nor bad. But, when out of control, fire can destroy this house and expose me to the cold. Like fire, feelings protect us if we handle them properly, and destroy us if we try to bury them with the rubbish. They just *are*.

We hide furnaces in dark, dusty basements away from the critical eye of others. We do the same with our feelings, especially with "negative" feelings. From the time we were children and heard, "Now quit crying like a cry baby," we were taught to smile and hide our angry feelings about being spanked or scolded. We learned that to get parental love and peer approval, we should bury fear, anger and other "negative" feelings in our dusty basement, the unconscious.

We also learned that we could deal with our feelings if we could name them. The feared Martian knocking on the moonlit window returned to Mars when we discovered the wind blowing a tree branch against the window. The more we can name what it is we really fear or feel, the better chance we have of dealing with the feeling rather than having it dealing with us. Naming a feeling is hard because we learned to mislabel our feelings. It sounded better to bellow angrily at a bully, "Watch out or I'll clobber you," rather than expose the real feeling of fear, "I'm afraid you are going to beat me up." As we grew, we became more sophisticated in misnaming feelings. Our fear of failing in math became voiced as anger at "that boring teacher." We learned to hide feelings behind "it" rather than "I." The feeling "I am bored in class" became another problem, "It is a boring class." The word "you" also could hide feelings. "I'm angry" became "You make me angry."

We could even pretend we were facing feelings with "I *feel* it's his fault." This is the same as saying "I *think* it's his fault." Whenever "think" can replace "feel" we are simply expressing a judgment (something is right or wrong) and not a feeling which just *is*. "I feel it is his fault" probably camouflages the feeling "I feel hurt." Feelings are usually the voice of our inner child not thinking but whining, giggling, or squirming to say "I want, need, wish, won't, can't, don't care, feel, etc."

Therapists like Dr. Eugene Gendlin find that repressed emotions are "acted out" in physical symptons such as tension, fatigue, headaches, or an upset stomach.[2] He suggests that we focus on the headache and then say interiorly, "You were an emotion but I swallowed you, so you became a headache. Now I want you to come back. I want to feel whatever emotion you are." With practice the physical reaction slowly becomes linked to a feeling of fear, or anger, perhaps with a fantasy like falling through space. After the feeling is pinpointed, I ask why I am feeling that way. When I finally locate the true feeling and the full reason for it, the physical symptom will begin to disappear.

Yesterday I began to write and fifteen minutes later tore up what I was writing. Something else was crying from within to be heard. I laid down on my bed and listened to my body with its tense forehead, tight neck, and set jaw. I began to build up a hunger for the physical tensions to reconvert into the feelings I rejected. At first I thought I was angry that I couldn't write, but anger didn't fit the tension. Slowly I began to feel as though I wanted to grip something. I wanted a better grip on where I should study next year. It felt like walking along a cliff in a dense fog wondering if the next step might be the last. Why was I anxious about next year? As I kept focusing on the tension, different reasons came to mind and then it became very evident. Deep down I feared that years of further studies might make me want to tear up everything I have written. My self-image was so attached to my workshops and writing that I couldn't risk discovering that I had built on sand. Since this fear of failure was too threatening, I repressed it, but it kept blocking my ability to write. As soon as I could accept and share with Christ my fear of failure, all tension drained out of me and I was able again to write because there was no need to bury my true feelings.

Burying my feelings not only choked off my writing, but also prevented me from praying. When asked what was most necessary for successful prayer, Martin Luther replied, "Don't lie to God." We lie to God by saying what we think we "should feel" rather than what lies within our hearts. "O heavenly Father, I come before your divine throne with the deepest sentiments of faith, hope and charity" is a pious lie unless I have met St. Peter and have an eternal smile. Christ didn't praise the religious clichés of the Pharisee, but the heartfelt prayer of the publican, "Oh God, be merciful to me, a sinner."

To discover my feelings, I must first want to face them rather than hide them in the basement unconscious. Feelings are always present but not always heard. Our "radio" for tuning in to feelings can be a good friend in whom we can confide our ups and downs. But since a good friend isn't always available, I frequently write out my feelings to begin my prayer. Writing pinpoints what is really felt. Sometimes speaking into a tape recorder and then listening to what I said can also help to locate what is really felt. Even just speaking my feelings out loud to Christ helps me catch what sounds sincere and what is phony.

The Old Testament saints scandalize us with their ability to pray aloud from the heart. Job curses the day God made him, Jeremiah storms at God for making a fool of him, and the psalmist tells God to crush the heads of his enemies. We skip these passages because we aren't at home with praying from our hearts. We may not like what is in our hearts, but if we are to pray and remain psychologically healthy, we must share it all with God. The gifted theologian-psychologist John Powell describes this psychological foundation of prayer:

> I hear Job cursing the day God made him, Jeremiah accusing God of making a fool of him, and the psalmist pleading with God to destroy his enemies; and I want to congratulate them for telling it like it was, for knowing how to pray. Modern psychology in a massive effort to release men from destructive, subconsciously repressed emotions is trying all sorts of therapeutic methods of sensitivity to put men in touch with their true feelings. The unwritten but practically certain promise is that, if one will learn to express his true feelings to others, he will in this communication deepen his relationships with others and through these deepened relationships find mental and emotional health. This is equally true of prayer. If I mask myself before God, I will never really communicate with him, never really pray, never really get to know him or feel that he knows me. The relationship of faith will be superficial at best, filled up with pious clichés, religious fantasies and delusions.[3]

St. Augustine honestly prayed: "Lord, give me the gift of chastity, but not yet."

Jesus wants to talk with us so we can give him what is in our heart. When I pray, I often picture Jesus sitting beside me as he did with the Samaritan woman at the well (Jn. 4). I see he is thirsty not just for water but to share the deeper part of myself. As I dangle the bucket down the dark well, I ask that I may be able to fill the bucket with water from the pools of those hidden, deep feelings that constantly shift and flow. Then I go down that dark well searching for a deeper, purer feeling free from surface debris. Beneath my anger at another interruption I may catch anger at myself for my impatience and beneath that a vague fear that what I write I still can't often live.

Then I draw up that bucket with my fear of being a hypocrite and share this with Christ, the Being of Light. He wants to talk about my life history and my need for his living water of acceptance to recover from past hurts. Gradually like the Samaritan woman I am able to accept my hypocrisy and myself and return, saying to those who hurt me: ''Come and see a man who told me everything I ever did. Could this be the Christ?'' I have met Christ, the Being of Light.

I don't have to wait until death to meet the Being of Light. I meet him like the disciples at Emmaus or the Samaritan woman every time I face with him my deepest feelings from being hurt and then absorb every detail of his loving, healing view.

Am I like the disciples at Emmaus willing to face with Christ the fears, frustrations, anger, rage, and self-hatred that I have buried through the years? Am I willing to let Christ show me through the Scriptures that I like to nurse grudges, feel sorry for myself, look down on another, feel taller, and have a narrow view of what another is doing? What I don't want to share with anyone else, can I still share with Jesus? Am I ready to be healed, or do I just want to smile and pretend everything is O.K.?

Part Four:
Five Stages
of Dying and Forgiveness

If we feel loved by God enough to share our feelings with him, then we can begin to share a painful memory to be healed. Just as Dr. Kubler-Ross has dealt with how the dying go through denial, anger, bargaining, depression, and acceptance, each of the next five chapters will deal with how a person goes through these five stages in healing a memory.

Each chapter will consider a given stage under four sections: (1) symptoms, (2) scriptural basis, (3) why the stage is healthful, and (4) how to work through the stage in prayer. The first section, concerning symptoms, will help us recognize feelings through which the Spirit speaks in that stage. The second section, dealing with Scripture, will examine how the Spirit has worked through similar situations, especially using the memory healing story of the prodigal son where what was death-giving became life-giving. The third section highlights why the stage's feelings are healthy so that we can accept and grow from the feelings at that stage rather than deny them and wish we were at another stage. The fourth section outlines how to pray through that stage, receive Christ's reaction and begin to forgive the hurt.

From this page to the last, don't just read this book! Recall a personal hurt and pray through each stage, checking what is said against your experience. Just as it is more fruitful to spend one hour praying over one's experience of a Scripture passage rather than quickly reading the entire Gospel, so too it will be more fruitful in these chapters to pray over one's own life experience rather than quickly read this book. This book is based on the *Spiritual Exercises*, and, like it, should not be read but experienced in thirty days of prayer. Most of what will be said is already known in the head but not yet prayerfully experienced in the heart. The participants who profit most from our healing of memories workshops are not those who take notes and try to remember everything, but those who pray and thereby experience much healing.

7

FIRST STAGE: DENIAL

As a hospital chaplain I have often been present when the doctor told patients that they had cancer. I can't remember a single patient who didn't deny it by talking about something else, pretending it was nothing, working harder than ever, or spending time applying cosmetics to recapture fading beauty. I do the same thing when I get hurt.

One time that I was hurt deeply occurred when I was sent out to teach on the wind-swept Rosebud Sioux reservation in South Dakota. I felt a bit wobbly because this was my first try at teaching and due to prefecting nights at the boarding school, I was never more than a page or two ahead of the students. I became an expert at making up historical facts (Napoleon had a six-footed horse that was one and a half times faster than any four-footed horse) that would make my Sioux students pay more attention to me than to carving their initials into a desk. I kept trying to prepare better classes but still felt a failure.

When I was feeling lower than a duck's instep, the priests with whom I lived asked me to give a talk on prayer. When I tried to tell them that I was no expert on prayer and hardly had a moment to pray, they convinced me that I could just share my struggle to pray. I reluctantly agreed, thinking that if I shared my struggle to keep praying, maybe they could get in touch with their own struggle and help me with mine. I tried to be honest and share everything— even my teaching struggles that entered my prayer. At the end I felt pleased because I had honestly shared my struggle to pray.

We filed out of the rec room to recover in the dining room with coffee and cookies. On the way as I paused to read the bulletin board, I could hear a conversation around the corner in the dining room. Two close friends were trying to recover from my talk. Every word is still etched in my memory. One said: "What did you think of that talk?" The other replied: "It sounded like a talk a novice (beginner) would give. It's hard to believe that he has been a Jesuit praying for six years. I wonder how long he will last as a Jesuit."

I was shocked and paralyzed. Did I really hear my close friend, Gus, say that I was never going to be a priest? My jaw dropped, my legs shook, and chills shot up and down my spine. I felt alone and abandoned in a world full of snipers, one of whom had just jabbed a bayonnet into my back and twisted it. I stood frozen at the board and pretended to read the notices even though they were all a blur. It's the crushed feeling a loving wife has when she hears for the first time that her husband will divorce her. Why go on?

I

SYMPTONS OF DENIAL

Then I began the process of screening out the hurt so I could go on. Denial brings in its wake the psychological defense mechanisms and patterns of sin that try to make me feel important again. My favorite defense is rationalization, an attempt to prove by reason that what happened is fine. My mind feverishly cranked out several: "He's just kidding. He would say that about any talk. That's just his opinion, and I can find six others who liked it." (Here I paused to fantasize whom I would talk with and how they would praise my talk.) "Anyway, he came late, missed the best parts and can hardly be a judge of the whole talk. What do I care what he thinks." At first I didn't believe my pep talk, but after a day of rewording, reworking, and rehearsing my arguments, I had convinced myself that all was O.K. I denied the pain with intellectualizations such as: "It could have been worse. It happens to everybody."

Through denial I was swallowing not just the pain (I was now uncomfortable rather than devastated) but also the fear and anger. At first I dreaded meeting Gus and getting another broadside. I would go out of my way to avoid him, but I gradually learned to sit next to him and avoid any conversation deeper than weather and sports. Gradually my hesitation to be with him vanished into a vague dislike and uncomfortable feeling I sometimes get with strangers. Eventually it was hard for me even to recognize that he had hurt me, except that I only half-listened to what he said, hid my feelings, spoke more cautiously, and was less grateful for him than for other members of the Jesuit community.

I also tried to swallow and repress my hurt feelings not with alcohol and drugs but with the more subtle escapes: work, TV, sleep and eating. I should have known it was compensation, the making up for frustration in one area by overgratification in another. I worked hard (my best emotional pain killer) reading that extra book that might make a better class. Yet my mind wasn't in my reading and I would finish a chapter not knowing what it said.

I went from one escape to another without even enjoying them. I watched more football games and at every commercial grabbed just one more handful of potato chips. I slept restlessly, dreamed more (often of being chased or chasing someone), and felt like taking another five minutes before facing a new day. I couldn't experience deep pleasure because I was compensating for deep pain. With these escapes causing more repression, the prevention of painful or dangerous thoughts from entering conciousness, I began to believe "it was nothing."

I needed approval not just from potato chips but from people. I went around asking the others what they thought about the talk, yet was still unsatisfied by their praise. I acted the opposite of what I felt (reaction formation), boldly smiling even at my critic Gus to prove nothing was wrong. I became a "yes" man—a Democrat with Democrats and a Republican with Republicans. I wanted a warm smile and not an argument. Because I needed everyone smiling, I really thought all the others were smiling. They weren't smiling more; I was projecting, attributing to others my desires.

I did the same thing with God in prayer. I came seeking to be comforted rather than with a readiness to listen and be challenged. Lest God challenge me, I spent 90 percent of the time speaking and 10 percent listening, and even then listening for insights rather than feelings. Rather than face my weakness and tender feelings, I told him all my great thoughts and got his nod of approval. I got tired of my great thoughts and had a distraction sandwiched between every insight. Prayer seemed to make little difference, so I spent less time in prayer. My own feeling of not being important was unconciously projected, so God became unimportant.

When God is unimportant and I am insecure, I try to hide my insecurity under the dark cloak of sin. Since all sin is an attempt to cover up the insecurity that I suffered from hurts, my old patterns of sin returned. Pride grew as I tried to lift myself up by looking down on others' failures and even being glad that some seemed to have a harder time teaching and praying than I did. I began to withdraw and treat others impersonally by avoiding them or just half-listening to what they were saying and missing what they were feeling. My feelings were hurt and I was too tender to face another's feelings.

This same set of symptoms (rationalization, intellectualization, repression, projection, fantasy, reaction formation, compensation, sin) returns whenever I am hurt. The deeper the hurt, the more I utilize these defenses and they become unconscious rather than caught by my consciousness. Others will have their own favorite defenses and patterns of sin. Many who go to prayer meetings utilize "Praise the Lord! Isn't everything great!" Sometimes I feel like following Dr. Carl Jung's suggestion to ask their spouse and kids.

II
DENIAL IN SCRIPTURE

Unfortunately, I'm not the only one who denies being hurt. Running from hurts by erecting a smokescreen of denial is as universal as the story of the prodigal son who took his inheritance and ran away from home (Lk. 15). We don't know what the real problem was—maybe the loss of his mother who is absent from the story. In any case, the son denied either that he had a problem or that the problem would get solved by staying home and facing it. The father also denied the little hurts that built pressure until it reached the point where the son felt he had to leave. All was not well even if the son did his job, never complained, and went to the synagogue. To the degree the father was surprised by his son's sudden departure and demand for money, he had hid in the fog of denial.

III
DENIAL CAN BE HEALTHY

About a year ago I was riding in a Volkswagen that was hit at a blind intersection. The little car was a wreck but I came out without a scratch. I started to climb out but a nurse from the neighborhood thought I was in shock and ordered me to sit down. I refused because I felt great. But she pushed me down and I sat right in the middle of a pecan pie. Then I was in shock!

When we have undergone a physical trauma like a car accident, our body goes into shock to conserve energy and keep us off our feet. We become pale, have a rapid pulse and shallow breathing, and may even faint. Every Boy Scout knows that these reactions should not be fought. Let the shock victim lie, and loosen the clothing for better breathing. Physical shock is part of the healing of a physical trauma.

When an emotional trauma occurs, like mine at the bulletin board, we go into emotional shock denial. Like shock, it is a necessary response to bring back emotional health and should not be fought. Breakdowns can come when we are forced to face something we need to deny. Until we can deal with a hurt, it is best not to face it. If we were aware of every past hurt that needed healing, we would feel swamped. We must at times be like the Alcoholics Anonymous member who takes only one day at a time and denies looking at all the hurts that will come in the future. In praying with another, we don't probe to bring out raw hurt but gently work with what the person is ready to face with Christ.[1] Denial prevents us from being overwhelmed by too much anxiety, disapproval or insecurity crippling our ability to bounce back.

Denial, like worrying or grieving, if moderately present, helps us to work through our fears. A recent study showed how a moderate amount of worry and denial helped patients recover from surgery. Patients were classified into those with excessive, moderate and no worry groups, depending on how concerned they were about upcoming surgery. After surgery the excessive worriers (with too little denial) had the slowest recovery. Almost as long in recovering were the no-worriers (too much denial) who were upset by the pain they hadn't expected. The quickest recovery was made by the moderate group (with moderate denial) who were content going through the pain they had expected. They also needed only half as much sedation for the post-operative pain because the proper combination of worry and denial had eliminated the emotional pain.

Moderate denial is just as helpful for spiritual health. After making a retreat, I usually find about five important things to do better. I'm going to pray more, spend more time preparing for Mass, be more grateful for all that happens, listen better, and find God in what I am doing. If I try to do all five, I fail at all five, since I have divided my energy five ways.

Through the centuries religious have practiced a "particular examen" focusing on correcting only one rather than five faults during the day. If I only focus on eliminating my ingratitude by thanking God for whatever is happening, my other four faults will disappear because when grateful I find God in what I am doing, listen better, want to pray more, and come to Mass prepared to give thanks. The particular examen is a form of healthy denial, a choosing not to look at all the ways I should be improving so as to put all my attention into one simple way. In like manner, if we use denial and just focus on the one memory of a hurt that Christ wants to heal, we have more success than in working with two or three memories at once.

Paul Tillich summarizes the extent and dynamic of denial as well as the price we pay for too much denial:

> Something in us prevents us from remembering, when remembering proves to be too difficult or painful. We forget benefits, because the burden of gratitude is too heavy for us. We forget former loves, because the burden of obligations implied by them surpasses our strength. We forget our former hates, because the task of nourishing them would disrupt our

mind. We forget former pain, because it is still too painful. We forget guilt, because we cannot endure its sting. Such forgetting is not the natural, daily form of forgetting. It demands our cooperation. We repress what we cannot stand. We forget it by entombing it within us. Ordinary forgetting liberates us from innumerable small things in a natural process. Forgetting by repression does not liberate us, but seems to cut us off from what makes us suffer. We are not entirely successful, however, because the memory is buried within us, and influences every moment of our growth. And sometimes it breaks through its prison and strikes at us directly and painfully.[2]

Too much denial cripples and can be healed in prayer. But how?

IV
DEALING WITH DENIAL

What happened at Emmaus is meant to happen to each of us whenever we are hurt and running. We are all running from the passion. The disciples ran from Christ's Passion, I from the bulletin board, and another from misunderstanding at home. Whatever the hurt, we too can be healed like the disciples at Emmaus by the same three steps: (1) tell Christ how we feel (Lk. 24:13-24), (2) listen through the scripture to how Christ feels (Lk. 24:25-27), and (3) with hearts burning live out Christ's reaction (Lk. 24:32-35).

The Emmaus way of healing by allowing Christ to absorb our reaction and then finally absorbing the reaction of Christ was the route the great mystic, Teresa of Avila, recommended for her novice sisters as well as those in the highest mystical prayer.[3] St. Teresa also assures us that this was the same road traveled by all the great contemplatives, especially St. Francis, St. Anthony of Padua, St. Bernard and St. Catherine of Siena.[4]

How do we judge if a person has reached this true contemplative prayer? St. Teresa emphasizes that true contemplatives may have many faults except one, the inability to forgive.[5] For Teresa true contemplation results in true forgiveness, the sign also of a healed memory. True contemplatives, as at Emmaus, gaze lovingly on the humanity of Christ until filled with their Savior's love and forgiveness, they too can heal a painful memory with his love and forgiveness.

1. *Tell Christ How I Feel*

To heal the memory of a hurt, I must be grateful enough for all my feelings to get past denial by sharing with Christ the hurt feelings that he wants me to heal. But when I am in denial, I usually want to thank God for everything—except my true feelings. In denial I think that this book was meant for others and not for me. Yet I and all of us have need for healing hurts that cripple us from giving and receiving love. Usually these are the times that come to mind when we lie in bed at night.

Asking Christ some questions can pinpoint the hurt that he wants shared. What in my life do I wish happened differently? What would it take to have everything feel perfect? What do I fear? Deep down I really feared that I didn't pray well and might lose my vocation with the Jesuits. I avoided speaking with Gus who criticized me even though I sought out reactions from all the others. For whose success is it hardest to thank God? Guess! Am I feeling any anger disguised as the inability to listen, or am I erupting in criticism? Discussing these questions with Christ brings me out of denial and ready to face what really hurt. Sometimes these questions are impossible to answer honestly unless I first share and pinpoint my feelings either in writing or in a bull session with an understanding friend. The more feelings are shared, the less they are denied.

Once I am in touch with what I am feeling, I share it with Christ, often aloud to see if it rings true. "Lord, things are going pretty well. Thanks for helping me to give that talk on prayer that most people liked. I can put up with the ones who didn't like it. But something is hurting me. I go around looking for approval. There's something I don't want to see in myself and that needs to be loved. What is it? What is making me feel tense like a wound-up spring? When was I hurt? Am I worried about my friend's criticism or something yet to come?"

After telling Christ how I feel, I ask Christ to get me in touch with the feelings he wants to heal. If we give Christ a chance (a few minutes of silent, reverent waiting), he will bring to mind the more painful and controlling hurt that needs healing.

Sometimes Christ takes us way back to past hurts that have crippled us through the years. Phil, for example, had such a fear of dentists that he couldn't see a dentist for twenty-three years and would faint when taking his daughter to the dentist. He sought psychiatric help but couldn't afford the therapy of six months to two years predicted to even uncover what was behind the phobia. But Phil came to our workshop and while we led the group in a healing of memories prayer, the Lord brought to Phil's consciousness a memory behind that fear. When Phil was thirteen, a dentist made verbal homosexual advances to Phil. When Phil protested, the dentist strapped Phil's hands and tried to inflict maximum pain by drilling his teeth without anesthetic. The dentist finished by slapping Phil and telling him this was the kind of pain he would experience if he ever told anyone. This had buried the trauma for twenty-three years until Jesus peacefully recalled the memory and in prayer helped Phil forgive the dentist. That week Phil tested his healing from the phobia when without any anxiety he had a dentist repair root canals, cap four teeth, and install a bridge.

Some hurts go back before age thirteen, even to birth and the months we were carried in the womb.[6] Barbara Shlemon cites a woman (we will call her Annette) who despite eleven years of therapy still lived with the obsessive-compulsive fears that would awaken her up to nine times a night to check the locks, stove and closet. She couldn't remember when her fears began. In prayer Jesus took her back to the womb and her mother's trauma at just losing a son and a brother. Back in the womb, Annette had absorbed her mother's fears that death might strike again. She also saw how her mother due to painful labor for three days, afterward unconsciously distanced herself from her daughter who had caused so much agony. Annette had no conscious memory of such events happening but still forgave her mother. To Annette's surprise she was healed and is still able to sleep straight through the night. Her mother later confirmed the three days of difficult labor and the deaths of her son and brother during the pregnancy.

Christ sometimes brings hurts to mind and at other times heals hurts when we are focusing on some other memory or even sleeping. One woman slept through a group prayer for healing of early hurts and awoke feeling freed but not knowing why. She went home and found that her nightmares had ceased and that she could relate well to her mother, a cranky invalid. Much healing occurs in dreams while sleeping, especially if we ask for healing before falling asleep.

How do I know what hurt Christ wants me to focus on and share? I pray for guidance and then simply tell Jesus what I feel and focus on the feeling until he brings a hurt to mind. Several might come. I take the one that hurts the most or goes back the farthest, since what gives me more pain or has remained, generally has wounded me more and still controls me. I pick the emotion that is strong enough to create a physical change, like a pounding heart, tense face, tears, turning cold or perspiring, relaxed jaw or a shudder. When I really feel an emotion, rather than just thinking about it, my body changes too. If I don't experience a difference in my body, I keep asking ''What else am I feeling?'' until I find the hurt deep enough to affect my body.

What if we ask Christ to bring a hurt to mind, spend a few minutes reverently and silently waiting, and yet nothing comes? Maybe we are feeling a deep loneliness that goes way back to being hospitalized for surgery at the age of three. If we have forgotten the wounding event, we can just take the feeling such as loneliness and then imagine the event that most fits the feeling. Maybe the loneliness we fear is not that of being in the woods alone in a log cabin but of being hurt in a car accident and bleeding to death with no one to help. If that scene fits more our fear of loneliness, it more closely matches our unconscious fear of surgery bringing death and permanent loneliness. When we walk through that constructed car accident with Christ, he can touch and heal the deeper loneliness from our fear of death at the age of three.

When describing to Christ my feeling of emptiness, different hurts came to mind: lazy students, too much work, my friend Gus' criticism, my brother John's death, and a superior's criticism. The one that most fit the empty, helpless feeling I had was Gus' criticism. The others were not as painful to recall, needed less healing and didn't seem to be Christ's choice. Thus I shared with Christ more of how it felt to be criticized. It felt like a friend thrusting a knife into my back and draining out my life. Finally I placed all that I expressed in Christ's hands and let go so I could focus on him and not on my problems. Now I could start to listen to Christ's reaction to me.

2. *Listen Through Scripture to How Christ Feels*

If my prayer is 90 percent speaking and 10 percent listening, I will feel almost the same at the end as when I started. How can I listen to a "silent" Jesus? Not the ears but the heart listens. Listening is not searching for words, but looking at Jesus with the loving gaze a mother has for her infant to whom she commits her life. Listening to Jesus is primarily an attitude of wanting only what he wants at any price even if it means the poverty and insults I fear most. Listening to Jesus comes not by sitting passively silent, but by gazing on him with so much love that I have to stop and ask him what he wants of me. The more I love a person, the more I listen to him. Any time I have taken a step toward deeper faith, hope or love, I have listened to Jesus.

When listening to Jesus, I ask what Scriptures Christ would share with me if I were walking with him at Emmaus. The disciples on the road to Emmaus felt the way I felt—confused and let down by a friend. Christ would probably respond to me as he did to them.

Whatever helps me to listen to a friend will help me listen to Jesus. I choose a quiet place, sit in a relaxed yet erect listening posture, and hold the Scriptures reverently until I sense a reverence for the power of each word. Then I slowly read the passage three or more times aloud until finally I can shut my eyes and relive the scene as if Christ were speaking each word directly to me.

To let Christ's word seep from my head into my heart, I close my eyes and get relaxed and centered on Christ. The more I am relaxed and centered on Christ, the more he can speak to my unhealed unconscious. To relax in Jesus, sometimes I concentrate on each part of my body, tense it up, and then let it loose, surrendering it to Jesus. As I feel his power entering and tensions driven out, I say "Jesus." Slowly I become like him, part by part, from the top of my head to my forehead, eyes, ears, and jaw, and all the way to my wiggling toes.

Then I take deep, slow breaths, breathing in and saying

"Jesus" with reverence and hunger since I need him as much as I need air.[7] Sometimes I will hold my breath to build up my hunger for Jesus. When I breathe out I give Jesus myself and hear him saying my name in the way he alone loves me and calls me. How I say "Jesus" changes because with each breath I open a deeper part of myself to Jesus and give him a deeper part of my life. If I get distracted, I simply return to saying "Jesus." I continue to do this until I sense how much he loves me and I have his mind and heart rather than the feelings I expressed to him.

Often the healing is deeper if I give Christ not just my body but my imagination too. Whatever I vividly relive in my imagination affects me as if I really experienced it. To activate my imagination I close my eyes and activate my senses.[8] I see Christ on the dusty Emmaus road adapting his gait to mine and listening intently as I share what hurts me. I smell the dust, the sweat, and the spring air punctuated by lilies of the field. I feel the warm sunlight, uneven stones under my feet and the bumping of our swinging hands as we walk close together to let a cart pass. I hear the squeaky wheels roll by, the birds chirp, and the plodding of our feet along the hard surface. Then when I am fully involved in the scene, I look at Jesus and see him wipe the dust from his squinting eyes so that he can look at me lovingly as my best friend. I watch his face—his gentle smile and especially his eyes until I can guess what he wants to say. It's easy to guess because Christ (Love itself) always says only the most loving words possible. When I get in touch with what I need most to hear, I am hearing Christ. As Christ looks at the hurt in my heart, he seems to say:

"Let me show you how I have been with you in your hard times. I hid in all those who broke bread with you and stood by you to bless you with a word of encouragement when your heart was heavy. I hunger to enter into you at the Eucharist and face everything with you even when it seems I have vanished. You have nothing to fear if you face Gus' criticism with me. Look at what I have struggled through—loss of friends, the passion . . . Look at what you have struggled through . . . Let me bring to your mind the growth that came in hard times so that we may thank the Father. Let me put my arm on your shoulder and fill you with my strength to face all I see ahead."

When I need to hear from others, "I liked that talk," I usually need to hear from Christ of his consistent, special care for me and really believe it. When facing a crisis, I do what the Jews did— review the history of the Lord's love. They could see Yahweh's love even in Joshua's lost battles that made them rely more on Yahweh then weapons, in famines that drew Joseph's family together, and in long days of slave labor that made them persevere while wandering through a desert to a promised land. If I can thank Yahweh not just for good times—friends, special moments in prayer, success in my work, health, moments of insights or deep peace—but also for the lost battles in the classroom making me prepare better classes, and the growth coming from the moments of slavery and wandering in a desert, then I am ready to face new crises rather than deny them. If I feel loved and secure, then I can face the hurts.

Like the disciples at Emmaus, I can return to the scene of the hurt if I have felt loved in meeting Christ and have his mind and heart rather than the feelings with which I started. If I don't feel more like Christ it is foolish and harmful to recreate in my imagination the bulletin board scene and its hurt and then expect Christ to walk up and heal my wounds. If the love of Christ isn't real for me at Emmaus, it won't be real for me when feeling the added hurt at the bulletin board. But to the degree that I have been stretched beyond my initial hurt feelings and have Christ's feelings and view, I can return in my imagination to the bulletin board and experience a new outlook, that of Christ. The Scripture not only opens me up to Christ's mind and heart but provides a test of whether I should look at my wounds with Christ or wait until his love and view are more real. If Christ's love is hard to find in the Scriptures, it will be harder to find looking at my wounds.

But because I experienced Christ's love as he spoke and put his arm on my shoulder at Emmaus, I feel different more loved, secure, ready to face suffering with him—and can return with him to the bulletin board where I was hurt. I enter the bulletin board scene just as I did at Emmaus, using all my senses until I can smell the coffee, see the notices on the board, and hear the death dealing words, "I wonder how long he will last as a Jesuit." As the waves of shock and disbelief roll over me, Christ walks over to the bulletin board, puts his arm around my shoulder, and begins to speak: "Don't worry. It's necessary that I should suffer in you so that you can share in my glory. It's not what he thinks but what I think that counts. You have nothing to fear if you face it with me."

What Christ says at the scene of the hurt, and what he says in the scriptural scene (Emmaus), may be the same or very different. If I have felt his love in Scripture, he may be able to say deeper, more challenging words. He does what I most need. Sometimes I am unsure of what Christ wants to say and I find myself going back to recall how he reacted at Emmaus and then returning again to the bulletin board when I understand his mind and heart. I am simply with him wherever I can best give him what I am feeling and absorb what he is feeling. Sometimes I talk with him, ask or answer questions, just admiringly watch him, or breathe in his feelings and breathe out mine. The Spirit knows best the depth of my wound and how to heal it.

Even if I sense no response from Christ, pinpointing what hurts and sharing it with him really helps. I receive many letters pouring out what is hurting and asking for advice. In expressing their feelings, the writers often pinpointed their real hurt and what to do about it. Often a letter closes with, "Thank you for reading all this. It sounds worse than it seems now. Take your time in answering this." Just in writing what they felt and thinking how I would respond, they received an answer.

Even the silence of Christ produces an answer if we really share what we are feeling and search for his response. It is evident that we have been talking not to ourselves but to Christ if the prayer creates deep faith, trust, love and surrender. To the degree we have the fruit of the Spirit (Gal. 5:22) we have been listening to Christ.

This process is not introspective psychoanalysis where an analyst helps us to figure out our problem. We meet not an analyst but Christ who calls us to see beyond ourselves until we have his reactions to love his Father and our neighbor. We do not dig and probe until we hit our deepest unconscious feeling, but calmly and prayerfully ask Christ to show us what feelings he wants us to accept and make into his reactions. Healing comes not by discovering the skeletons in the closet but by discovering Christ in the closet and putting him on (Rom. 13:14). We don't figure out our problem but absorb Christ's love until we can trade hearts.

Healing occurs not by rigidly following a method but by getting to the mind and heart of Christ, whether it comes by scriptural prayer, the stations, the rosary, or just actively imagining what Christ would do and say to me when I am hurt.[9] The essential steps are to face the hurt (tell Christ what I am feeling), get stretched by Christ's mind and heart (listen to Christ's reaction) and then live out Christ's reaction.

3. Living Out Christ's Reaction

How can we live out Christ's reaction?[10] The main thing that Christ seems to say when I am in denial is, "Don't be afraid but share with me whatever is hard to face. We both have faced worse and grown through the cross." Seeing the past from Christ's viewpoint helps me to turn from denial and face anger. The more I know how Christ has loved me and has loved through me in all the years of my life, the more I will be able to find his love even in angry times of hurt. I begin to see that the times I was angry—my brother John's death, an impossible assignment among the Sioux, leaving old friends—were the times of great gifts. These are all healed memories that make me at home with facing anger and further hurts, for I know that they, too, can be gifts. But when I see only a time of hurt (my friend's criticism) and no gifts coming from it, that memory needs healing, so I don't keep fearing criticism and denying it by burying my anger. Every unhealed memory makes it easier to remain in denial and more difficult to be at home with angry feelings. If we have been hurt by angry parents, peers or friends, we don't want angry feelings in us or around us. The next chapter shows how to bring those hidden, angry feelings to Christ so that we can be freed rather than run from angry people or be controlled by buried anger.

8

SECOND STAGE: ANGER

Even "nice old ladies" usually become angry patients once they stop denying that they have cancer. They criticize the food, ring every other minute for the nurse, blame the doctors for not having found the cancer sooner, and find fault with friends who visit without bringing flowers.

When we are hurting, we become like cancer patients, ready to blame another. Very few drivers in a car accident admit that it was their fault. We blame the other driver, the blind approach, the slippery pavement, or the car's poor brakes. Anger needs a target.

I
SYMPTOMS OF ANGER

But I am an expert at denying my symptoms of anger. I have been raised as an American tending to repress anger the way the Victorian age repressed sex. I learned that anger is a capital sin, that I shouldn't raise my voice, and that angry parents spank me while angry peers beat me up or call me names. I learned to hide my anger from my friends so that I wouldn't lose their affection, and eventually, with practice, I even hid my anger from myself.

Thus for a long time I never allowed myself to feel angry at Gus' criticism of my talk, but rather felt frustrated, tense, judgmental, irritated, disappointed, edgy, let down, less loving, or a dozen other euphemisms for "anger." Sometimes I wasn't even in touch with my negative feelings but only felt less joy, creativity, spontaneity and love. I was angry, but afraid to name my anger and risk losing a friend, getting hurt, or losing control.

But swallowing my anger made me lose friends as I became more impatient and critical. Impatience made me a clock watcher shifting feet and tightening my jaw when people came late. I found myself rushing what I was doing (eating fast) to get on to the next event (reading a newspaper) and rushing that too. I even helped people finish their sentences so I could get on to what I wanted to say or alter their insight with a "Yes . . . but . . ." When I took time to talk with someone, I would only half listen, hearing what he said but missing how he really felt. I began to teach subjects, not students, and look forward to classes ending, not beginning. I impatiently worked harder and alone, seldom delegating a task because I felt that others didn't want to help or because I didn't think that they could do a good job. I became a "constructive" (because I was the critic and not the target) critic of everyone—those who didn't know I needed help, those who were late, and those spreading injustice by their apathy. When I prayed, I treated God as I did others—half listening, talking about my work, complaining about injustices (like Gus's criticism) that needed changing and venting impatience at God's timetable. Much of the day my anger expressed itself in continual wishes that something would change and go faster or better.

Ways of expressing anger depend on how deeply we are hurt and how readily we express anger. Anger has as many shapes as people have. When angry, children wet beds and forget to do what they just promised, husbands withdraw behind work and newspapers, wives gossip on the phone, religious force a smile and practice self-control. Workers sometimes call in sick and recover at home, puffing out their anger, drowning it in drink and swallowing it with food and pills.

If anger is swallowed long enough, the body may rebel with ulcers, asthma attacks, hypertension, hyperthyroidism, rheumatoid arthritis, colitis, neurodermatitis, migraine headaches, coronary disease, and mental illness. The symptoms of anger match perfectly the symptoms of Type A Behavior responsible for heart attacks.[1] Unresolved anger is equally as destructive to emotional health because swallowed anger often results in self-hatred and depression. If we say, "I never feel angry," we probably will convert our anger into illness.

II
ANGER IN SCRIPTURE

Anger festering from some hurt probably drove the prodigal son to demand his inheritance, run away into a distant country, and drown his problems in the pleasure of loose living (Lk. 15:11–32).

These actions didn't heal his smarting anger but rather he returns home angrily thinking, "my father's hired servants have bread enough to spare, but I perish here with hunger!" His anger or ours is neither good nor bad, but judged by whether it makes us run away from our compassionate father or return to his healing embrace.

The prodigal returns to his father who seems to have no trace of anger but only a compassionate embrace. Was the father of the prodigal son ever angry and wishing things were different? Such a compassionate father was not indifferent but probably felt the pain of the departure. The pain of anger may have helped him keep one eye on the road with hope that he could glimpse his missing son. Maybe his anger at whatever drove the son away made him dream of correcting the situation with a welcoming party which gets planned with no hesitation.

But unlike the father and younger son who chose in their anger to experience love and compassion, the elder son chose in his anger to experience hostility. "He was angry and refused to go in," but instead answered his father.

> These many years I have served you, and I never disobeyed your command; yet you never gave me a kid, that I might make merry with my friends. But when this son of yours came, who has devoured your living with harlots, you killed for him the fatted calf! (Lk. 15:29–30).

The elder son's anger turns to hostility that attacks his brother's presumed "living with harlots" and his father's unearned forgiveness. It is not feeling anger that makes the elder son differ from the father and prodigal but rather his hostile demand that forgiveness be earned by good behavior before compassion kills the fatted calf. The capital sin should not be feeling *anger* but nursing unresolved anger resulting in *hostility*, the attitude leading to hurt another by negative humor, destructive criticism or other unloving behavior. Feeling anger is healthy; acting hostilely is usually unhealthy and sinful.

Like the compassionate father, we are to feel anger and respond with love rather than the elder brother's hostility (the wish to hurt). Because hostility, not anger, should be the capital sin,

Ephesians exhorts, "Be angry but sin not . . ." (Eph. 4:26). Anger can be constructive if it leads us to help the person who hurt us or another. Christ angrily told Peter to "get behind me" (Mt. 16:23) because he loved Peter and wanted him to grow by facing the approaching suffering in Jerusalem. Where people are hurt by greedy temple sellers (Mt. 21:22ff), demons (Mt. 1:25), hypocritical pharisees (Mt. 15), unmerciful men (Mt. 3:5), unbelievers (Jn. 8:44), or wicked masters (Mt. 18:34), Christ's anger blazes forth. Christ doesn't just silently withdraw, swallow his anger and hope injustice will disappear. Anger drives him to correct injustices quickly even before night falls (Eph. 4:26).

But for centuries artists have painted the peaceful Good Shepherd Christ who says: "Blessed are the meek, for they shall inherit the earth" (Mt. 5:15) rather than the angry Christ correcting injustice by casting out the temple merchants. Perhaps we don't understand "meek" (Gk. *praotes*) meaning "angry at the right time" and midway on the spectrum that runs from *orgilotes* (excessive anger) to *aorgesia* (excessive angerlessness). Anger has its right occasion if it fulfills "Love your enemies, pray for those who persecute you" (Mt. 5:44).

Like Christ, Yahweh is at home with anger. Terms for anger and rage are attributed to God five times as often as to man.[2] Of all the targets for Yahweh's anger the most frequent is Israel, the people Yahweh loves most. Among all Israelites Yahweh is angered by those he most loves: Jacob (Gn. 32:23ff.), Moses (Ex. 4:24ff.), and David (2 Sm. 24:1ff.). To love is to risk being hurt and angered.

Likewise, those who can get angry at Yahweh are those who love him most. David is angry at Yahweh for striking Uzzah dead when trying to catch the ark as it fell, and he even refuses to bring the ark into the city (2 Sm. 6:8). Job, covered with boils, spends chapters angrily asking variations of "Why dost thou hide thy face and count me as thy enemy?" (Jb. 13:24). Because these men love Yahweh, they expect more from him and are more easily hurt when they do not understand his ways. The Old Testament forces us to ask: Do we like Yahweh, love people enough to get angry at them? Do we like Job, expect enough of Yahweh to get angry at him when he hides his face?

III
ANGER CAN BE HEALTHY

Something is wrong if we never feel anger. We should love ourselves and others enough to hate violence, selfishness, prejudice, sexual chauvinism, and other injustices. Anger energizes us to change what should be changed so that we can live in a better, more loving environment. When I am detached from the suffering of the Sioux—poor, unemployed, trapped by alcoholism, victims of white and red violence—I sit back and let others correct these injustices. I "hunger and thirst for justice" among the Sioux only when I am angered at injustice. Anger also helps me to fight against what I fear. When a car swerves into my lane on the freeway, I get angry, and instantly my body, triggered by epinephrin and norepinephrin, releases sugar and pumps blood toward the muscles so that I can react and overcome the accident I fear. Anger can pinpoint a fear I need to face and overcome. Burying anger can build fear that may lead to depression and suicide.

Just to allow myself to feel angry means trying to overcome my fear of losing a friend, not being accepted, getting hurt, or losing control. When Gus criticized my prayer presentation, it took much healing before I was secure enough to even recognize my anger. Initially I tried to bury my anger as if it weren't Christian. Sometimes I wonder how much of Christian forgiveness is only reaction formation concealing hate behind a smiling facade. But pretending anger wasn't there only made it grow and get displaced to hurt the wrong targets—my students, those drinking too much, and others needing not anger but extra care. Denying my anger so I wouldn't lose control and lose friends backfired, as I found myself uncontrollably more critical of my students and eventually of even Gus. Burying anger plants an angry harvest of whatever is buried.

In German concentration camps, for example, angry prisoners were punished until they learned to fear and bury their anger in order to survive. But frustrated anger initiated regression to patterns of immediate gratification (fighting for food and wolfing it down), fantasy (dreaming of miraculous rescues), and identification with the aggressor (helping the guards to intimidate the new men), and ended in apathy. Victor Frankl, psychiatrist and founder of logotherapy, relates how his fellow prisoners chose either to feel the concentration camp horrors and become angry or to feel none of the brutality and bury their anger in apathy. The inmates who continually chose to insulate themselves from feeling any hurt became totally listless and refused to move for roll call, dinner or even the bathroom, until eventually they died. Nothing frightened them any longer and they hardly seemed to feel a bloody beating.[3]

Thus denying anger is unhealthy and can destroy us. Feeling anger, on the other hand, is as healthy a reaction to being emotionally hurt as feeling pain is to being physically hurt. When emotionally hurt, people who love themselves get angry; people who don't love themselves get depressed and even suicidal as in Frankl's concentration camp. Because depression is often displaced anger turned against oneself, a good psychotherapist treats the depression by helping the client express anger in a healthy way and at the proper target. Many depressions begin to lift when answering, "Who or what makes me angry?"

Feeling anger enables me to identify the hurt and heal it in a healthy way. When the emotional hurt isn't felt, it becomes like a cancer that grows wildly until it is exposed and its hidden dimensions are cut away. Anger's warning that I have been hurt and am in danger of closing myself off from God and others can alert me to share with a friend and God all the hurts that prick my anger. Anger like pain pinpoints what gets under my skin and most needs healing. I only have to ask who or what is bothering me most and properly express this. Healing can begin when I ask God or a friend to help me because I am angry at that policeman for giving me a ticket; not when I punch the officer in the nose.

Anger not only helps me love myself by pinpointing what hurts and beginning to heal it, but it also helps me love the person who hurt me. Once I am able to recognize my denial and begin to get in touch with my hidden anger and my need to forgive, I can choose either to forgive little by denying another's weakness and saying, "you're not so bad; I forgive you," or to forgive much by allowing my anger to see another's weakness and saying, "I see the worst that is in you, the hurts in myself and yet I love you as Christ does." Anyone can love the smiling side of a person, but anger allows my love to deepen into forgiving even the wounding side of another. I can accept the anger and weakness in another's wounding side only to the degree I can recognize and accept my own angry feelings and weaknesses as does Christ. Anger, therefore, stretches me to love more as Christ until I can forgive even the weakness in myself and in another.

Not only can feeling anger lead to a deeper love but also a deeper love can lead to feeling anger. A loving wife has reason to feel more angry when her husband forgets her birthday than when her neighbor forgets. The more we love a person, the more we can get hurt by their lack of love, and we can feel anger. The deepest hurts come from those closest. That's why when trying to heal deep hurts in clients, psychotherapists often focus on relationships with mother, father, and spouse.

Therefore thank God for feeling anger, often a sign that we love either the person hurting us or we love ourselves enough to dislike getting hurt. To be in touch with our angry feelings is always healthy, but how we deal with our angry feelings can cripple us or give us new freedom to walk boldly. It's human and not wrong to feel pain or anger. What becomes right or wrong is how we express our pain or anger.

IV
DEALING WITH ANGER

Anger must be dealt with or it will deal with us. Dr. Floyd Ring studied how reactions to anger influence our health. Dr. Ring, of the University of Nebraska Medical School, asked his colleagues to send him four hundred patients (all unknown to him) already diagnosed with fourteen ailments.[4] He tried to diagnose the four hundred patients solely on the basis of a fifteen-minute personality interview with each patient, who was covered by a linen sheet. Two observers stood by, making sure that the doctor neither saw nor asked anything that might reveal medical symptoms.

Solely on the basis of their personality, he diagnosed correctly 100 percent of the hyperthyroids, 71 percent of the coronary occlusions, 83 percent of the peptic ulcers and rheumatoid arthritis and 60 percent or better of those with asthma, diabetes, hypertension and ulcerative colitis. His first or second diagnosis was correct for 87 percent of the patients. He found the best diagnostic question to be: If, before you became ill, you were sitting on a park bench and a stranger, who was about the same size as you, kicked you in the shins, what would you do?

The "excessive reactors" wanting a verbal or physical showdown tended to suffer from coronary occlusion, degenerative arthritis and peptic ulcers. The "deficient reactors," suppressing their fear or anger and doing next to nothing, suffered from neurodermatitis, rheumatoid arthritis and ulcerative colitis. The "unrestrained reactors," those aware of fears and anger but rarely expressing them, tended toward asthma, diabetes, hypertension, hyperthyroidism and migraines. Obviously how we deal with anger is just one of many stress factors that lead to illness, but it seems to often be a significant factor.

It seems that any way a person reacts to a kick, he gets sick. It's too bad that Dr. Floyd Ring didn't interview some healthy people to see how they deal with anger. But psychiatrists have done that and have found that healthy people both recognize their angry feelings and find the right way to express their anger.

There are as many ways of constructively dealing with anger as there are angry people.[5] Some find it helpful to divert their anger into work by chopping wood, scrubbing a floor, or getting even with a dirty wall. Anger needs tension (try getting angry without getting tense), so anything that drains away tension, whether a hot shower, a hard run or a relaxed walk, will diminish anger, too. But though these activities usually drain out the present anger, they fail to heal past hurts that fester and cause continuous anger.

Many find that when they can pin their feelings down into words and then share how they feel, the anger from past hurts begins to heal. A friend who sympathizes can offer us the love and understanding we crave when hurt if we say: "I really feel angry now, so help me in working with it." A warm friend's acceptance of my anger makes it easier to experience in prayer Christ's acceptance of my anger and vice versa.

Besides sharing with a friend or with Christ, sometimes we can directly tell whoever hurt us exactly how we feel and why we are angry. This takes much trust and openness for both to be honest without leaving wounds. Very few people can be open to constructive criticism from an angry man. At first anger usually makes us exaggerate the harm we suffer and closes us to another. Healing occurs to the extent that we can confront another in love rather than angrily striking back. Anger should be expressed, but in a way that ties people closer together.[6] To test this closeness in a community, simply ask: Are people trusting enough to express anger in a loving and upbuilding way? Loving correction demands a loving community.

Christ strongly encourages loving correction: "If your brother sins against you, go and tell him his faults, between you and him alone. If he listens to you, you have gained your brother" (Mt. 18:15). But this advice is preceded by how we should come—humble as a child (Mt. 18:1–6), knowing how we scandalize with our sinfulness (Mt. 18:7–9), and like a shepherd seeking a lost sheep (Mt. 18:10–14). Most people cannot reach this ideal when initially angry, but only later when they recognize their own responsibility in getting hurt and therefore come both forgiving and asking for forgiveness from a brother.

We approach our *brother* in a way that will help him listen and be reconciled. Peter understands this and asks: "Lord, how often shall my brother sin against me and I forgive him?" (Mt. 18:21). The time to confront someone with our angry feelings is when we can forgive seventy times seven because, unlike the unforgiving servant, we know how much we have been forgiven (Mt. 18:21–34). The time to talk is when we know our own weakness and are asking forgiveness rather than just demanding forgiveness and projecting our weakness angrily on another. Too often when I angrily accuse my students of not working, it's a projection of my weakness in not working to prepare better classes.

Frequently, before angrily expressing myself to Gus or my students, I find it helpful to heal that anger by sharing it with Christ. He is the only one who can completely understand, since he was persecuted in every imaginable way and was hurt in all the ways we were hurt. But, more importantly, he can do more than listen. Jesus Christ can bring to mind all the hurt we have denied and touch every painful area with his healing that reaches into the past and future. He knows our hidden wounds and our insecurity that craves his love and care. Healing will come as it did to the disciples on the road to Emmaus if, once again as in dealing with denial, I do the following:

1. Tell Christ how I feel (Lk. 23:13–24).
2. Listen through Scripture to how Christ feels (Lk. 23:25–30).
3. Take on Christ's reaction and live it out (Lk. 23:31–35).

1. *Tell Christ How I Feel*

The first step is to do whatever helps me to prayerfully come into the presence of Christ and share what I am feeling. The questions that helped in the denial stage will often help delineate the dimensions of the anger I feel. What would it take to have everything perfect? What do I fear or avoid? What do I wish had happened differently? Whom do I wish were different? Whom do I fear, avoid, half listen to, or love less than previously? For whose success is it hardest to thank God? Writing or speaking aloud the answers usually generates a deeper response and helps me catch anything sounding shallow or insincere.

What we are feeling often has deeper levels. When I was criticized, I felt angry at students who were less interested in my anthropology classes than in the wasps diving from the classroom lights. I could talk to Christ about my anger toward my students, but this was displaced anger and not the deeper level needing healing. When did I feel most like this? That question brought me back to the deeper hurt, my friend's criticism. Maybe there was another time further back. I want to talk to Christ about the situation that most hurts. That's the one from which I am still running to avoid the pain.

Once I have located the situation where I was most deeply hurt, I reconstruct it in my imagination so that I can hand over to Christ my memory of all the hurt and destruction. The more the senses are involved to reconstruct the hurt, the more I can hand it over for Christ to heal. Christ asked the disciples on the road to Emmaus to unburden all that was going wrong. Christ wants us to come as we are—crippled and hurt and not with the smile and halo we wish we had. The most frequent barrier to healing a memory is that we cannot face and share with Christ all the anger of a deep hurt.

My prayer might sound like this: "Lord, show me what I felt like saying and doing. Let me share all its ugliness and hurt with you so that it will all be in your hands. You were present and hurt when I was hurt. Bring into my memory every detail that I have buried. Let me keep telling you what it was like until I can add no more to the pain and there is no more to say. Let me keep sharing with you as long as I feel the hurt even if it takes months. Absorb from me everything: every memory, every word that stings. You had many things said behind your back and know how I feel. Let me share with you everything that is wrong and how it hurts. Help me in my imagination to reconstruct every detail of the destruction at the bulletin board.

"Lord, I'm standing with you back at the bulletin board. I can see its notices of deaths and the Mass schedule, smell the aroma of coffee coming from the dining room, I really feel good. The talk went well and people are laughing as they drink coffee and munch oatmeal cookies. Then I hear: 'What do you think of that talk?' 'It sounded like a talk a novice would give. It's hard to believe that he has been a Jesuit praying for six years. I wonder how long he will last as a Jesuit?'

"Lord, I feel drained and scared, yet I'd like to rush in and embarrass Gus by asking if he really means what he said. Should I reveal his hypocrisy by asking him what he thought of the talk and then confront him with his own words? Would anything really help? What difference does it make? It's only his opinion and he is critical of everything. All the others liked it. I'll show him that he's wrong by maturely letting it bounce off. I'll just talk to the others and see what they think.

"Lord, as I talk to others and hear that the talk was good, I begin to feel anger. Here he criticizes me for the way I pray, and yet his Mass is a twenty-minute race to finish early and have more time for dinner. Why do you keep him as a Jesuit? Look at the people he has hurt with his demeaning comments and destructive criticism. Why don't you send him someplace else where his comments won't demoralize good people? What can I do that will keep others from getting hurt?

"He wounded me too. Because of him I just seem to be growling at my students and finding fault with everything. I'm beginning to wonder what people are saying behind my back and whether they really mean any positive comments that come my way. I'm even beginning to question whether I really am a Jesuit or a good teacher. So take all this destruction that he started. Just let me rest a few moments in your arms and breathe in your strength. (Then I just rest and ask Christ to do for me whatever I most want and need.)

"Look, Lord, you can tell me that you love him and died for him, but you can't tell me that you want him the way he is. You may love the sinner but not the sin. You confronted Peter and the Pharisees so that they might change and stop hurting the people. Now do something about changing him, since you cared enough about him to die for him and can do all things. What are you waiting for? You told me to "pray for those who persecute you." I'm doing my part and praying, and now it's up to you to do the changing or let me know how I can change him. He needs to apologize to some of the people he has ripped apart. Could you teach him the difference between criticism and compliments? Could you get him praying so you have a chance to love him? But it sounds foolish to talk this way with you, because you know his needs and love him. I want what you want. Show me how he needs your care and healing touch so that I can ask you for it and give it when I have a chance. Forgive him and help him. If he is hurting so many people, he must be hurting inside and needing you. What would you do and say to heal him?"

2. *Listen Through Scripture to How Christ Feels*

"Lord Jesus, when did you feel criticized unjustly? You must have felt a little like me when the Pharisees invited you to dinner and then criticized you for not washing. Show me as I read Luke 11:37–44 how you want me to treat this Pharisee before he hurts more good people. (I then relax, get in a listening posture and prayerfully read Luke 11:37–44 slowly several times until I can think and feel like Christ and know just what he would say and do without having to read it again. I then picture Gus smiling and dunking a cookie in his cup of coffee just as he drowns me in criticism. I watch Christ enter the dining room and see what he says and does. I keep watching Christ until I have his mind and heart. I then imagine myself saying and doing what Christ would. What I can imagine of Christ's response becomes easier, and what

I can't imagine and feel shows me where I need Christ's love and power to grow.)

"Lord as I listen to you, Gus doesn't sound as bad as your Pharisees. Gus is talented and has been given four jobs in the last three years because he does well. But it must be frustrating for him to always be moved into a more difficult job just when he feels he is succeeding on the old job. Each job is harder and less successful. You seem to say that he is more angry at his lack of success than at my talk. Thanks for letting me see that his criticism is only a smokescreen of stored-up frustration from other failures, and that I shouldn't take it personally.

"Lord, put into my mind the hurts he has suffered so that I may ask you to heal those times. Who hurt him in a way that made him hurt me? For what has he been criticized? I see him buried behind his desk piled high with papers. You seem to put your hand on his shoulder, wanting to give him the time and patience to answer all his mail. Maybe I could even ask to help with that. But, Lord, help me to see the hurts deeper than the pile of mail. Why does he see himself as a failure? Help me to see what he needs and then place him in your hands so that you may give it. Let me watch what you do and say so that I can do the same.

"Lord, I can now catch a glimpse of his good side, too, although Gus still seems to have ten faults for each virtue. He has had four jobs in the last two years because he does well and is then given more responsibility. It must be frustrating to always face a bigger challenge without seeing results. Use his gift of adaptability to help him know how to change and have courage to try new ways in his own life just as he has tried new jobs. What else do you see in him that my anger hides from me? Show me the good you want to build upon.

"Lord, how did you react to the Pharisees so that you could build upon whatever good they had? You keep getting hurt by Pharisees, yet you always eat with them (Lk. 7:36; 11:37; 14:1). I think that is what you would do with Gus. You would keep all the doors open to him. Help me to share meals with him as you would, trying to build trust, trying to reach out to whatever hurts in him.

"Lord, you also respond to Pharisees by doing good. As they criticize, you heal on the sabbath a man with a withered hand (Mk. 3:1–6) or run to the protection of a woman whom Simon the

Pharisee is demeaning (Lk. 7:36). Help me to quit being tied up with criticism so that I can heal those who are hurting—the students I criticized and the teachers Gus criticized. What would you do for them? Maybe you would just quietly point out their strengths and goodness as you did for the woman at your feet. I've been running around and looking for approval of my talk, and I'm sure that they could use positive encouragement too.

"Lord, you also keep fearlessly speaking out. We are to not be concerned about the reactions of Pharisees but of God (Lk. 12:4–7). I should fear Gus' criticism only if it is the truth in your eyes. In the days ahead, keep showing me your view. And when it is time to speak out, let me speak the truth fearlessly without anxiety, 'for the Holy Spirit will teach you in that very hour what you ought to say' (Lk. 12:11). So let me put all fears in your hands now. I see your hand lifting all fear from my shoulders. Thank you."

Usually when I can admit I am angry, the Lord shows me the destruction I detest, whom I am blaming, why the person is that way, the hidden side I can't see and what he wants to do and say through me to bring this healing.[8]

3. *Living Out Christ's Healing Reaction*

Anger is a motor that can drive us to love like Christ when we are free enough to acknowledge anger and then steer it toward loving, non-hostile action. But unacknowledged anger chokes action because I either get angry at myself and quit trying, or get angry at God and try without him, or get angry at others and work alone, or get angry at the wrong target and try the wrong solution. Freedom to act doesn't come overnight. It begins by acknowledging my anger and using its energy to build a better environment reducing the occasions of anger. My resolution to build a bridge to my critic by eating meals with him lasted for three unenjoyable meals featuring salty sarcasm on every subject. I found myself becoming more tense, and argumentative. As a result I began eating with the students and teachers, trying to offer a few positive words. I was free enough to love them and build them but not to love my critic.

Freedom from hostility grows as I relax to share my anger with Christ, with another who can listen and pray with me, or with a sheet of paper that won't talk back. When I am angry I become tense and negative, and my world narrows to what happened at the bulletin board. Anger loosens its tense grip when I relax and manage to laugh at myself—a martyr hanged, drawn and quartered by two sentences. I can't remain scowlingly negative for long if I start praying for those who are hurt (including my critic) and start to thank Christ for the growth in my life that has come from critical people who helped me to honestly face my faults and correct them. If I can ask Jesus to heal my critic's weaknesses and thank Jesus for strengths that can grow, I also grow. I find it hard to be hostile while thanking the Lord for the critical people and asking that I may grow from them. If I also can broaden my world by visiting a hospital or home for senior citizens, my corner of the world doesn't look so dark.

Christ doesn't just feel anger and then sit with it or shout his woes against the Pharisees and move on to fishing. Christ uses anger to confront injustice and change it. When Christ enters the synagogue and finds a man with a withered hand (Mk. 3:1–6), he also finds an unjust situation—no healing permitted on the sabbath day. His anger moves him to confront and change the injustice that others have avoided by swallowing their anger:

> And he said to them, ''Is it lawful on the sabbath to do good or to do harm, to save life or to kill?'' But they were silent. And he looked around at them with anger, grieved at their hardness of heart, and he said to the man, ''Stretch out your hand.'' He stretched it out, and his hand was restored. The Pharisees went out and immediately held counsel with the Herodians against him, how to destroy him (Mk. 3:4–6).

Both Christ and the Pharisees were angry. Christ uses anger to confront injustice with love and healing. The Pharisees respond angrily with injustice, an unforgiving heart, and hostility against the healer.

Healing the wounds of anger begins in little ways, but healing with prayer has big results. A close friend was in church praying that she might be healed of her alcoholism and begin caring again for her four small children whom she would abandon when drinking. Nothing seemed to help—AA, long talks with counselors, or even the cries of her hungry children failed to keep her sober. As she prayed for sobriety, she was flooded with waves of love for the man who had killed her husband two years ago. For the first time she no longer felt hostile toward the man who made her a widow. She forgave him and prayed that the Lord would care for him. Since that day she has remained sober and a devoted mother. As this forgiveness deepened over the next years she was also healed of migraine headaches and a pinched nerve in her wrist injured in a fight long ago. Physical healings of migraine headaches, ulcers, high blood pressure, insomnia, colitis, asthma, arthritis and even cancer frequently occur as Christ takes our anger and gives his forgiving healing response and all this can happen by taking the three steps of Emmaus.

9

THIRD STAGE: BARGAINING

After a patient facing death quits blaming the doctors and God, he begins to realize that he needs the doctors and God if he is to escape death or at least postpone its hour. He begins to make bargains with them in return for help. "If I quit smoking, take all my medicine, and keep struggling to live, then help me to live longer and even recover." God hears proposed bargains such as: "If I make this novena and pray every day for the rest of my life, give me another chance." "Yes, I will give up drinking, but first get me out of here healthy." "Yes, I will accept death but first let me see my daughter happily married." The variations are endless, "I am willing to . . . only if you . . ."

Bargaining is a common reaction to hurts other than death. We are tempted to talk the highway patrol officer out of a ticket by kindness, promises to stay under 55, and maybe a little cash. If someone scratches our car, we are willing not to report the accident if he produces the cash for repairs. If our neighbor spreads some unfavorable gossip, we are willing to forgive her if she makes a public apology. We forgive criminals if they go to prison. The variations are again endless, "I will forgive him if he first tries to change (or apologizes, or gives up drinking, or suffers for what he did, or promises never to do it again, or . . ."). Bargaining is easy to rationalize. We are just helping a person to do what he should.

I
SYMPTOMS OF BARGAINING

Since bargaining is primarily a mixture of anger (blaming another and wanting him to change) and depression (blaming myself and wanting to change myself), the symptoms vary depending on whether I am more angry or depressed. When anger dominates, I have the energy to redecorate my room all the colors of the rainbow. When depression reigns, the yellow walls look grey and I can scarcely make my bed—or get out of it. Bargaining is a stage of measuring-cup love—always measuring what I get (because anger says he should change) against what I give (because depression says I should change).[1] Bargains come in many varieties of "If (*and only if*) you change, I will forgive you."

When bargaining, I say "If Gus changes, I will forgive him." I really mean "only if he changes, I will forgive him." The alternative to bargaining is loving a person unconditionally—just the way he is. In most of my relationships I can usually find some symptoms of bargaining, since only a totally unscarred and free person can consistently give unconditional love.

Only long after Gus inferred I would lose my vocation did I reach the bargaining stage. As I began to see the pressures on him, his good points, other targets of his anger, and how striking out at me was a cry to be loved and helped, I began to bargain. My bargains were, of course, for his good, to help him change. "I will forgive Gus if he shows me he really does respect me and especially my prayer." "It will be all right if he just quits talking behind my back." "He would be O.K. if he could just admit his own inadequacies." "If he can simply say to my face he didn't mean it, then I'll forget it." "Even if he can't admit he is wrong, if he does me a favor then I'll know he is sorry."

I had come a long distance from feeling that Gus couldn't possibly change. I could now recall the original time of hurt, word by word with less pain and distortion. He wasn't so bad, even had a couple of good points, and blew up at me because he was wounded by other hurts. In trying to care for him as Christ cared, I was getting closer—but still I wanted him to earn my forgiveness. Christ wanted to forgive him not because he deserved it but because he needed it. I wanted him to change so that I could love him again. Christ wanted to love him and thereby give him power to change. If I were to drop any of my bargains, I needed the mind and heart of Christ.

St. Francis of Assisi described the mind and heart of Christ sought during the bargaining stage. It is a handy measuring stick since only a person who has moved out of anger into bargaining can honestly pray this prayer and give up his desire to be consoled and understood first:

Lord, make me an instrument of thy peace.

Where there is hatred, let me sow love;
Where there is injury, pardon;
Where there is doubt, faith;
Where there is despair, hope;
Where there is sadness, joy;
Where there is darkness, light.

O Divine Master, grant that I may not so much seek to be
    consoled, as to console;
Not so much to be understood, as to understand;
Not so much to be loved, as to love.
For it is in giving that we receive,
It is in pardoning that we are pardoned,
It is in dying that we are born again to eternal life.

II
BARGAINING IN SCRIPTURE

The prodigal son story reveals the dynamics of bargaining.
The younger son returns thinking his father will be bargaining to
accept him back only if he returns to be treated as a hired servant
(Lk. 15:17). But the father is beyond bargaining and wants to
receive his son unconditionally. He doesn't wait to see if his son is
coming back to borrow more money but "while the son is still a
long way off" he "runs" out to welcome and love him even if the
son hasn't changed. The father does not focus on his own hurt
feelings, wait for an apology, or even allow the son to continue his
planned confession. Rather the father celebrates the return of his
son by preparing a banquet and making this offending son more
honored than ever. The father is like God. He doesn't know how to
bargain but only how to forgive unconditionally.

Like the father of the prodigal son, Christ's forgiveness is also
unconditional. He never places conditions on forgiveness by saying, "I will forgive you only if you change, apologize, or earn it
first." Whether a man is unable to follow him (Mk. 10:21), denies
him as Peter, betrays him as Judas, or nails him to a cross, Christ
still unconditionally forgives him and hopes his forgiveness will be
accepted.[2] Christ is ready to be hurt seventy times seven times

(Mt. 18:22) and still forgive us, as he does in confession. Jesus gave his life for us, and he repeats this offering daily in the Eucharist for the forgiveness of sins (Mt. 26:28). "Greater love than this no man has than that he lay down his life for his *friends*" (Jn. 15:13) is surpassed because Jesus dies even for his *enemies*. Christ loves us not only if we change but just as we are, thereby giving us power to change.

The problem then is not twisting Christ's arm so that he will give us more forgiveness but being open enough to receive his infinite forgiveness offered even to the worst offenders. We are as open to Christ's forgiveness as we are open to Christ present in our offender. If we say to our offender, "I can't love you much by forgiving much," we are saying this also to Christ, present in our offender. In whatever way we don't love the *least* (even offenders in prison) of our brothers, we don't love Christ and block receiving his forgiveness (Mt. 25:41–46). Christ can offer forgiveness but he can't force us to receive it any more than we can force our offender to accept our forgiveness. Like Christ we are to offer this total forgiveness even if it isn't received. As Ephesians sums up, "Forgive as God has forgiven you" (Eph. 4:32).[3]

This is the key to healing a memory. When we can forgive our offender as completely and unconditionally as God forgives us, then we no longer experience the past hurts as painful times but as times of growth. We become like Christ, not focusing on the self-centering pain, but saying, "Father, forgive them, for they know not what they do" (Lk. 23:34). The time of hurt transforms into a time of forgiving love. It can't remain a wounding time closing us up if it becomes a time to forgive and reach out even to those who hurt us. This happens when we get stretched way beyond our limited forgiveness by experiencing how Christ thinks and feels. Memories are healed not only by psychologically thinking things through but by putting on the mind and heart of Christ and, with his power, giving his forgiveness.

When we can forgive with the mind and heart of Christ, our prayer gains new power. Too often we feel that the power of prayer depends only on our faith, but Christ insists on both faith *and forgiveness:*

Therefore, I tell you, whatever you ask for in prayer, believe that you have received it, and it will be yours. *And whenever you stand praying, forgive*, if you have anything against anyone, so that your Father also who is in heaven may forgive you your trespasses (Mk. 11:24–26).

John repeats the same promise, with emphasis on asking in Christ's name:

Whatever you ask in my name, I will do it, that the Father may be glorified in the Son; if you ask anything in my name, I will do it (Jn. 14:13–14).

To the Jew "name" was not a word like "Jesus" but the whole person of Jesus present with his mind and heart. Therefore we pray in his name not when we use "Jesus" but when we pray as he would with his same thoughts and feelings. Prayer is heard and answered to the degree that we are praying as Jesus would pray. That's why healing of memories takes place not simply by digging up the past and sorting it out in prayer but by growing in putting on the mind and heart of Christ and forgiving the person who hurt us just as Christ would forgive him. Philippians states that our minds are healed to the degree that they become Christ's memory, and we forgive as he did on the cross:

In your minds you must be the same as Christ Jesus. His state was divine yet he did not cling to his equality with God but emptied himself to assume the condition of a slave, and became as men are; and being as all men are he was humbler yet, even to accepting death, death on a cross (Phil. 2:5–8).

III
BARGAINING CAN BE HEALTHY

Bargains are like x-rays highlighting hidden areas where I am unlike Christ. They pinpoint where my strengths have become weaknesses and where my weakness is not yet a strength. For example, why did I demand that Gus quit criticizing others and show in some way that he had changed his mind about my weak prayer and vocation? I demanded that he quit criticizing others not just for their sakes but because I really believed that he could easily do that. I presumed he could do it because I had successfully ceased criticizing my "slow" students. If I could do it, he could do it too with a little effort. I didn't consider that it was easier for me since I am naturally quiet or that Christ's power was responsible for the victory. What I was seeing as my virtue was really my pride. I demand of another what I have become proud of being able to do. Bargains locate my sinful pride.

Bargains pinpoint not just strengths that have become swollen with pride but areas of weakness that are tender and easily hurt. When I dreamed of what I would most like to hear from Gus, it was, "Thanks for your talk on prayer. At first I didn't like your talk because it wasn't the way I prayed. But now I see that your way of praying really helps you and makes you a good Jesuit. I think I will try some of the ways you mentioned." I wanted most to hear that I prayed well and would not lose my vocation. Why? Deep down I had fears that in the frantic pace I was not taking time to pray and would lose my vocation as had others who stopped praying. What I want most to hear is often what I need most to change and correct in myself. As I get more in touch with my power to love as Christ does, I can begin to even cancel my demands for change in Gus and see the possibility of forgiving first. "He must change" becomes "I can change and love even the unloving."

Ironically when I forgive and thereby extend new life by accepting another, he often does change. God promises to offer new life to anyone we forgive and who is open to God's offer (1 Jn. 5:16). At an inner healing workshop, several in a second marriage spent the weekend trying to forgive their former spouse. They went through all the stages of forgiveness until they were even grateful for ways in which they could grow from the wounding separation. A year later we returned and asked the group what difference the workshop made to their lives. Out of the seven who forgave a former spouse after years of resentment, five found that their former spouses had suddenly made an effort to forgive and build a bridge towards them. One suddenly called a week after the workshop, another traveled two thousand miles to see his family, and another wrote his first letter in ten silent years. All five of these people did nothing but prayerfully forgive and were asking the

Lord how to build a bridge when their spouses unexpectedly responded. Even when we can only forgive and don't know how to build a bridge, the Lord uses our new love to offer growth to the person we forgive. Agnes Sanford tells her workshop participants to forgive and then return home and expect to see a difference in the person forgiven.

Just as our forgiveness can touch persons miles away, so too it can reach across time to love those who have died. Both the dead and living are part of the body of Jesus Christ, and by forgiving can help each other through Jesus, just as my right hand can help my left hand to remove a burden (Rom. 14:9; 1 Cor. 12:12ff.; 2 Mc. 12:44–45). Every time we forgive the dead and accept their forgiveness, we give them more of Jesus's love and lighten their judgment which is based on how they loved Christ in those they met on earth (Mt. 25:31–46). No longer do they exist needing purification for the ways they hurt us. As we forgive them, they experience our love which frees them to love with greater power.[4] Our dead also wish through Jesus to forgive us for any way that we may have hurt them. Having seen Christ face to face, they desire to love Christ in himself and Christ in us. They want to forgive us so that Christ's love in us might grow and we can share eternity with them.

Although the living like the dead often respond when they are forgiven, we don't forgive to make them respond. That's bargaining again. Like Christ I must love people not because they are good or so they will be good, but simply because they are sinners.

> Why, one will hardly die for a righteous man—though perhaps for a good man one will dare even to die. But God shows his love for us in that while we were yet sinners Christ died for us (Rom. 5:7–8).

Bargaining pinpoints where we just want to love good people. Canceling our bargains deepens our love until, like Christ, we can love not the sin but the sinner.

In helping people to forgive a deep hurt, since it is difficult to love a sinner, I strained to disguise sinfulness. I insisted that: most hurts are unintentional; anyone who hurts you is reacting to times he was hurt and not to you personally; you need to see his good points, and anger blinds you to the ways he may have changed. I utilized every theory of determinism: he was reacting to his poor health (biological), a zero IQ (genetic), mistreatment in childhood (psychological), being raised in a slum (ecological), and bad friends (social). I tried to get them to say like Christ: "Father, forgive them, for *they know not* what they do" (Lk. 23:34).

For example, I insisted that an accountant should forgive his boss for firing him because his boss was reacting to other pressures at work and at home rather than maliciously intending to hurt him. Then I tried to get the accountant to be like Christ and say for his boss, "Father, forgive him, for he knows not what he is doing." I sat back waiting for forgiveness but was startled to hear him say, "But he did know what he was doing!" He was confident that his boss deliberately and maliciously intended to hurt him by firing him.

Then he taught me a new depth of forgiveness. "But I forgive him. Father, forgive him, for *he knew* what he was doing." The accountant didn't have to bury any of his anger behind half-true rationalizations such as "my boss is reacting to something else." He was able to face the worst, the part that was sinner, and extend him the same forgiving love that Christ gave to sinners. When we cancel the ultimate bargain, "I could forgive you if you were just reacting to other pressures," we find a deeper love—Christ's love not just for good men but for sinners. Like Christ we are called to love sinners whether they change like the good thief or die cursing us as the bad thief.

But shouldn't we want others to change for the better, be sorry, and accept forgiveness? Yes, but this can't be a condition for love any more than a mother refuses to love her creeping child because he can't walk. It is the mother's love that eventually gives the creeping child confidence to try and walk towards her arms. As we formulate our bargains and cancel them, we love a person who creeps, and by our love we give him the power to take new steps. The first impulse to change comes not so much from being challenged as from being loved.

Adults also often need unconditional love before they face the challenge of walking rather than creeping. I have a friend, Joe, who has been in and out of prisons for twenty years and charged with every crime from theft to murder. Many have told me that he is a hopeless and hardened criminal, but I have tried to stand by him for years.

In dealing with Joe I learned much about what Alcoholics Anonymous calls unconditional "tough love." When I first met Joe fifteen years ago, I did everything I could do to help him. When he landed in jail, I tried to find a smart lawyer or a lenient judge to get him out of jail. But Joe would steal something again and expect me to get him out again. Thus I found that unconditional love doesn't mean hurting someone by doing everything for him, but only unconditionally doing what is loving and growthful for him. Now when Joe lands back in jail, he knows that I will do nothing but visit him. We have an agreement that if he gets himself into trouble, he must get himself out of trouble. I found that the best way for me to love him was to start treating him as an adult who was responsible for all his actions. Because I finally learned to offer unconditional "tough love" that won't give up loving him no matter what happens, Joe today is free and growing more responsible each day.

To help Joe grow more responsible, I also asked Joe to report weekly to a reformed alcoholic friend so that problems could get handled before they built up. Like Joe, my friend had struggled against alcohol and could help him fifty times better than I could. We are called to love unconditionally, but often this means stepping back and finding the person who can best love. This is especially true when we find ourselves getting worn out and exasperated in trying to help another. We may have to avoid some people for a while until we are strong enough to grow while reaching out for them. It is always hard to say "no" to people asking our help, but unless we do, we can end up exhausted and needing help. The "no" must come not from a desire to be inconvenienced but from a desire to be a healthy person able to pour out more unconditional love. Jesus could heal crowds only because he said "no" and went off to pray and regain his strength.

Like the crowds seeking Jesus, we are instinctively attracted to the goodness in people who don't bargain. While other religious groups die out, Mother Teresa of Calcutta attracts hundreds of young girls who want to follow her in serving Christ dying among the poorest of the poor.[5] They take in those facing death alone without friends or hospitalization. The sisters can ask the dying for nothing except to have the privilege of caring for Christ. Although she is a Catholic nun, Mother Teresa doesn't even bargain to have the dying man accept Christ but simply loves him unconditionally because he is Christ. If a dying Moslem desires to hear passages from the Koran, Mother Teresa reads the Koran as reverently as she would read the Old Testament to Christ. Yet who today has done more to change hearts than Mother Teresa with her unconditional love for the dying?

Today many aspire to be like Mother Teresa serving the poorest of the poor in a foreign land. Since Jean Vanier gathered the first L'Arche community to help those physically and emotionally crippled, over fifty of his houses receive a steady stream of visitors and volunteers eager to join his work.[6] His philosophy is simple: the handicapped and healthy need each other. Those who are crippled give much because, in order to overcome their pain and limitations, their love must be deeper, and their needs call others to a new depth of being able to offer love and care. Community members learn to love one another for who they are, not for what they can give. In the Haiti community, Jolibors, who cannot speak, fears everyone, and spent his life in an asylum, also inadvertently calls everyone to offer a genuine, deeper love that goes beyond words and banishes fear.[7] The most wounded stretch the community toward the most growth where there is no bargaining but only unconditional love.

As Jean Vanier sees life, in order to love themselves, the healthy need the handicapped:

> I have learned more about the Gospels from handicapped people, those on the margins of our society, those who have been crushed and hurt, than I have from the wise and prudent. Through their own growth and acceptance and surrender, wounded people have taught me that I must learn to accept my weakness and not pretend to be strong and capable. Handicapped people have shown me how handicapped I am, how handicapped we all are. They have reminded me that we are all weak and all called to death and that these are the realities of which we are most afraid.[8]

The handicapped also need the unconditional love of the healthy:

> An alcoholic is told he must stop drinking; it's bad for his health. But he doesn't need to be told that—he's been vomiting all day. He doesn't need someone to proclaim the law to him, for he knows the law. What he wants is to find someone who will give him the force, the motivation, the thirst for life. It is not because you tell someone not to steal that he will not do it. He needs strength, he needs to be attached to someone who will give him the life and the courage, the peace and love, which will help him not to steal, or not to take drugs, or not to drink, or not to fall into depression.[9]

Do those who wound us most offer us any less growth? Do they need any less our unconditional love? Why are we all dreaming of running off to live with Jean Vanier when the handicapped live among us in those we most want to change?

IV
DEALING WITH BARGAINING

To walk rather than creep is risky. The world of soft, patterned carpets is left behind for the strange upright world of shelves and table tops. Many falls, tears and a bruised nose testify that two feet don't offer the stability of creeping. It's a world of more "no's" and "don'ts" as things get pulled off tables and a stove is explored. There must be times when a child wishes he never learned how to walk.

We experience many of the same feelings in working through the bargaining stage. It's risky to leave the black and white world of anger where we are right and our assailant is wrong. Christ's upright perspective of loving and forgiving our enemy feels strange because we come from a world where people are loved more if they are loving and are expected to earn love. As we take a couple of steps towards forgiveness, we will hit bottom many times. In forgiveness we say, "I am willing to absorb all the ways you can hurt me and I will try to return the love you need until your hostility disappears or my kindness heals you." Eventually the day arrives when we can't angrily blame hard floors for our aches and pains but start blaming our own wobbly legs. There are many days when I wish I could keep blaming another and hadn't taken my first steps in the new world of seeing my enemy as Christ sees him.

Taking our first steps through bargaining involves our same three major steps of Emmaus:
1. Tell Christ how I feel.
2. Listen, especially through Scripture, to how Christ feels.
3. Live out Christ's reaction.

1. *Tell Christ How I Feel*

The first step comes when I tell Christ how I honestly feel rather than how I wish I felt: "Lord, I can now see the pressures on Gus and some of his good points, but he still needs changing for his own good and so that others don't get hurt. I would be able to forgive and really accept him if he could just quit criticizing others. And if he could in some small way show that he accepts me (a good word, a new responsibility), it would be much easier to accept and really forgive him. Most of all I want to hear from him that I am a good Jesuit and not ready to lose my call to the priesthood. That's not asking so much. I'm going more than half-way in no longer demanding that he first make a public apology, an attempt at praying himself, or even a private apology to me before I totally accept him. Now get him to change as much as you have helped me to change. It isn't fair that I should get all the help."

2. *Listen to How Christ Feels*

The second step is asking: When did Christ feel the way I feel and how did he react? When was Christ hurt most by a friend? Peter's denial that he knew Christ reminded me of my friend's denial that I had a call to be a Jesuit priest. I then decided that Christ's response to Peter on the lake shore (Jn. 21) would help me discover how to respond to Gus' denial. I therefore read the passage several times, closed my eyes, became relaxed with every muscle surrendered to Jesus, and began to breathe in and out: "Jesus." After about ten minutes, when I sensed his love, I sat in my imagination with Peter and Jesus around the fire on the shore with sand between my toes, roasting fish over the flickering fire.

The scene may be peaceful but there was a subtle argument. Christ took the initiative to forgive: "Simon, son of John, do you love (*agapao*) me more than these?" Before his denial Peter would have shouted "yes" because he wanted to be first even if it meant being first to walk on water toward Christ. Christ was asking for *agapao* love, total love that gives all even to the point of dying. But the new Peter knows his weakness in denying Christ and cannot promise *agapao* but only *phileo*, the ordinary love of friend for friend.[10] Nevertheless, Christ loves the impetuous side of Peter that could lead to leadership and risk-taking as easily as it did to an impetuous denial. He takes Peter's greatest defect and makes it a gift for leadership, "Feed my lambs."

A second time Christ tests to see if Peter's love measures up to *agapao*.

> "Simon, son of John, do you love (*agapao*) me?" "Yes, Lord; you know that I love (*phileo*) you." "Tend my sheep" (Jn. 21:16).

Once more Christ accepts Peter just as he is without changing and measuring up to his hopes for *agapao* love. Christ accepts not just the weak, impetuous Peter but the sinful Peter who knowingly denied him not just once but three times despite time for reflection and change.

The third time Christ uses Peter's word for love (*phileo*) to show Peter that he accepts him just as he is, a sinner, without heroic *agapao* love. Peter wins:

> "Simon, son of John, do you love (*phileo*) me?" "Lord, you know everything; you know that I love (*phileo*) you." "Feed my sheep" (Jn. 21:17).

Because Jesus can love Peter as he is with his weak *phileo* response, Peter will grow in loving Jesus even to the point of finally giving *agapao* love as a martyr in Rome. Growth in love comes not by wanting to grow or figuring it out but by being loved.

Even though Christ didn't say an audible word to me, he spoke to my heart while speaking to Peter. Jesus seemed to be asking me many questions. Could I take the initiative to forgive Gus as Christ did when he came to Peter, filled his boat with fish, fed him, and then offered love and responsibility three times to heal the three denials? Could I see Gus' impetuous criticism the way that Christ saw Peter's—a gift for honesty and leadership? Like Christ could I love Gus even in his sinfulness with an affirming love that would help him to feel secure enough to make change possible? Could I tear up the IOU I demanded and write a blank check with the selfless love of Christ who focuses only on what he can give and not on the return? Can I love Gus even if he keeps criticizing and thinking that I am ready to lose my vocation?

3. *Live Out Christ's Reaction*

It's easier to *say* "Yes, I will be to Gus what Christ was to Peter" than it is to *do* what Christ would do. It's easier to watch what Christ says and does to Peter than to see in my imagination what Christ would say and do to Gus. Thus I watch what Christ would say and do to Gus—perhaps getting him more coffee, helping him focus on what he is doing well, draining his heart of anger by listening with understanding, helping Gus to focus not on his words about me but on the deeper hurts, helping him to see his strengths, adding hope where there was darkness, and loving him with a smile that brings deep healing. Next it is my turn to do in my imagination with Gus what Christ did and have Christ do all the hard parts until I can allow Christ to use me to say and do to Gus all that Jesus wants.

How do I know I really have Christ's mind and heart toward Gus and am not just rehearsing reactions? If I have, I will be able to cancel my two remaining bargains: (1) If you quit criticizing others, I will forgive you. (2) If you feel differently about my vocation and prayer life, I will forgive you. In forgiveness, I can say, like Christ: "Gus, I forgive you for everything you did and didn't know what you were doing. I want to love you even if you keep criticizing others and think I am ready to lose my vocation."

Besides canceling my bargains, I will see more good in Gus and become less critical even when hurt again. If my love is like Christ's and my bargains are truly canceled, I won't be demanding a return before I can give. There will be times when I again will feel critical and angry because in forgiving I am becoming healed and allowing room for more buried feelings to surface. But these feelings will be healed more deeply because I have decided to love, not criticize. Love is a decision, not only a feeling . The feelings will also change as they are recognized, shared with Christ and given to him in return for his feelings. It helps me to sigh deeply and breathe out into his hands what I am feeling while absorbing what Jesus is feeling.

As I see more good in Gus, I may start to blame myself. Why did I react like that? Why am I so easily hurt? Why does it take me so long to forgive? Others can receive criticism. Why can't I? When I really forgive, I quit blaming the other and start to assume the depression stage's responsibility for my own reaction. My bargains switch from demanding another change before I can forgive him to demanding that I myself change before I can forgive myself. I may feel worse than ever because I am asking a deeper question. "What's wrong with him?" is now "What's wrong with me?"

Maybe by now forgiving another until I can say "What's wrong with me?" sounds hopelessly complex or perhaps possible for the minor hurts in life like insults but not for those needing years of psychiatric care. We don't always have to consciously form bargains and cancel them but we do have to give the Lord's unconditional forgiveness. Corrie Ten Boom discovered to her surprise that the Lord's forgiveness can heal hurts as deep as her own imprisonment and deaths of her father and sister, Betsie, at the hands of the German Gestapo. She summarizes simply what has taken a chapter to say.

It was at a church service in Munich that I saw him, the former S.S. man who had stood guard at the shower room door in the processing center at Ravensbruck. He was the first of our actual jailers that I had seen since that time. And suddenly it was all there—the roomful of mocking men, the heaps of clothing, Betsie's pain-blanched face.

He came up to me as the church was emptying, beaming and bowing. "How grateful I am for your message, Fraulein," he said. "To think that, as you say, He has washed my sins away!"

His hand was thrust out to shake mine. And I, who had preached so often to the people in Bloemendaal the need to forgive, kept my hand at my side. Even as the angry, vengeful thoughts boiled through me, I saw the sin of them. Jesus Christ had died for this man; was I going to ask for more? Lord Jesus, I prayed, forgive me and help me to forgive him.

I tried to smile, I struggled to raise my hand. I could not. I felt nothing, not the slightest spark of warmth or charity. And so again I breathed a silent prayer. Jesus, I cannot forgive him. Give me your forgiveness.

As I took his hand the most incredible thing happened. From my shoulder along my arm and through my hand a current seemed to pass from me to him, while into my heart sprang a love for this stranger that almost overwhelmed me.

And so I discovered that it is not on our forgiveness any more than on our goodness that the world's healing hinges, but on his. When he tells us to love our enemies, he gives, along with the command, the love itself.[11]

10
FOURTH STAGE: DEPRESSION

As the dying patient feels his strength ebb away, he knows he won't be saved by his bargains, a better doctor, or promises of prayer, tithes, or angelic behavior. Eventually his anger lashes out hostilely. In a gloomy silence he broods over questions like, "Why didn't I go to a doctor sooner before it was too late? Why didn't I get the best doctor right away? Why didn't I take that family trip and spend more time with my children and grandchildren? Now it is too late. I should have . . ." If the dying patient values his life and his friends, he frequently becomes depressed.

If I value my life and friends, I too will experience depression. I became depressed over my reaction to Gus' criticism because it meant the loss of a friend I valued and the possible loss of my goal to become a priest. If I didn't care about Gus or about growing in prayer and priesthood, I wouldn't become depressed. I don't get depressed when I am indifferent to everyone and not reaching toward any goals. Only when I don't take risks to love and grow do I remain free from failure and symptoms of depression.

I
SYMPTOMS OF DEPRESSION

The dark cloud of depression strikes with recriminating thoughts of "I should have . . ." Usually I don't know I am depressed but sense that both sides of the bed are the wrong side for getting up and that it's best just to lie there another five minutes. Two ironclad laws keep me in bed: the law of gravity and Sam Dude's law of duality, "Of two possible events, only the undesired one will occur." I finally tell myself, "You should have been up an hour ago," slide out of bed and yawn my way listlessly through the day's projects. I put off whatever can wait and come late for whatever must be faced. When depressed, I don't take on new projects but try to resurrect an old lesson or homily. I'll ask more often "What did you think about the homily?" but really can't hear the compliments and don't want any criticism. I volunteer to give a homily, even though I'd rather passively sit through the worst of homilies, because it's harder to say "no" when depressed and needing to please. Never saying "no" leads to overextension and more reason to kick myself for having too much to do and no time to do anything well.

Never saying "no" and thus becoming overextended is just one of the sinful *patterns of depression*. The depth of my depression can be gauged by how many times I react to hurts in a sinful way. Any sin makes me more vulnerable to getting hurt. Any bruising hurt makes me more vulnerable to sin. If I sin by pride, I am more vulnerable to criticism's bruises and cover these with more prideful boasting. If I sin by clinging to things, I am more vulnerable to getting deeply hurt when my things get taken or abused, and I cover this loss with a tighter grip on what I still have.

It's a vicious cycle. When I am down on myself because I am feeling guilty (I should have . . .), I do all the wrong things that make me feel more guilty. My most sinful years were also the years I was most depressed. When I was kicking myself for teaching six subjects so poorly that half my students quit coming to class, I was also criticizing my students, boasting about my heavy load, praying less, hoping that other teachers were struggling equally hard, and wilting under Gus' criticism. When I become depressed, I become a sinner, and more depressed, and more a sinner.

I try to break the cycle of depression by coming to prayer as a sinner needing Christ's help but end up plotting how to try harder on my own. I keep focusing on my problems rather than on Jesus and then wonder why my prayer makes me more depressed. For every time I say "thank you, Lord," I say ten times "Lord, help me change the way I . . ." My attempts to hate the sin and love the sinner end up hating the sin and hating the sinner. Not liking myself, I eventually believe that God doesn't like me, and I soon stop praying or cut it short. In depression my mind is on my troubles, not on the Lord, and it is a struggle to do more than simple vocal prayer or singing of hymns.

When I can think or pray, I begin to glimpse that I am also at fault for allowing myself to get hurt. Publicly I may still justify and defend my reaction, but in my guts I wish I had reacted differently. I now see two problems: Gus' criticism and my overreaction. Now I no longer simply blame Gus for my response. I begin to ask questions like: How did I and others hurt him previously so that he struck back? Why does it take me so long to forgive and help a person who is hurting? Why didn't I see the pressures he was under? Why don't I pray more? He was wrong, but why can't I still love him?

"He was wrong. . ." echoed what I shouted in the anger stage because I still carried some anger into depression stage. Anger and depression symptoms often surface together. Much psychological depression is really swallowed anger and will disappear if I can answer the question "Who or what is irritating me?" and then deal with my anger. I am seldom really angry at another (anger stage) without getting angry at myself (depression stage) and vice versa.[1] When I don't like my anger, I usually feel guilty about my anger. But in the depression stage I mutter more often "I should have . . ." than "He should have . . ."

II
DEPRESSION IN SCRIPTURE

In Christ's forgiveness story of the prodigal son (Luke 15), the father's forgiveness and desire to celebrate are contrasted with the elder son who is angry when his brother returns home. The elder son, overlooking his own cold heart, sees only his brother's guilt. In his anger he can't give or receive love from the father or younger son.

The younger, depressed son is in better shape than his brother because he knows he is a sinner in need of forgiveness. He hangs his head for good reasons: he has paid more attention to unclean pigs than to his God, wasted his gifts, and renounced his loving father. Filled with sorrow, he says: "Father, I have sinned against heaven and before you. I am no longer worthy to be called your son" (Lk. 15:21). He breaks the vicious cycle (depression—sin—more depression—more sin) by confessing his sin and accepting forgiveness. Depression's "I should have . . . (never run away)" brings more growth than the elder brother's angry "He should have . . . (stayed away, and remained rejected)."

One of the surest symptoms of healthy depression is a desire to beg for forgiveness. Because the prodigal son was depressed enough to return and beg for forgiveness, he becomes closer to the father than ever before and receives new gifts (the best robe, ring and shoes). The very sin, running away, becomes the source of many new gifts: in the future it is unlikely that the father or the son will take each other for granted again, they probably will be less critical and more affirming of each other, the son may be more sensitive to sharing with the starving, and both will want to reconcile the elder brother lest he runs and makes the same mistake. The parable shouts that recognition of depression and its symptoms can lead to a deeper love and opening into new life.

Wanting to confess sin and accept forgiveness is also the striking difference between Peter and Judas. Both men denied Christ and fell into depression over their actions. But only Peter is eventually able to accept his sin and seek reconciliation with our Lord. He returns to serve Jesus wholeheartedly. Judas, on the other hand, cannot face his own sinfulness, and does not seek eventual reconciliation with the one he has betrayed. His failure and depression lead to suicide. Peter, of course, is forgiven for his denial and he remains deeply loved and trusted to "feed my lambs" by leading the church. But of Judas, with whom there has been no reconciliation, Jesus later says, "It would have been better for him had he not been born" (Mt. 26:24).

Depression brings symptoms of despair or new hope depending on whether we focus on our problem or Christ's love for sinners. Judas focused on his problem and hanged himself; Peter focused on Christ's forgiveness and hanged his problem. Judas thought that some sins were too great to forgive. Peter knew that the greater the sin, the more eager Christ was to forgive five hundred rather than fifty. In Scripture the depressed people who grow are those who confess sin and accept God's love. They are the ones who understand that confession is not a time of changing God's mind so that he will accept us with our sin but a time of changing our mind so that we will accept God's forgiveness given on Calvary for us as sinners (1 Jn. 1:8–9).

For years I believed that Christ did love weak people like the prodigal son and Peter but that he loved more those who could "be perfect as your heavenly Father is perfect" (Mt. 5:48). Trying to become perfect made me focus on my efforts and become a self-centered Pelagian rather than a sinner needing a Savior. Finally, I reread Matthew and discovered the passage (Mt. 5:43–48) asks us to be perfect like the Father in only one area—loving and extending mercy to our enemy. In his parallel passage Luke substitutes "be merciful" (Lk. 6:36) toward our enemy for "be perfect." Luke 6:36, "Be merciful as your heavenly Father is merciful," is possible. The Lord simply asks me to be merciful to Peter and the prodigal within me and within another. We are most like the Father and Christ not when we are perfect but when we forgive. Our Father loves us not because we are perfect adults never making mistakes but because we are infants learning to walk through falls and needing extra care. His love for his weak children is reflected in a mother's love for her weak baby: "Does a woman forget her baby at the breast or fail to cherish the son of her womb? Yet even if these forget, I will never forget you. See, I have branded you on the palms of my hands" (Is. 49:15–16).

III
DEPRESSION CAN BE HEALTHY

Although there are as many definitions of depression as people depressed, this book is using "depression" in the classical sense of anger turned against oneself. In the depression stage my anger turns inward producing guilt over allowing myself to be hurt or over hurting another. Whether I am angry at myself or at my actions makes the crucial difference between unhealthy and healthy depression. As healthy anger leads me to be angry at Gus' unloving criticism while still loving and forgiving him, so too healthy depression leads me to be angry at my unloving actions (so I can correct them) while still loving and forgiving myself (so I see and use my gifts to correct them).

I must love and forgive myself for ways I have hurt myself or another whether it was intended (sinful) or unintended (evil). Most of the times I must forgive myself are times of unintended evil when I meant well but made mistakes, e.g. gullibly trusting another who misled me, not succeeding despite real effort, or failing to notice another's need. Usually I can more easily forgive myself for what was unintended (e.g. if I didn't intentionally let myself get hurt by Gus's remark or try to hurt him) than for what was intended (e.g. if I did intentionally dwell on Gus's remark or decide to strike back at him). If I didn't intend the evil, I can usually forgive myself easily with a simple, "I am human like everyone else and entitled to make a few mistakes." Usually then I find myself more in the anger stage saying "It's his fault and not mine." But when I remain depressed and hear guilt's "I should have . . ," then some part of me probably feels responsibility for more than unintended evil. When I can't forgive myself with "I had good intentions and meant well," then I am called to a deeper level of loving and forgiving myself as sinner. I should as St. Augustine said, "Hate the sin and love the sinner."

Hating the sin and loving the sinner helps me change what needs to be changed. For example, if I am in a car accident, I can rationalize that the accident was just an unintended evil because I drove carefully. But if I didn't fix the brakes as warned, then deep down I probably feel guilty for not braking in time. It's helpful to discover ways I feel that I am a responsible sinner so I can change the situation rather than have another accident due to not braking in time. I must also forgive and love myself or I can become accident prone in unconsciously trying to punish myself. Thus depression is healthy when it leads to hating the sin and loving the sinner.

Dr. Karl Menninger, psychiatrist and founder of the world famous Menninger Clinic, in *Whatever Became of Sin* points out that to deny I am a sinner is a very unhealthy attitude.[2] For Menninger and for this book, a sinner is one who is *responsible* for his unloving actions and *can change*. If I am hurting myself or another, I have a choice of ignoring it and letting the patterns continue or of recognizing the evil and correcting it. Dr. Menninger says I have three choices of correction: prison because I can't reform, a mental hospital because I am mentally ill and don't know the evil I am doing, or facing that I am a sinner because I am not mentally ill or a hardened criminal but responsible for my actions. If I am a healthy person who has hope for changing, I am a responsible sinner who wants to turn away from sin. If I do not hate my sin, I become insensitive to my destruction rather than correct it. If I fail to love the sinner, I become depressed and scrupulous with no power to correct my destruction. For Dr. Menninger and for St. Augustine, a healthy person is one who hates his sin and loves the sinner.

The chart below summarizes this difference between healthy and unhealthy depression.

HEALTHY AND UNHEALTHY REACTIONS TO SIN AND SINNERS

	Healthy	Unhealthy
My Sin	Hate my sin— See the destruction Admit my responsibility Take steps to change	Love my sin— Deny the destruction Deny my responsibility Take no steps to change
Myself	Love myself as sinner	Hate myself as sinner

Depression is healthy when hating the sin involves three essential steps: 1) see the destruction, 2) shoulder responsibility, 3) take steps to change what can be changed. These are the same attitudes Dr. Menninger proposes for health in *Whatever Became of Sin.*

Healthy Depression: Hate the Sin—See the Destruction

We should hate the sin and love the sinner not only because sin put Christ to death 2000 years ago but also because sin snuffs out Christ's life within us today. Sin's wake of destruction extends beyond me to cripple Christ in everyone. Watergate graphically illustrated how one lie spread to poison a nation and destroy voters' confidence in being heard and served by the democratic process. One lie began a process that kept the congress preoccupied and ignoring legislation for world hunger, the aging, health care etc. I have a tendency to think that only a President's sin can be so destructive. Yet my lies (such as exaggerating or belittling my gifts) spread distrust making it easier for a President to lie like everybody else.

Sin's destruction spreads not just across a country but also across time. Americans celebrating the 1876 centennial spurred Custer on to wipe out the Sioux opposition. Instead Custer was wiped out and the Sioux were corralled to ever shrinking reservations breeding poverty and apathy. Decades later as a beginning teacher I get worn out trying to overcome the apathy and help the Sioux help themselves. Because I am worn out, I allow myself to get hurt by a trifling remark and I further wound my students. How am I to blame rather than Custer?

Hate the Sin—Shoulder Responsibility

I can throw up my hands and say that I am not responsible for what Custer and other whites did to cripple the Sioux and for the situation that ultimately crippled me. Custer could say the same thing and we would all end up blaming Adam or rather poor Eve. To the degree I can yet neglect to create a more loving environment, I add to the destruction of Adam's original sin. Sin isn't just the destruction I do; it's the good I knowingly neglect and leave for another to do. I may not be guilty of Custer's sin but I am guilty if I fail to help my Sioux brothers who are still suffering from Custer and others. Today we are recognizing this in communal penance services emphasizing our *social* (shared or "ecclesial") sin in a world filled with poverty and prejudice. We must call ourselves sinners, people responsible for a better world and gifted to heal it so even the air breathes justice, love, and forgiveness. To the degree I know I can heal but don't heal, I am a sinner.

Our list of sins, therefore, should not be a list of our faults but a list of our gifts which are not being used to heal. Sin is found not so much by surveying where we have broken the ten commandments but by surveying our gifts to love God and neighbor and where we have abused or buried them as the servant who buried his talent (Mt. 25:14-30). By burying his money he didn't break one of the ten commandments but he did neglect to use his gift and so he hears, "You wicked and slothful servant. . . ." and is cast into the darkness (Mt. 25:26–30). My sins too will be not just the ways I hurt others but the ways I let myself bury or abuse my talents for healing others. For example, one of my sins is failing to discipline myself to sit down and use my gift of writing and another is writing too much until irritable and exhausted. On the other hand since I have no gift for singing, it is not sinful but an act of charity when I fail to exercise my ear piercing voice. The same standard applies to Peter and Judas who sinned more than the crowd denying Christ because as apostles they knew Christ intimately and had a greater gift for loving and serving Christ. Because great saints have great gifts to love, they have great potential to sin.

I am responsible not only for using my gifts to love but also for developing new gifts to love. Perhaps because long ago I had been criticized by a first grade teacher and lived a life full of unhealed hurts, I readily feel fearful and angry when criticized at the bulletin board. Sin enters not in feeling fear and anger but when I notice my fear and anger and decide to bury them again or act with hostility rather than heal my reaction by prayer, sharing with a friend, seeking psychological help, or in rare cases praying for deliverance from demonic influence. I may not be responsible for feeling irritable, but I am responsible for whether I react by drowning my anger in work until I am exhausted and critical of my students, or whether I take time for prayer and recreation so I receive new strength to deal with the situation. It isn't sinful to feel anger but it is sinful to feed my anger by refusing to use my remaining gift of freedom to grow closer to Christ and heal my wounds. Sin can come when I passively sit back and let the past control thus excusing myself from using my remaining gifts to grow.

Dr. Karl Menninger hopes that more of us will say, ''I'm a responsible sinner and can change'' rather than blame our actions on a first grade teacher, bad genes, an absent father, an evil spirit, a wounding word, or peer pressure. All these influence us and reduce our responsibility, but, if we are healthy, we choose how we respond to their influence.

We will be able more often to make the healthy statement, ''I am a responsible sinner and can change,'' if we examine the thoughts we harbor when hurt. These thoughts make us responsible for how we continue to feel and are the key to changing our sinful reaction. Change comes when we can make conscious our ''irrational'' thoughts and replace them with Christ's thoughts. For example, the hostility I felt toward Gus was not due just to his words but to the way I irrationally interpreted his words. Remember Gus' comment about my talk? ''It sounded like a talk a novice would give. It's hard to believe that he has been a Jesuit praying for six years. I wonder how long he will last as a Jesuit.''

The event (comment) itself didn't wound me; my reaction did. I could have thought, ''Maybe Gus is right because his criticism hurts. I've been working too much and praying too little. I'm glad he alerted me to the danger before it's too late to correct." If the comment were wrong, I might have thought, "Poor Gus, he must be hurting and really angry at something else. I wonder what I can do to help him." Both reactions would get me closer both to God and Gus and leave me a happier, richer person.

But instead of rationally viewing how the event could help me grow closer to God and Gus, I was threatened and began irrationally viewing the event. When I saw Gus' destructive criticism from the irrational view that certain people are bad (not just badly acting) and deserve severe blame and punishment to make them change, I became angry and thought, "Gus is a vulture. He deserves to be punished so that he will change. Never trust him again."

Anger left and depression arrived when a new irrational view, "I must be loved and accepted by those who are important to me and live up to their expectation," led me to focus not on Gus changing but on myself changing. This belief kept telling me, "You'll have to change everyting, immediately, right now, so that those important to you will love you and consider you a success." Not the event alone but my irrational view of the event crippled me with unhealed anger, bargaining, and depression.

Dr. Albert Ellis, the founder of rational emotive therapy, clinically confirms that emotions are not caused by the event alone but also by my view of the event. He has formulated ten irrational ideas (views) that lead to destructive feeling and even to mental illness.[4] Ellis concludes that health returns when these irrational viewpoints are replaced by rational ones, likewise in healing a memory new health comes when we abandon our irrational viewpoint and begin seeing them from Christ's viewpoint. In these ten irrational views lies our responsibility for being crippled rather than gifted by hurts.

The ten irrational ideas (views) of Ellis are listed slightly simplified and with a scriptural passage indicating Christ's view that brings healing. If any ring true, they clarify our responsibility for being hurt and the road back to health. They spell out where we have been wounded by Satan's attack against the fruit of the Spirit. "But the fruit of the Spirit is love, joy, peace, patience, kindness, goodness, faithfulness, gentleness, self-control; against such there is no law" (Gal. 5:22). If we are lacking one of the Spirit's fruits, we can recall our hurt feelings and ask, "With what thoughts did I justify remaining angry at whoever hurt me? What thoughts kept me angry at myself?" We can then confess these irrational, unforgiving views, and can look at Christ to absorb the gift of his life-giving view.

TEN IRRATIONAL IDEAS

I am responsible for getting or remaining hurt if I kept irrationally thinking . . .

1. Against love (without return)—I must be loved and accepted by those who are most important to me and live up to their expectations.
   Mt. 5:11—Blessed are you when men revile you and persecute you and utter all kinds of evil against you falsely on my account.
2. Against joy—I must be perfectly competent and successful in achieving before I can be happy with myself.
   2 Cor. 12:9–10—"My grace is sufficient for you, for my power is made perfect in weakness."
3. Against true peace (present in the midst of trials)—It is easier to avoid certain difficulties and responsibilities rather than face them. If I ignore them, they may go away.
   Lk. 9:23—"If any man would come after me, let him deny himself and take up his cross daily and follow me."
4. Against patience—I must find the quick and perfect solution to my problem.
   Phil. 4:5–6—"Let all men know your patience. . . . Have no anxiety about anything, but in everything by prayer and supplication with thanksgiving let your requests be made known to God."
5. Against kindness—Certain people are bad and they deserve severe blame or punishment for their sins.
   Lk. 23:34—"Father, forgive them, for they know not what they do."
6. Against goodness—I must be prepared for the worst by constantly dwelling on what may be bad, dangerous or feared.
   1 Jn. 4:18—"There is no fear in love, but perfect love casts out fear." (Put energy into evaluating fears and focus on the

Lord's loving power to act against them.)

7. Against faithfulness (through the years)—I have been shaped by the past and it is too late to change.
   2 Cor. 5:17—"If anyone is in Christ, he is a new creation; the old has passed away; behold, the new has come."

8. Against gentleness—It's terrible when things do not go the way I had planned.
   Mk. 14:36—"Father, all things are possible to thee. Remove this cup from me; yet not what I will, but what thou wilt."

9. Against self-control—I have no control over my own happiness; what happens to me determines my happiness.
   Mt. 6:22–23—"The eye is the lamp of the body. So, if your eye is sound, your whole body will be full of light; but if your eye is not sound, your whole body will be full of darkness." (Not the event but how I see it makes me happy.)

10. Against freedom (no law)—It's easier to keep doing things the way I am doing them without taking on new commitments.
    1 Cor. 13:4–7—"Love does not insist on its own way. . . . Love bears all things, believes all things, hopes all things, endures all things."

Hate the Sin—Change What Can Be Changed

If I really hate the sin, I need to not only locate the sinful attitude but also to change it, just as I need to reduce my telephone bill by cutting down the number of long distance calls. Yet I will keep making calls as I enjoy hearing a friend's voice or wish to avoid the pain of waiting endlessly for written replies. The pleasure and pain are the "secondary gains" that make me comfortable and unwilling to change. They may be conscious or unconscious. Healthy depression prods me to change even at the cost of giving up the more destructive secondary gains.

The above ten irrational ideas point out not just the unhealthy view leading to sin and Christ's healthy view but also the secondary gains that block change and that can also be confessed and traded for Christ's view with the Spirit's power. These are often false fruits that look like the fruits of the Spirit but are unloving views. If I were to forgive Gus, I would have to give up the following secondary gains:

TEN BLOCKS TO CHANGE

I don't want to change and forgive Gus because of . . .

1. False love—It's nice to get sympathy and be loved as a persecuted martyr having Gus's enemies as friends. I don't want to face ways that my love for Gus fell short and left him wounding others.
2. False joy—I can be happy with myself by blaming failure on Gus rather than on not praying well enough to give a talk on prayer.
3. False peace—Things are peaceful now, so don't rock the boat by taking on the difficulty and responsibility of building bridges to Gus. There is nothing much to forgive.
4. False patience—Gus is wrong, and maybe if I am patient he will change. (This is an easier solution than changing myself.)
5. False kindness—I can feel superior and kind when I look down on Gus and see how unkind he is.
6. False goodness—For the good of everyone Gus has to change and quit criticizing people. Until then I had better not trust him and get hurt again because I have enough pain in my life right now.
7. False faithfulness—I can faithfully tolerate Gus the way he is. He's too old and set in his ways to change, so why waste energy reaching out to him rather than to another?
8. False gentleness—If I can be gentle and kind to Gus until he feels sorry, then Gus will want to make reparation and do all I plan.
9. False self-control—I am in control of my own happiness and don't need Gus in my world. I can't help him. He has to help and control himself. If I help him, he will become dependent.
10. False freedom—I don't have enough time and energy now, so I can't commit myself to building bridges to Gus and losing my freedom to do better things. Give him an inch and he will take a mile limiting my freedom.

Similar secondary gains make it just as difficult to forgive myself.

A healthy depression uncovers the irrational ideas that keep me from shouldering responsibility for my sin and the secondary gains that sap my desire to change. Change comes not by gritting my teeth and summoning up more willpower to be nice to Gus but from seeing what irrational ideas opposed to Christ's healthy view made me vulnerable to being wounded by criticism, and what secondary gains kept me nursing my grudge. Then I can hate my sinful views and actions, confess them to Christ, and use the gifts for growth Jesus gives in loving me as sinner.

Healthy Depression—Love the Sinner

When giving retreats, I found the key time of growth was not so much when a retreatant figured out his irrational ideas or the answers to all his problems but when he could see himself as the sinner he really was with all his irrational ideas or problems and that, as a sinner, Jesus loved him and therefore he too could love himself as a sinner. If he just saw himself as a sinner, he grew discouraged. If the retreatant just saw himself as good and gifted and therefore loved by God, he never saw the depth of the Father's love given freely and not earned by good behavior.

> Why one will hardly die for a righteous man—though perhaps for a good man one will dare even to die. But God shows his love for us in that while we were yet sinners Christ died for us (Rom. 5:7–8).

We know the depth of God's love only when we know the depth of evil and sin in us that turns others away but makes Jesus give his life. If we really are depressed, we are on the verge of discovering that we are really loved.

God's infinite love is limited only by our need and hunger for his help. He has a reservoir of love that never runs out and that can be given only to the degree we have an empty vessel because we know our weakness and need. That's why, when the saints are closest to God, they feel most distant and really do see themselves as sinners. Great saints like Paul and Peter became great saints when they saw that they were great sinners. The test for sanctity is not how close I feel to God but how much I hunger for God. That's hard for me because I'd like to feel close to God rather than experience depression's need for God. When St. Ignatius wanted to feel close to God, he recalled all his sins and soon became filled with loving gratitude for God's rescuing mercy. Saints are people who hate the sin and love the sinner.

How does looking at our sin and weakness get us in touch with a self that is lovable?[6] Sin makes us unloving, not unlovable. We are sorry for the unloving side of us that caused destruction. But we can be grateful for the growth that comes from sin, the resurrection that follows the destruction of the cross. First, it is a gift to be depressed, to feel that we aren't all we should be. When we say "I should have . . ." we are complimenting ourselves with "I have higher values and the potential to reach them." The more I saw the destruction of criticism and that I had been freed previously from criticizing, the more disappointed and depressed I was at again falling into my old critical pattern.

Depression from the sin in us can be present only when there is a deeper recognition of our gifts. In the story of the prodigal son, the younger son probably would not be depressed if his father were a tyrant and sent him off penniless to avoid feeding another mouth. He would be angry, not depressed. But because he had a loving father, fortune, and food, he gets depressed at seeing his sinfulness and is eager to return. Only when we see our gifts and how we have misused them do we get truly depressed and call ourselves a sinner. When there is little awareness of sin, there is usually little awareness of God's gifts. Recognition of gifts is the beginning of recognition of sin; recognition of sin is the beginning of recognition of new gifts.

What gifts come from sin? We sin in the ways we are most gifted. If we are gifted speakers, we monopolize conversations and fail to help the timid come out of themselves. If we are too critical, it is the misuse of our gift for finding and repairing what is wrong in the world. If we are gifted at listening, we sin by listening too much and failing to speak up against injustice.

In grade school I gritted my teeth and told myself that I would recite. But I had a deep fear of speaking out because I had been laughed at when reciting in the second grade. Since then I let others speak out and became a good listener, even though others were being criticized behind their backs. I was able to break out of this sinful pattern not by developing more willpower but simply by using my gift for listening, which I did carefully for fear I would have nothing to say if called to express an opinion. As I listened carefully to people, I grew to understand their view and love them until I found myself irresistibly speaking out and defending them when they were criticized. My sinful silence disappeared because I discovered the gift given when I was hurt.

Sin goes away not by gritting our teeth and saying, ''No, I won't do that again,'' but by smiling and using our drive as gift. For example, rather than get discouraged for having strong sexual feelings, it is better to thank God for them. Sexual temptations go away not when we say, ''I don't want to feel this way,'' but rather when we thank God for strong sexual feelings when they come and then use those feelings creatively to be more intimate with Christ, with friends, and with those whom others ignore. Thus many prostitutes, by rechanneling their strong sexual desires, develop an intimate love for Christ (Lk. 7:37) (Lk. 15:1).

Not just strong sexual desires leading to prostitution, but any drive leading toward sin can be rechanneled and become a gift. Thus Christ rechannels Peter's drive to become first into a gift for leadership. After meeting Christ, Paul's driving anger which persecuted Christians also becomes a gift as that anger drives him out even to Rome to preach the good news. Not only for Peter and Paul but also for us, our present sin and our worst past sins can be the source of gifts if we ask Christ what good he can bring out of the times we most hurt people.[7]

But can every sin become a gift? How do you begin to love yourself if you have killed another in a car accident, if your drinking destroyed your family and psychologically crippled your kids, if you had an abortion killing an innocent life, if you failed to help a depressed person who committed suicide, if you mixed drinking and driving with an accident that paralyzed you for life, if you ran away from home and never had a chance to tell a dead mother you were sorry? I have known a depressed person in each of the above situations. We all have. But each of these persons began to be healed of his depression when he could begin to confess his guilt, accept Christ's love and see how he had new gifts from his sin.

Is this possible? One of the most wounded was a teacher who had fears of driving a car, was scrupulous, constantly rechecked doors and lights, wondered whether past confessed sins were really forgiven, and found herself constantly repreparing well-done lessons. The earliest time she could remember being down on herself was when as a beginning teacher she had corrected a misbehaving student by striking his head. As a result, the student lost some of his hearing. After days of prayer, she discovered that Christ loved her even then.

She began to see that this event was not only the source of her problems but the source of her gifts. Her guilt at hurting the child helped her work with handicapped children, prepare classes thoroughly so she wouldn't have any discipline problems (she was an excellent teacher), become a math and typing teacher where carefulness paid off, and have excellent rapport with teenagers who felt down on themselves (as she did); it also kept her praying and dependent on Christ and kept her going to school to improve her skills.

Even though she hurt one child, she helped so many others through gifts from her depression. Rather than feeling guilty, she began to feel grateful even for her scruples which she saw as a gauge alerting her to tension that needed to be dealt with before it found a destructive outlet. As she became more grateful, her fears and scruples began to disappear. When she saw how her gifts came from her disasters, she stopped trying to be perfect and allowed Christ to bring good out of mistakes. She could love herself as a sinner as she saw the visible ways that Christ had loved her as sinner.

Test For Healthy Depression:
Do I Love Myself as a Sinner Enough To Love Another Sinner?

How do we know if we really hate our sins and love ourselves as sinners? How can we tell whether we really accept Jesus' love for us as sinners or whether there is still a part of us that we can't love as Jesus does? When retreatants tell me, ''Now I really know how much God loves me as a sinner,'' I ask them, ''Who in your whole life hurt you the most?'' Then I send them off to spend a day in prayer trying to love that sinner as much as Jesus does. Only those who understand how much God loves them as sinners can give that same acceptance to whoever most hurt them. The test of how deeply we have experienced God's forgiveness is simply how deeply we can forgive our neighbor and vice versa. ''Forgive one another as God in Christ has forgiven you'' (Eph. 4:32). We love

Christ and ourselves as much as we love the person we love the least.

One retreatant, Joan, tried to love and forgive a mentally ill woman who would insult everyone who entered their home. Joan lived with this woman in a nightmarish world of constant insults to herself and her friends. During the retreat Joan couldn't experience her own sinfulness until she struggled for four days unsuccessfully to forgive the mentally ill woman. Nothing helped her until she realized that the inability to love was not present just in the mentally ill woman but also in herself because she could not love and offer forgiveness. What she most disliked about the woman was in herself too. For a day Joan struggled to see how God had forgiven her own unforgiving heart and loved her in her weakness. When she experienced God's acceptance of her weakness, she was finally able to forgive the same weakness in the mentally ill woman.

Often I can forgive only when I realize that what God accepts in me is what I can't accept in another. When I discovered that I was as critical of my students as my friend was critical of me, it was easier to forgive Gus. I often wondered why God didn't make forgiveness easier and quicker when praying for it. Now I see that the struggle and difficulty I experienced in trying to forgive another makes it possible to accept the other's struggle and difficulty to come closer to me. When I see how God accepts both of us the way we are, I too can accept both of us the way we are. This forgiveness is deeper because I am then giving God's forgiveness toward me and not my limited supply of love. God's forgiveness toward me and my forgiveness toward another are like the voice and the echo.

When I can confess, "I am a sinner loved by Jesus," I hate the sin and love the sinner, thereby opening myself to spiritual, emotional, and physical healing. Calling myself a sinner loved by Jesus means that I want to heal those hurt by my destruction, can change with Christ's love, know a deeper dimension of his love, have more control over my own happiness, desire to live rationally with the Lord's healing view, have a chance to discover new gifts, and have new power to love and forgive other sinners like myself. That's why depression can be healthy.

The chart below summarizes the test for healthy depression.

TEST FOR HEALTHY DEPRESSION STAGE—I'M O.K.;
              YOU'RE O.K.

	SIN	SINNER
MYSELF	Hate my sin	Love myself as sinner—I'm O.K.
ANOTHER	Hate another's sin	Love another as sinner—You're O.K.

Other unhealthy options:

1. If I do not hate my sin; I may deny or project my guilt and become fixated in the denial, anger or bargaining stage. "I am not responsible," so you are. I'm O.K.; you're not O.K.
2. If I do not love myself as sinner, I may identify my guilt with myself and fall into unhealthy depression. I'm not O.K.; you're not O.K.
3. If I do not hate another's sin, the anger meant for another may get turned toward myself and I get emotionally depressed. I'm not O.K.; you're O.K.
4. If I do not love another as a sinner, I may remain in the anger stage. I'm O.K.; you're not O.K.
5. If I love neither another nor myself as sinner, I may alternate between anger and depression. I'm not O.K.; you're not O.K.

IV

DEALING WITH DEPRESSION

If we don't deal with depression, we can end up mentally ill or even physically ill. Dr. Loring Swaim, an instructor in arthritis at the Harvard Medical School and with fifty years of experience in orthopedics, found that the first attacks of rheumatoid arthritis almost always followed unhappy events where the patients felt great emotional strain.[8] When patients could get beneath bitterness and resentment and began to forgive those responsible for the unhappy event (anger) and when they could finally forgive themselves for "unsatisfied selfish demands" (guilt), the active disease frequently was arrested. The attack would remain quiescent until the patient again failed to deal with his anger or guilt. Forgiveness again made the attack subside. If we don't deal with our negative emotions, they deal with us.

If the hurt is deep, it may take months to deal with depression and reach the acceptance stage. When depression is long term, involving suicidal thoughts, or bringing major changes in patterns of sleep or appetite, then professional help is also needed. With less serious depression, the process is speeded up when I can share with an understanding friend and be affirmed by those around me. I need another's acceptance to concretely experience Christ's acceptance and begin to accept myself. When hurt by Gus, constant acceptance from my fellow teachers made me secure enough to receive Christ's acceptance offered in prayer. I need to use all of God's gifts whether they come packaged as professional help, medication, the warmth of a friend, or acceptance found in prayer.

How can I deal in prayer with my guilt feelings? The process is the same as for dealing with the feelings present at any stage. Like the disciples on the road to Emmaus:

1. Tell Christ how I feel. Tell him about the evil destruction and how I feel responsible and want to change.

2. Listen through Scripture to how Christ feels. How would Christ react to me and to the person who hurt me?

3. Live out Christ's healing reaction.

I am healed when I enter the mind and heart of Christ and am able to live as he would. Talking and praying with an understanding friend can also help with these steps.

1. Sharing with Christ How I Feel

When I am depressed, often it helps to make the stations of the cross or to pray over a passion scene to get a sense of how Christ understands and has experienced what is happening to me. I ask Christ to help me see and share what is making me depressed. Am I really angry at someone else or at myself and all I wish I had done differently? Then I simply tell Jesus as honestly as I can what I am feeling. Usually it begins as self-pity, how I have hurt myself, and then grows to ask help in acknowledging my irrational views and repairing the destructiveness of my reaction. If I am really honest I often find some left-over anger disguised as anger at myself. Reviewing the ten irrational views often helps to pinpoint my sinful view so that I can tell Christ how greatly I feel in need of his forgiveness and his view. My prayer might be the following:

"Lord, Gus has a problem, but I do too in overreacting. Why do I irrationally believe that I must have everyone's respect? Why do I keep saying 'yes' until I am overextended and vulnerable to the slightest criticism? Why am I more concerned about what Gus thinks than about what you think of me? Why am I talking about Gus behind his back yet self-righteously blaming him for doing it to me? Why do I fear angry criticism and bury it until it builds up and explodes? Here I am sent to help the Sioux, thinking that I can really understand another culture, and I can't even understand my fellow Jesuit's cry for help. Why didn't I see the pressures Gus was under? Why do I have to get most angry at the·people who most need help? Why is my love so selfishly given only to people who are good to me? Maybe I'm really not meant to work out here or to even be a Jesuit priest. Maybe I don't pray enough to become a priest. Why can't I start praying rather than just pretend he is wrong? Why can't I forget the untrue and do something about the true criticism? Lord, my love and forgiveness fall so short of your steadfast love for me and for Gus. Heal me and stretch me.

"Lord, even what I've said is self-centered. I'm all concerned about the way I've hurt myself and didn't even see that I hurt you too. The real tragedy is not how I hurt myself but how I hurt you in myself and others. You said, 'Whatever you did to the least of my brothers, you did to me.' Every time I hurt myself or a student by my remarks, I hurt you.⁹ Somehow you seem remote and I don't feel as sorry about hurting you as I do about hurting myself. Forgive me for not being more sorry and for being more concerned about what I suffered than about what you suffered because of me. Lord, I need healing of my cold heart. I can't even tell you that I'm really sorry.

"Lord, I am surprised at how much evil my cold heart can do after just a slight criticism. Why doesn't this happen more often? I see now it's not my strength that keeps me from being shattered by remarks but rather your forgiving love and power constantly protecting me. Forgive me for my self-pity and for focusing on my weakness rather than thanking you for realizing I need you and have your protective love to avoid these falls. I keep feeling that I must recognize all my sin and get rid of it when really I must accept your love before I have the power to do anything. Help me to quit kicking myself and drawing up my solutions rather than thanking you for how I feel and how you will help me grow from it. My worst sin is not anything I've done but my lack of faith in what we can do together to build a new future and repair my destruction. Jesus, show me my sin so I may proclaim your healing love and forgiveness which is even greater than my weakness. Let me focus not on analyzing my sin but on praising your healing love and forgiveness that strengthen me to grow.

"Lord, I place in your hands all these things I wish I had done differently because I want your forgiveness and healing. I give you all the ways I have hurt others and ask that you may heal us all in whatever ways we are still suffering from my actions or lack of action. I don't want to hide from you anything that needs healing. Bring to mind all that you want to touch."

2. *Listening to How Christ Feels*

After I have put into Christ's hands all that I wish I had done differently and all the destruction that needs his healing, then I watch Christ to see what he would do and say to me. Like the disciples on the road to Emmaus, when I share what I am feeling and listen to him explaining another view through the Scriptures, then my heart burns within me.

What would Christ say and do to heal me? How did Christ react to a person who felt the way I do? There are many sinners in the Gospels, but the one who seemed closest to how I saw myself was Simon the Pharisee who inwardly criticized the woman at Christ's feet only to find out that he was the greater sinner (Lk. 7). I read the passage several times, relax as a sign of surrender, get centered on Christ, imagine each detail of the scene, and then begin to listen with my heart.

Christ seems to be saying to me, "Yes, you have behaved like Simon the Pharisee looking down on your brother and ignoring my needs in the Sioux. But Simon didn't even know he was a sinner. Be grateful that you do know. I gave Simon time to answer correctly and discover on his own that he was a sinner. I did not tell you immediately that you were critical and oversensitive because I wanted you to discover the depth of weakness I forgive in you so you could forgive the same depth of weakness in another. Now you can come with a debt of five hundred rather than fifty and with me forgive another a debt of five hundred rather than fifty. I forgive you much so that you will be able to love and forgive much. You can love and forgive more people like yourself now that you know how much you are forgiven. Be grateful that you can see your own faults in those you are to forgive.

"You fear losing your vocation. Who is clinging to my feet? Simon who tries to be perfect is criticizing me, while the woman who knows she is a sinner loves me and remains close to me. The weaker you are, the closer we can become because you need me more and I can then give more. Don't worry about whether you are perfect but about whether you are at my feet and allowing yourself to be loved. I call weak instruments who rely on my strength and give me the credit.

"But you keep wishing that you didn't have faults. You feel that you would be closer to me if you were perfect. That's bargaining. You have looked through my eyes and been able to love Gus just as he is. Now look through my eyes and be able to love yourself with all your weakness. Cancel your unspoken bargains: 'If I were less critical, less sensitive, better able to change rather than making the same mistakes, then I could forgive and love myself.' You are to hate the sin and love the *sinner*, not just the 'nice guy' in yourself.

"I too want you to grow, but growth comes not when you dislike yourself and try harder to change, but when you love yourself as much as I do and use my love to grow. People change when they fall in love and want to live up to the love they are being offered. See yourself not as the person you want to be but as the sinner you are so that you will see how much I love you. Anyone can love the person you want to be, but only I can totally love the person you are. Cancel your bargains and love yourself just as you are with my forgiving love. I made you not an angel but a man designed to make mistakes and learn from them. I don't want a Hollywood hero who never gets tired or never runs out of bullets.

"You keep asking for my forgiveness like the woman at my

feet who didn't know she was already forgiven. You would not be here asking to love more unless you were forgiven. You just have to accept the forgiveness I gave when I died for you. Take my hand and feel the wound opened for you. What more can I do to love you? Put your other hand in mine to show me that you want to be closer than ever. Let me place my hand on your shoulder and fill you with my strength to show you how to fill empty people and not just those who can love you in return.

"You tell me that you don't feel sorry enough. Again you are thinking that you have to earn my forgiveness—this time by feeling right. I didn't love the woman at my feet because she poured out an expensive ointment but because she was coming to me empty. Your lack of feelings is part of the emptiness I love. Come to me with the faith that you don't have to feel forgiven in order to be forgiven. Simon didn't feel like a sinner but was one, while the woman at my feet felt like a sinner but was loved much. Being forgiven and loved doesn't depend on feeling forgiven or even sorry. Forgiveness is a deeper reality than feelings that come and go. Don't focus on feeling sorry enough (you can't ever) but focus on my great love for sinners. Contrite feelings are good, but the important thing is to accept my great love for you whether you feel sorry or as dry as dust. Continue to breathe out with a deep sigh all your unwanted, depressed feelings and fears. Breathe in my peace and healing power. Now just silently rest in my embrace so that I can heal you and fill you with my love. . . . Your faith has saved you. Go in peace."

Then I watch myself doing all the things I just told Christ that I didn't like—getting wounded at the bulletin board by a few critical words, self-righteously criticizing Gus and my students, and saying "yes" to every project until I crawl into bed exhausted with no time to pray. In each scene I watch Christ put his hand on my shoulder, smile and then embrace me because he can forgive a debt of five hundred rather than fifty to bring greater closeness from the sin. I rest in his arms until I can feel loved and able to smile and accept myself in those sinful situations just as Christ accepts me. This isn't just an imaginary acceptance. To test whether I have really experienced Christ accepting my weakness and gifting me, I picture Gus and see whether I can accept in him the sinner that

Christ embraces in me. If this was a real experience, I will want to give Gus the same acceptance and gifts that Christ gives me.

What Christ says and how he heals can't be put into words because he speaks in heart language and heals especially when I just rest with him.[10] Usually a time comes in prayer when Christ speaks to my heart and I just want to silently rest in him and be loved. This is hard for me to do, because when I am not talking it feels as though I am doing nothing. But when I get to know someone well, I can just be with him and enjoy him without saying or doing much. Prayer's healing moments are not so much the times I get new insights but the times I just rest in Christ's loving embrace.

3. *Living Out Christ's Reaction*

The third step, acting healed, starts with prayer. I ask Christ to put into my imagination his ways of acting and into my heart his power to repair the damage in myself and in others. Failures still occur, but they mostly come when I am either angry at myself and quit trying, or am angry at God and return to doing things my way with my strength. My prayer was like the following:

"Lord, as I come before you and see you touching the woman at your feet and healing her with the words, 'Your faith has saved you; go in peace,' I know you want to do the same to me. Put into my mind how you want me to live with your mind and heart. . . . It seems what you want most is for me to forgive Gus completely now that I see how I am like him and how you accept me. Help me to love him the way he is. Help me to take my gift for criticizing and put it to constructive use by helping him to write the student handbook—a job he dreads. Put into my mind the ways you most want to heal him and work through him so that I can ask you, Lord, and do what I can, to help him grow. Show me how you love him as I want to love Gus more. . . .

"Lord, I thank you for helping me give Gus your love. My forgiveness is deeper when I can love him the way he is and start to build the bridges you want. I feel ready to get closer to him. Let me find the best time and situation when he is ready, and let me be just as patient with him as you were with me. Show me in the days ahead how I can repair the harm I caused him and my students by talking behind their backs. Make me alert to times I can spread a compliment.

"Lord, I don't want to block your healing love toward all those around me. Show me how you want to use what I most dislike about myself. . . . Take my sensitivity to criticism and make me sensitive to the criticized. Let the criticism about my prayer life sensitize me to what the Sioux feel when their prayer with the sacred pipe is criticized. Make me more sensitive to the criticism in the air when I live with the Sioux family this summer. Take my sinfulness that I want to hide and keep it before my eyes so that I may hunger to pray more and won't lose my vocation. Take my self-pity at not being accepted and make it a drive that helps me build a community here where we really accept and support each other. Show me the ways in which you want to heal me and gift me so that I may give you thanks."

When I can begin to pray, concentrating on my gifts and not on what is wrong with me, I can not remain depressed. Depression is largely a matter of choosing to remain down on myself. It's often the simple choice of whether to keep getting discouraged at my penchant for criticism or use it as a gift for changing what needs to be changed in building a better world. Every conflict can bring either sin or virtue. Doubts about faith can either destroy faith or make it stronger than ever. We aren't born with virtue but we develop it in facing temptation and in bouncing back from falls to become more reliant on Christ's strength. What we have done wrong shouldn't get us down; it should get us leaning on Christ. Saints aren't people who never sin. Saints are human beings whose sin brings them closer to Christ.

Living Out Christ's Reaction by Confession

Many things help to heal a depression—saying "I'm sorry," making restitution, talking and praying with a friend, making the stations of the cross, visiting the sick, getting rest and recreation, and especially confession. I have seen the Lord heal many times during our retreats and workshops, but his favorite time seems to be confession. In just minutes the Lord begins to heal deep hurts driving a person toward suicide. It doesn't take a special confessor but only a willingness to answer with the Lord these questions:

1. How has the Lord gifted me?

2. How do I need forgiveness for my sins of failing to use these gifts?

3. Who, needing my forgiveness, has hurt me so I react as an insecure sinner?

4. From this hurt, what growth do I see coming for which I wish to thank the Lord and ask him to increase?

The new rite of reconciliation was redesigned to make the sacrament a time of healing through these steps of accepting forgiveness, offering forgiveness, and giving thanks for growth and possible growth. The new rite of reconciliation recognizes more than ever that confession of sin brings healing and so is no longer called "confession" with its emphasis on enumerating sin but "reconciliation" with God, others, and our deeper self.

Every part of the new rite is meant to be a healing of memories with its Scripture reading to see situations as Jesus sees them, the face-to-face conversational format getting beyond the list of sins to their roots in past hurts, the freedom to choose a healing penance rather than "three Hail Mary's," the laying on of hands (an ancient sign of healing), and the new absolution formula "May God grant you pardon and *peace*. . . ." The closing words, "Give thanks to the Lord for he is good and his mercy endures forever," reminds us that healing continues forever as Christ's mercy deepens in us to the point of giving thanks for the good gifts from the hurt. Confession is so healing that every sacrament begins with a brief rite or reconciliation.

Praying and confession, however, are not substitutes for personal reconciliation but only a preparation for it. Telling Christ that I'm sorry for criticizing Gus is only a preparation for telling Gus: "I was wrong; will you forgive me?" To ask for forgiveness is harder and takes a deeper assertiveness that heals. When I say "I'm sorry" rather than "I'm really angry at you," it's easier for the other to say "I'm sorry too." Be reconciled to your brother not when you have something against him but when you look again and see also what he has against you. Marriages get broken when a wife passively accepts her husband's adultery. Marriages get repaired when a wife sees how she is part of the reason that her husband looks for another woman.

The depth of forgiveness is measured not by words but by actions of reconciliation. The new rite of reconciliation suggests penances that repair the damage of sin. Rather than say three Hail Mary's, a more healing penance would be to repair the damage with a letter, compliment, phone call, visit, gift, favor, fasting, or service to the community such as taking a senior citizen shopping. An impatient father of a rebellious child might choose a penance of spending time alone with that child. One hour given alone to a child is worth ten given to him with others.[11]

Too often I forget about repairing myself. If I see myself as a lovable, forgiven sinner who is a temple of the Spirit and son or daughter of the Father, I should treat myself with love. Rather than select a self-punishing penance, I should ask, "What would I do if I really loved myself?" Maybe I would read a stimulating book, get the sleep I crave, take the invigorating exercise I enjoy, or treat myself to a good time with a friend. It's easier and unhealthy to keep kicking myself than to celebrate with a party my return as a prodigal son. Our book, *Healing of Memories*, might be helpful if confession has become not a celebration of new freedom but a routine time of saying the same sins and experiencing little healing and power to change.[12]

Despite doing all these suggestions I may still feel depressed. This especially happens when I want to feel differently and have not surrendered to Christ my desire to be in charge of my feelings. Rather than tell the Lord how I want to feel, maybe the Lord wants me to say, "I want to grow from whatever way I feel so please help me to grow." Deep love and forgiveness are rooted in a decision to love and forgive even when I don't feel like it. Rather than dwelling on these unhealed and lingering depressed feelings it is more helpful to search for the healed feeling of being loved.

This is like a man who has lost an arm; although he may still feel as though the arm is there, he can't feed himself with it. If I have followed the steps in this chapter, I am forgiven whether I feel like it or not and can act grateful rather than depressed. Slowly the forgiveness will deepen until I begin to also feel loved and loving. If I continue to feel depressed, I start to visit others with bigger burdens—an unemployed father, the pain-riddled sick, a grieving widow living frugally, an elderly neighbor lonely and awaiting death. It's hard to remain depressed by my burden when I see theirs.

If I still feel depressed, the real problem is possibly not depression but anger. If I look at my sin and don't feel forgiven and gifted, it isn't because I am too great a sinner but because I am angry at God and can't accept his love. Anger at God has many subtle forms: feeling like working rather than praying, expecting little change from prayer, feeling that God might ask too much, shortening prayer time, and promising total surrender but keeping one little area of compromise. When these happen, I must go back to the anger stage and sit next to Job asking God why he allowed the dead family, burnt barns, and ulcerous boils. If I begin to see his love even in these tragedies, then I am approaching the acceptance stage.

Perhaps this sounds hopelessly complex and unreal. Working through depression is as complex and as real as working through alcoholism. When we get hurt, some of us drink, while others choose another of the capital sins. But the road back is the same trail of admitting that we have a problem, asking for forgiveness, and getting the Lord's power and view of how to love ourselves and others. This chapter could be summarized by the twelve steps of Alcoholics Anonymous.[13]

THE TWELVE STEPS OF A.A.

1. We admitted we were powerless over alcohol—that our lives had become unmanageable.
2. We came to believe that a Power greater than ourselves could restore us to sanity.
3. We made a decision to turn our will and our lives over to care of God as we understood him.
4. We made a searching and fearless moral inventory of ourselves.
5. We admitted to God, to ourselves, and to another human being the exact nature of our wrongs.
6. We were entirely ready to have God remove all these defects of character.
7. We humbly asked him to remove our shortcomings.
8. We made a list of all persons we had harmed, and became willing to make amends to them all.
9. We made direct amends to such people wherever possible,

except when to do so would injure them or others.

10. We continued to take personal inventory and when we were wrong, promptly admitted it.

11. We sought through prayer and meditation to improve our conscious contact with God as we understood him, praying only for knowledge of his will for us and the power to carry that out.

12. Having had a spiritual awakening as the result of these steps, we tried to carry this message to alcoholics, and to practice these principles in all our affairs.

When my alcoholic friend, Joe, walked along the twelve steps, his depression dirge became a song of gratitude for his alcoholism. He saw his alcoholism as a gift to experience God's power, to experience being loved much because forgiven much, and as a gift through which he could help other alcoholics. The gifts of the reformed alcoholic belong to each of us as we reform through the depression stage and enter the acceptance stage.

11
FIFTH STAGE: ACCEPTANCE

Walk into any hospital room and you usually find get-well cards, flowers, candy for the visitors, and a smiling patient. Even if the patient is facing surgery or death, if you ask him how he feels, he smiles with confidence like Jimmy Carter campaigning. A moment later when the visitor leaves, he is back to complaining about the nurses never bringing ice water. How do you know whether a smiling patient really has accepted his fate or is just denying it?

I too feign acceptance. Because I was blaming myself for overreacting to Gus' criticism, I thought I had completely forgiven and accepted him. But about a week later when he asked to see me in his office, I immediately began to grow tense and fearful. What is wrong this time? Nothing came to mind, yet I was shaking. Before being hurt by his remark, I never feared being called in to his office. But now I feared getting hurt again because the wound wasn't healed, and I hadn't forgiven Gus to the point of acceptance and trust. As I found my forgiveness deepening in the following weeks, my fear of dealing with Gus vanished.

1

SYMPTOMS OF ACCEPTANCE

If it is easy to feign acceptance, how do we diagnose true forgiveness? Denial and acceptance seem almost alike. When I first heard Gus' criticism at the bulletin board, I felt denial. "That's all right. Others liked the talk." In the acceptance stage I also said, "That's all right," but I wasn't hiding a raw wound. Denial's wounds are camouflaged by rationalization, patterns of sin, escapes, hunger for approval, and all the other ways by which I cover up insecurity. In denial I may smile at Gus but my anger still gnaws away until I growl at myself or my students or feel that God is unfair. But in acceptance I am free from these symptoms and instead experience gratitude for growth from the hurt, an ability to grow from new hurts, an openness to feel all my emotions, a reaching out to others, and a commitment to Christ not possible in denial. Rather than denying my experience, I am asking, "How can I more fully experience, enjoy, and profit from this day, person, and challenge?"[1] Forgiveness and healing are proportionate to the new openness to God, neighbor, and myself in each of a day's events.

What might happen on a day of acceptance? Days of total acceptance are as rare as a rainy day when I want to get up immediately. When in acceptance I awake rested and eager to start the day even if planning a picnic in a downpour. I can remember dreams and recall that in last night's dream I sold the Brooklyn Bridge. Successful dreams and new dreams can occur and be recalled because old hurts are healed and make way for other hurts to get attention. On my way to breakfast I walk past the bulletin board and break into a rare 8:00 A.M. smile that says, "I'm glad it all happened." Everything seems good, even the lukewarm coffee at breakfast. I find myself enjoying the breakfast and conversation, rather than eating to get recharged and on to the next activity. Throughout the day I enjoy doing what I'm doing rather than hurrying to finish.

After breakfast it is time for teaching. We again start class with half the students present, but this time I am grateful that half came rather than complaining that half stayed away. Because I have been criticized, I am left more sensitized to the harm I do when I criticize my students. Before this, I would criticize them when they would say, "I'm just an Indian and can't do that math." Now I know the criticism they have experienced and the depression that saps initiative. I don't have the ready answers on how to change, but I fit more their definition of a friend, "One who carries my sorrows on his back." My suffering now gifts me to understand the suffering in others. As the classroom banner proclaims, "You cannot touch the wounded until you have scarred hands."

Scarred hands cannot only make me more open to my students but also more open to Christ. I find myself praying more honestly—even sharing my anger towards Christ's slow pace in healing me. I have a hunger to give Jesus my feelings and be further healed as I take on his mind and heart. As a memory is healed and I begin seeing it with Christ's mind and heart, I don't want to forgive and forget. Rather I want to forgive and remember what Christ sees—the growth and possible growth that he promises: "We know that in everything God works for good with those who love him" (Rom. 8:28). Thus I allow Christ to show me the growth that came from being criticized such as how that criticism probably saved my religious vocation. If I hadn't been criticized, I probably wouldn't have started to pray again, and I could easily have lost my vocation, as happened to half of those teaching with me.

As I become more grateful for the gifts that came from being criticized, I also become more forgiving. I don't try to forgive my critic on my own energy but ask Christ for help so that my forgiveness will be as deep as his acceptance of me. After the depression stage shows me the depth of my weakness, it is hard to criticize another's weakness. Gradually I throw out my lists of all the ways in which I or another should improve, and I become more concerned about asking God's help to grow from failures. My prayers that I will never again get hurt by criticism now change to asking that I be able to grow from future criticism.

God's patience with me gifts me with a new patience to help others grow. People are like plants, needing time, warm sunlight, and daily watering to grow. I quit asking shy violets to be assertive roses. I quit giving advice, listen until I see through their glasses, and let them make mistakes to learn the same way I learn. I invite others to share their fear, anger, and depression because they sense I am at home with my negative feelings and won't look down on them. We start talking about struggles rather than weather and sports. In the warm sunlight of affirmation we can laugh at our mistakes and try again.

In acceptance I can even affirm my critic Gus. When he tells me about giving a successful retreat, I don't feel a competitive "Why does he always get to go away and do all the things I would like to do?" Instead, I'm glad that he succeeded. I want the best for him. Sure, that means that I would like him to grow and be less critical, but I don't wait in the corner until he changes before I reach out to him. I begin to build bridges to him by really listening until I can understand his views even if I don't agree with them. I can get called into his office without wondering what is wrong and rehearsing my defense. I can listen to his anger without tuning him out for fear of being hurt again. When I meet him in the hall, my smile flashes more readily. I want him to feel forgiven and accepted, not wrong.

Finally, in accepting another I can also accept myself at new levels. When I hear a rare compliment, I say less often "But . . ." and more often, "Thank you." "I should have . . ." becomes "How can I grow from that failure?" I am ready to take risks and fail—and even to try another talk on prayer. I begin to persevere with more patience at difficult projects, such as trying to reach a problem student whom I wanted transferred out of my class. Because I am trying new risks there is more failure, but the difference is that now I grow more often from the bad times.

All the above can happen in therapy, resulting in an admiration for the therapist. But when it happens by putting on the mind and heart of Christ in prayer until I have his reactions, then I end up deeply committed to Christ. I will know a power to love beyond any therapy because I can give only what I have received, and I have received Christ's unconditional acceptance in a way that no therapist can begin to accept me. True acceptance is best measured by the degree to which I can say, "I am loved by Christ and want him to be the center of my life." Only a totally unscarred and free person can consistently give this unconditional, healing love. Too often my own needs and hurts close me to my God, my neighbor, or my deeper self. How can I remain in acceptance? Scripture's answer is to suffer as St. Paul and those living the beatitudes did.

II
ACCEPTANCE IN SCRIPTURE

To the degree that we live the Beatitudes (Mt. 5:1–12), we live acceptance, and we live happy, healthy lives focusing not on the pain from hurts but on the growth from hurts. Psychiatrist James Fisher sees mental health encapsulated in the Sermon on the Mount which the Beatitudes introduce and summarize.

If you were to take the sum total of all the authoritative articles ever written by the most qualified of psychologists and psychiatrists on the subject of mental hygiene—if you were to combine them and refine them and cleave out the excess verbiage—if you were to . . . have these unadulterated bits of pure scientific knowledge concisely expressed by the most capable of living poets, you would have an awkward and incomplete summation of the Sermon on the Mount.[2]

The Beatitudes don't promise that we will masochistically enjoy the evil and suffering when poor or insulted but that we will be happy over the growth which with acceptance can always be present. For example, Christ took one of the greatest tragedies, a prodigal son running away from home, and showed how even it could be a time of the Beatitudes' happiness over growth (Luke 15). In returning home to forgive and be forgiven, the prodigal son experiences the Beatitudes' acceptance of God, his father, and himself. His poverty in spirit allows him to admit that he is needy and can't continue without a God and father. To the degree that the prodigal really mourned that he has sinned against heaven and his father, he will never run away again. Instead of running away, he returns meekly asking to be only a servant and not a son, yet he has all his inheritance returned as symbolized by the ring and the best robe offered by the father. He will probably hunger and thirst for justice toward his servants because he knows the hardships of being a starving worker. Each of the Beatitudes call the son to joyful growth if he focuses not on the hurt but on the growth possible from the hurt.

The father too accepts the hurt and hears the call to grow from it, especially as a peacemaker. Because the father is in acceptance, he confronts his elder son not out of a hostility that ventilates and manipulates but out of love that says ''All that is mine is yours.'' At peace with his own anger and worth, the father hears and understands the elder son's anger even though he doesn't agree with the hostile way it is expressed. Because the father has worked through the depression stage, he sees his own failure to help the younger son work out the conflict rather than run away, and he tries harder to avoid any similar conflict that may make the elder son run too. The Gospels tell us not to avoid confrontation but to wait until we are peacemakers and can confront in love and acceptance rather than in hostility. We must ask, ''Am I confronting you because you bother me or because I love you?''

The Beatitudes call us to love even when hurt so we feast not on sour grapes but on the fatted calf. We can choose in any situation to be either the elder son, angry and focusing on the hurt, or the father forgiving and accepting the growth from the hurt. Acceptance gives power to grow whether the person changes, like the prodigal, or remains the same, like the angry son.

The Beatitudes' call to grow in the midst of suffering is not just an ideal reached in a story like the prodigal son but the reality lived in the life of St. Paul. Through experience Paul discovered that he could face all suffering and grow from it with Christ. He boasts about Christ's love for him not because his life has been free from hurts but because he grew in the midst of shipwrecks, beatings, being stoned, imprisoned, robbed, and starving (2 Cor. 11:23–27). Since "we know that in everything God works for good with those who love him" (Rom. 8:28), Paul insists that no hurt or tribulation can keep us from growing closer to Christ.

> Who shall separate us from the love of Christ? Shall tribulation, or distress, or persecution, or famine, or nakedness, or peril, or sword? . . . No, in all these things we are more than conquerors through him who loved us. For I am sure that neither death, nor life, nor angels, nor principalities, nor things present, nor things to come, nor powers, nor height, nor depth, nor anything else in all creation, will be able to separate us from the love of God in Christ Jesus our Lord (Rom. 8:35–39).

After exhorting the Thessalonians to be confident that they can grow from the coming suffering of the expected Parousia. Paul reveals his secret for growing in situations. "Rejoice always, pray constantly, give thanks in all circumstances; for this is the will of God in Christ Jesus for you" (1 Thes. 5:16–18).[3] We too can always grow like Paul if we take a hurt and prayerfully thank God for its possibilities for growth in light of the following questions raised by the Beautitudes' promises.

MATTHEW 5:1–12: BEATITUDES—
THANKING GOD FOR GROWTH FROM HURTS

1. "Blessed are the poor in spirit, for theirs is the Kingdom of heaven."

Did being hurt make me ready to admit that I am needy and must trust more in God who can then use me more? Pray more? Better?

Did my neediness make me deepen friendships? Better know my limitations?

2. "Blessed are those who mourn, for they shall be comforted." Did being hurt and comforted make me desire to do the same, especially for those hurt in the same way?

Have I been comforted? Is the recall less painful than the event?

3. "Blessed are the meek; they shall inherit the earth." Did being hurt make me more gentle, enabling others to grow and be grateful for their gifts, less ready to hurt?

4. "Blessed are they who hunger and thirst for what is right; they shall be satisfied." Did being hurt make me more ready to act and meet the needs of those who are suffering?

Did the hurt drive me to develop new skills, desires, or knowledge for serving?

5. "Blessed are the merciful; they shall have mercy shown to them." Did my struggle to forgive the hurt help me to accept others who are struggling to forgive me? Can I be forgiven easily because I forgive easily?

Have I experienced my need for Christ's help if I am to forgive seven times seventy times, immediately, unconditionally? Is my forgiveness closer to Christ's?

6. "Blessed are the pure of heart; they shall see God." Did being hurt by men make me act more for God and less for men?

Can I give more with less thought of return? Deal better with failures?

Is it easier for me to thank God for his work in every situation?

7. "Blessed are the peacemakers; they shall be called sons of God." In trying to forgive and make peace, have I become a better peacemaker?

Did not being heard and receiving disrespect make me a person who listens better and tries harder to respect each man?

Am I more apt to catch myself and others not listening and building bridges?

8. "Blessed are those who are persecuted in the cause of right; theirs is the Kingdom of heaven."

Has my suffering helped me to develop patience and perseverance, in following Christ despite setbacks and criticism?

Do I believe that my suffering can be the time I am most like Christ and nearest to him? A time of making reparation for my sins?

To the degree that I was wronged, have I tried to bear it patiently, knowing that as the injustice grows, so does the eternal reward and Christ's love?

III
ACCEPTANCE CAN BE HEALTHY

Is this stage of acceptance the basis of health and growth not only for Paul but also for modern man? Yes. The Freudian school of psychoanalysis tried to surface and then accept the hurts buried deeply in the unconscious. Third force psychology adds another dimension, the importance of values (especially of love) in shaping behavior. Choosing to love even those who hate you is central to Maslow's self-actualizer, Adler's creative self, Allport's altruism, Rollo May's will to love, Rogers' non-directive therapy, and Frankl's logotherapy.[4] For all of these thinkers the psychologically healthy person accepts himself and offers the same acceptance to others.

Frankl asked himself why some could take the brutality of his concentration camp and become healthy people who gave away their food to the sick while others stole food, gorged themselves and apathetically collapsed. In watching his fellow inmates, he discovered that some grew not because they suffered less but because they had a reason to accept the suffering. Despite torture they clung to life because they clung to finishing a book, returning to their children, or to helping others bear suffering.

Frankl also discovered that what seemed his greatest tragedy, the Nazis' destruction of a manuscript containing his life's work, was really responsible for his survival of the concentration camp ordeal. Stronger than the pain of Nazi torture was his desire to reconstruct daily the lost manuscript. Even in the midst of a delirium from typhoid fever, he clung to life and wrote his thoughts (later *The Doctor and the Soul*) on prison scraps. Where loss of a manuscript made others give up life, Frankl made it the reason to endure all and live. As Frankl concluded, everything can be taken from a man but one thing—to choose one's attitude in any given set of circumstances, to choose one's own way.[5] Even in a concentration camp we remain free to choose whether to hate or offer the forgiveness of acceptance. When we see the growth possible from the loss of a manuscript or any hurt, we are giving ourselves a *why* to accept suffering and forgive.[6]

Those who accept suffering and forgive become healthy saints with power to relieve the suffering around them. In reading a *Time* (Dec. 29, 1975) article, "Saints Among Us," dealing with a dozen modern living saints like Mother Teresa of Calcutta, I tried to discover what made these ordinary people extraordinary saints. They all were people who did two things: suffered and used their suffering as a gift to relieve suffering. Yaeko Ibuka, for example, was sent to a leprosarium to die but later discovered that she didn't have leprosy. She may not have known leprosy but her heart knew the leper's ostracism, and for the last fifty-five years even at the age of seventy-eight she cares for lepers. Another modern saint, Schwester Selma Mayer, chose to remain single and dedicate her seventy years to nursing the sick in Jerusalem. Why? At the age of five she lost her mother and determined to give to others what she has missed—a mother's love and concern for human beings. Living at the hospital and often sitting up all night with a critically ill patient left her little time, but she still adopted and raised two daughters who had been orphaned like herself. Hermann Gmeiner also lost a mother and thus felt the pain of World War II's homeless refugee children. He too remained unmarried to give undivided commitment to 1500 orphans in his SOS villages. The modern saints are ordinary people who used as gifts the hurts that would have psychologically crippled those not forgiving the hurt and finding its gift.

Forgiving to the point of being grateful for the possible growth from the hurt is not a magical bromide painlessly bringing psychological and spiritual health. Another modern saint, Martin Luther

King, didn't find that the police dogs bit less or the jail doors suddenly opened when he could forgive the Birmingham police. Forgiveness to the point of gratitude for growth is not a way to manipulate God and have things our way but to bring healing his time and way. God doesn't promise to eliminate our problems but he does promise to help us face them and grow from them until at last we can pray the serenity prayer. "God grant me the serenity to accept the things I can not change, the courage to change the things I can, and the wisdom to know the difference."

IV

DEALING WITH ACCEPTANCE

To reach a serene acceptance of death, a dying person wants to silently hold the hand of an accepting friend. We too reach acceptance of our hurts when we hold the hand of a friend, especially Christ's hand. The steps, as at Emmaus, are the same as for any stage:

1. Tell Christ how I feel.

2. Take on Christ's feelings—his mind and heart, especially through scripture.

3. With Christ's mind and heart live out his reaction.

1. *Telling Christ How I Feel*

When on the verge of acceptance, I am conscious of how Christ has accepted one in ways I haven't accepted another. My prayer went like this:

"Lord, I know that you accept me just the way I am. The more I am weak, the closer we can be. But I know that more with my head than with my heart. I really don't feel as close to you and to Gus as I did before I was hurt by his remarks. Just yesterday I asked him how he liked my talk on prayer, and he changed the subject. It's still not easy to live with him. I don't see where I am any better off because he criticized me. I don't even know how to care for him. Nothing seems to make much difference to him. So show me what you see—how I am growing and how I can use your gifts to keep reaching out when there is no response. Make me grateful to him and to you."

2. *Take On Christ's Feeling*

Next I ask Christ how he wants to respond to a person feeling like me. How did he spell out to his disciples what was to make them grateful and gifted when people didn't respond? Matthew heard him speak of many gifts coming from being hurt, and he summarized these in the Beatitudes. As I listened to each with my heart, Christ seemed to be stretching me to see growth where before I had seen only pain from being hurt.

"Lord, thank you for showing me how I have grown from being hurt. Thank you for making me poor in spirit with an empti-ness driving me to pray again so I won't lose my vocation. Thanks in the midst of my mourning for comforting me with new friends as I spoke with people about how that talk sounded. Thank you too for the gift of meekness making me more gentle by giving me a desire to affirm others rather than criticize them behind their backs. You have also made me a better peacemaker because I now want to speak up when I hear another criticized, and I also want to help heal Gus' wounds. Thanks also for showing me other gifts, and that even struggle is a gift helping me to accept others. Since during struggles I see how you accept the worst in me, I can be more merciful. I've had a hard time forgiving students I catch cheating. Let me imagine that happening and show me how you want me to react to them. What would you do? . . . Now help me to do the same. How can I heal all that makes them insecure and needing to cheat . . . What would you do for them?"

3. *Living Out Christ's Reaction*

We don't have to imagine ourselves doing well in every possi-ble situation. Take one situation and watch Christ's reaction. The healing part is not watching ourselves but getting stretched by Christ's reactions. Then we can watch ourselves react as would Christ until we really begin to think and feel like Christ. As one retreatant said, "I no longer get Christ to walk with me, but now I walk with Christ."

Walking with the mind and heart of Christ at his pace must be a daily exercise if we are to know the reactions of Christ for any situation. To think and feel like a Sioux I spent a summer living with an Indian family speaking Lakota, eating dog soup, and doing all that they did. To think and feel like Christ I must live in a Christian community and daily watch Christ in Scripture, in the sacraments, in prayer (private and with others), and in those most like him until I can live my day as he would. How would Christ eat a meal or wash dishes? How can I allow others to make mistakes and learn from these as Christ did with Peter? How can I approach people as Jesus does in the Eucharist—as nourishment to build and not to tear down.

Christ enters bread and wine that he may enter us and through us enter and heal our world. Prayerfully reaching the stage of acceptance should not lead to sitting in a corner and healing more hurts. If we really love those who hurt us, we want to make our home and environment a place where their wounds can heal and where others will not be hurt as we were. Thus when I could finally forgive Gus, I found myself not only trying to make the school a place where people would not be hurt by criticism but also trying to do kind things for Gus.

Hurts such as Gus's criticism may cripple us, but when healed they give us power to build an environment more conducive to life. Like the reformed alcoholic helping another alcoholic in Alcoholics Anonymous, we have power to build a more loving environment in whatever way we were hurt and healed. Thus a friend of ours, who was the victim of a rape, leads other victims of rape through the agony of anger and guilt to acceptance of themselves and of men. Experiencing the violence of rape has made her fight against the causes of violence by raising a loving family, boycotting violent movies, voting intelligently, joining Bread for the World to eliminate world hunger, and joining Common Cause for more responsive government. If we don't have the desire to form a healing environment, we are still crippled and not healed.

Often forming a healing environment means reaching out for the very person who hurt us. The challenge is not to go to Africa to love the poor but to love the guy next door who plays loud African music all night. Doing something kind for another heals me, heals our environment, and often heals him. Even if he doesn't change, it is impossible for me to do something kind for an enemy without being healed. I can't dust another's room or sharpen his pencils without dusting away some anger and sharpening my desire to forgive because I love him rather than because he is wrong. The world will change when I start asking: "Who hurt me? What can I do to make him happier and more secure so he doesn't have to hurt another?"

But the more I step out to others, the more I become aware of my own need for healing. For instance, being criticized gave me a desire to reach out to alcoholics who received so much criticism. But I found myself at first very repulsed by inebriated men staggering around out of control. I needed to first heal my own wounds from the times when I was hurt by people drinking or out of control. When in the process of being healed and thus of taking new risks, it at times seemed as if I was not making progress because new risks opened me to new hurts for healing.

Healing a hurt has at times dramatic steps that can be seen and applauded, such as when I was able to face Gus with no fear of criticism. But most of the time healing a hurt is a process hidden as deeply as some of the hurts. Healing a hurt often begins with one prayer but continues every time I act with the mind and heart of Christ and become grateful for the growth from the hurt. It took Christ himself three years to heal Peter of the hurts that made him boast and fall. Others like Paul were healed overnight. I have seen deep hurts healed both ways, but Peter's process is more common. Healing a memory should really extend over a lifetime if our gratitude grows over a lifetime.

The deepest healing is neither to be able to walk again nor even to forgive a parent and find a depression lifted. When Christ sends ten lepers to the priests, ten lepers are physically healed but only the Samaritan returns with the deepest healing, praise and thanks to God: "Was no one found to return and give praise to God except this foreigner? . . . Rise and go your way; your faith has made you well" (Lk. 17:18–19). Healing is not the lifting of a foot that never moved or the lifting of a depression of ten years, but the lifting of our minds and hearts to God. We are not healed unless we love Christ more and he loves more through us. We are in the final stage, acceptance, only if we have a grateful heart given to Christ for his love to touch those we touch. The answer to "Have I been healed?" is another question: "Am I reaching out like Christ to heal?"

Part Five:
Eucharist—Summary of Five Stages
of Dying and Forgiveness

Two thousand people jam Our Lady of Mercy parish in New York every First Friday. They overflow even into the basement where they can only hear the upstairs Mass. People flood into the church an hour early because they don't want to miss the opportunity to receive the Eucharist which has power to heal everything from strained marriages to even illnesses such as cancer.

Yet, in other parts of New York, churches remain empty. Adults have given up on the Eucharist as they watched their marriages fall apart despite their continual Mass attendance; teenagers refuse to attend Mass because they see adults, even after receiving the healing Body of Christ, continue to gossip and treat their children impersonally.

That the Eucharist brings healing to some and not to others ought not surprise us. Even Christ's Eucharist didn't heal Judas. Whether Christ celebrates the Eucharist in New York or Jerusalem, whether with Judas or with gossiping adults, more healing occurs when participants allow their memories to be healed. This chapter will show how the five stages for healing a memory are also the pattern of a healing Eucharist.

12
EUCHARIST: HEALING A MEMORY

Why doesn't more healing happen at the Eucharist? The pious Catholic mafia never miss a Sunday Mass and never miss killing a person who knows too much. Priests can receive the Eucharist daily yet find no healing from alcoholism and depression. If the Eucharist is a time of healing, why aren't lives changed?

Not only today, but even when Christ celebrated the Eucharist, healing didn't always happen. After Judas received the Eucharist, he had Christ put to death; after Peter received the Eucharist, he went and denied Christ three times. But usually when Christ celebrated the Eucharist, healing did occur as when he broke bread with the Emmaus disciples or later with Peter on the lake shore (Jn. 21). When Christ celebrated the Eucharist, healing happened to the extent that the participants allowed their memories to be healed.

In the final eucharistic story of Luke,[1] Jesus healed the memories of downcast Emmaus disciples so that they could forgive the chief priests and themselves for Good Friday. The disciples did not forgive and forget but forgave and remembered Good Friday from the healing, scriptural viewpoint of the risen Jesus. Once the healing of the memory was culminated in the Eucharist, they could return to Jerusalem, the home of the enemies that they had fled (Lk. 24:47). The breaking of the bread was healing because broken-hearted feelings were given to Christ in exchange for his forgiving view and his heart burning within.

Not only the Emmaus disciples, but Peter also had a downcast face when he met Christ. Discouraged by his own threefold denial around a charcoal fire and events of the past days, Peter wanted to go fishing and get back to the way things were before he met Christ (Jn. 21). Unlike Judas who felt his betrayal made him deserve the death sentence, Peter through the Eucharistic meal would slowly understand how his threefold denial could make him a compassionate leader of the Christian community.[2] While breaking bread with Christ around another charcoal fire which recalled the denial scene, Peter admitted three times that he was incapable of loving (*agapao*) and only capable of caring (*phileo*) for Christ. But that admission allowed Christ to seriously invite Peter to head the Christian community as it expanded among the gentiles. Peter, at home with his own weakness, came to accept the alleged weaknesses of the gentiles who were looked down on by many because they didn't keep the Jewish customs of Christianity (Acts 10). Through healing a memory at the Eucharistic meal, Peter found himself no longer a downcast fisherman, but rather a powerful leader of the Church.

Christ continues to heal memories through the Eucharist today, just as he did with the Emmaus disciples and Peter. Agnes Sanford, whose schools of pastoral care have trained many to pray for healing, uses the Eucharist to heal memories that happened years ago.[3] She likes to spend some time each Saturday reviewing a given year of her life. On Sunday she brings all the hurts of that year, gives them to Jesus in the Eucharist, and walks home with that year no longer crippling her but gifting her to spread his eucharistic love.

Sometimes we cannot go back to a given year but need to deal with the sharp pain of the present. I remember an Indian grandmother unable to forgive a drunken man who shot her fine husband. She brought that painful memory to the Eucharist and walked with the Lord through the days following the shooting when she felt so alone and deserted. She then asked the Lord to help her forgive and bring new life out of that tragic situation. Next, she asked the community to also forgive with her the man who shot her husband. Finally, she asked forgiveness of everyone for being so turned in on her own sorrow that she had forgotten how alone and deserted the sobered up man and his family now felt. Today she continues to reach out especially to children and the elderly who feel alone and deserted.

When we, an Indian grandmother, Agnes Sanford, Peter, or the Emmaus disciples heal memories with Christ during the Eucharist, we accept Holy Thursday's Last Supper invitation to "do this" with Jesus. "This is the cup of my blood of the new and eternal covenant which shall be shed for all so that sins may be forgiven. Do this in memory of me" (1 Cor. 11:25; Mt. 26:28). "Do

this'' means not just to repeat the motions of offering bread and
wine, but to give ourselves to one another to the same extent that
Christ did at the Last Supper, at Emmaus, or on the lake shore "so
that sins may be forgiven." In forgiving ourselves and others to the
extent of seeing painful memories as gift, we try and give ourselves
just as unconditionally as Christ gave himself even to Peter and
Judas. Christ could share Eucharist with Judas plotting his death,
because Jesus accepted even the painful memory of death as a gift
through which he could prove his great love for sinners (Rom. 5:8).
When we heal a memory during the Eucharist to make life-giving
what was death-giving, we declare with Christ that we can die and
also rise with him. How can we celebrate the Eucharist in such a
way that we accept his invitation to "do this in memory of me" and
thus receive the same healing as did Peter on the lake shore or an
Indian grandmother?

How To Make the Eucharist More Healing

Perhaps we have attended the Eucharist dozens of times and
yet haven't experienced healing like Peter did. Perhaps we feel like
someone in the crowd when Jesus healed the woman with the flow
of blood (Lk. 8:43–48). Why did she find healing when she pressed
against Jesus yet most others in the pressing crowd probably didn't
find healing? The woman differed from the crowd because she
brought not just her pain but a high expectancy that touching Christ
would make a difference. She was not just a spectator in a pew but
a person hungering for healing and expecting it.

Unlike the healed woman perhaps we have found ourselves to
be little more than spectators in a pew with little happening besides
our watch advancing an hour. But when we come with our pain
making us hungry for healing and expecting it, we touch Christ and
hear, "Your faith has made you whole, go in peace." Besides
bringing the pain of past years like Agnes Sanford or the sharp pain
of present situations like the Indian woman who lost her husband,
we can also bring the pain experienced at the Eucharist itself.
"Eucharist" means "giving thanks." To discover what the Lord
wants to heal at the Eucharist, we just ask, "For what is it most
difficult to give thanks?" Sometimes we might find it difficult to
give thanks for certain people or certain styles of the Mass.

None of us are equally grateful for everyone. With whom would we least like to be on a deserted island? Would it be the senile lady who prays her rosary out loud or the barefoot teenager who wouldn't touch a rosary? Sometimes it may not be the people but the celebrant that irritates us by giving an hour homily or no homily. Perhaps there is someone absent whom we feel needs the Mass more than anyone present. If we can discover one person with whom we feel distant, we discover an opportunity for healing and coming closer to the whole Christ.

Perhaps more than people, the style of the Mass puts us most in touch with hurts. We may need healing to attend a conservative Latin Mass or a swinging guitar Mass. In our parishes we have the quiet eight o'clock Mass that draws older people who don't relish a handshake of peace. In contrast, about noon the young people wake up to attend the folk Mass noted for its songs and embraces of peace. Because at the Eucharist we neglect to heal the hurts between generations, we are beginning to have a church split into two congregations. Whatever makes the Mass difficult, also makes the Mass an opportunity for healing.

Whether we are hurt by the people, style of the Mass, or something else, we heal the hurt by simply telling the Lord how we are feeling and then listening to how he responds through a given part of the liturgy. Recently I attended an 8:00 A.M. Mass that offered me infinite possibilities for healing. The Mass opened with the organist dragging out "Holy God" into a dirge that made me gasp for breath after every other word. My performance was a solo since the congregation were octogenarians and fortunately couldn't even hear the organ. The portly pastor waddled out and, without even looking at us, raced through the Mass as if he had to finish in fifteen minutes to eliminate a parking lot jam. I kicked myself for not choosing another Mass and glanced at the nearly deserted church to see if others were also edging toward the door. I angrily asked Jesus, "Why do you let him drive away all your young people? Why don't you heal him so he is a better instrument communicating your love?"

Just as these thoughts raced through my mind even faster than the celebrant's prayers, we were saying the penitential rite which begins every Eucharist. This was the time to give Jesus all my anger and pray, "Lord have mercy" toward me and all who have hurt me. When I can bring to the opening penitential rite a memory of someone who has hurt me and tell the Lord how I feel, then reconciliation and healing can begin.

After I angrily told the Lord in the penitential rite how I wanted the celebrant to be healed and changed, I could listen to the Lord's view in the readings. That Sunday's reading was Luke 4:16–30 where Jesus reads in the synagogue that he was sent to proclaim liberty to the captives and is rejected in his home town. So I asked Jesus to fill this impersonal pastor with the Spirit of the Lord so he could proclaim liberty to all the captives in his parish. But just as I smugly sat down for the homily, I thought, "Am I as blind to God acting in this pastor as the Nazareth citizens were to God acting in the carpenter's son?" However as the pastor launched into a twenty minute homily on giving more to the building fund, I felt in need of the Spirit of the Lord to free me from my growing irritation. Fortunately his homily was so boring that it offered no distraction to further my healing by formulating my bargains into the one way I most wanted that pastor to change. My final bargain went, "Jesus, I could forgive him if he cared for his people as much as he cares for his building fund. Heal him so he doesn't build a new church that is even more empty."

At the offertory I tried to get Jesus' mind by offering not my own gifts but the hidden gifts present even in those who build empty churches. What gift did this pastor have? As he hurriedly offered the gifts, I thanked Jesus for giving us a priest who could offer Mass in just ten minutes, just in case anyone had only ten minutes to live. But as I joked with Jesus, my anger began to evaporate; I saw a pastor wounded and frightened of being himself. I thanked Jesus that the pastor's fear hadn't driven him out of the priesthood and that he still struggled to say Mass and to build a church where others could pray. He was like the unpolished raised chalice offering a place for Jesus to come. If I have faith, Jesus can come whether the chalice is new and polished or old and scratched. I thanked Jesus for the faith of his old, scratched pastor still saying Mass and dreaming of a larger church.

By the time I briefly thanked Jesus, the pastor was well into the Eucharistic prayer, the time to receive healing by taking on Christ's desire to be bread. Christ leaps into bread so that he can come to even scratched and impersonal communicants just as they are. At the first Eucharist he accepts Judas and his disciples even when they have one foot out the door ready to flee. Jesus is completely vulnerable, willing to be hurt again and again as bread. In bread he gives his total self, enters the communicant's world, and just doesn't demand that the communicant enter his. I heard the Eucharist calling me and the congregation to love the old pastor just as he is, until he experiences so much love that he will be secure enough to return love. Slowly I cancelled my bargain, "Jesus get him to care as much for his people as he cares for his building fund," as it evolved into "Jesus get us to care as much for him as you do in the Eucharist so he will know how to care. Forgive us and heal us."

The closer we get to communion time, the more the liturgy focuses on my need to be forgiven and healed. We bring our depression over being a sinner and pray the "Our Father" requesting forgiveness, followed by "Deliver Us From Evil," then a prayer for peace, then "Lamb of God who takes away the sin of the world have mercy on us," and finally "Lord, I am not worthy that you should come to me, say but the word and I shall be healed." During these prayers I asked the Lord to reveal my own need for healing and forgiveness. Why was I so upset over the pastor's emphasis on money? Isn't part of the reason because I have difficulty asking people for money and for help even when I really need it? It's easier to dislike him rather than admit I need to be a bit more like him. Didn't I also impersonally respond (wishing I were at another Mass rather than facing him) to the pastor's impersonal way? Was I seeing the speck in another's eye but ignoring the beam in my own? From the "Our Father" to communion I prayed the liturgy's prayers asking Jesus to forgive me and to heal me from the wounds that made me insecure, impersonal, and unable to ask for help.

At communion time I simply rested in Jesus and thanked him for his healing love for me and for the pastor. As Jesus took on my life, I gave him my feelings and asked to take on his mind and heart until I could live out his reactions. Slowly I began to thank Jesus for creating my new hunger to say Mass reverently and with real love for the people, for forgiving my own impersonal treatment of an impersonal and wounded pastor whom I could now love, and for revealing my own need to love myself enough to let others love and help me. I then silently adored Jesus and let him love me. I often do this at communion because when I look at Jesus lovingly, my prayer often goes a new direction with new dimensions of healing. Sometimes Christ may bring to mind a past hurt I need to forgive with him while other times we just silently adore the Father. Healing happens to the degree I use the love of Jesus within me to love not only the Father but myself and whoever irritates me.

When celebrating Mass in this healing way, people are healed not only interiorly but also physically (I Cor. 11:17–34). The eucharistic prayers expect healing of the whole person. Before Communion the priest prays, ''Let this not serve unto condemnation but unto health of mind and body.'' This prayer for healing is followed by the centurion's, ''Lord, I am not worthy to receive you but only say the word and I shall be healed.'' Even St. Augustine, who believed that the physical healing occurred only in earlier times, had to retract his views because he saw the Eucharist, as well as other means, bring physical healing.[4] As a chaplain bringing the Eucharist, I too have witnessed physical healings even recorded on heart monitors.

Whether speaking about healing that can be recorded on heart monitors or healing that involves a change of heart toward a pastor, Eucharistic healing occurs when we give Christ our hardened, unforgiving hearts and receive his heart of flesh opened on Calvary. There he released to us his forgiving Spirit as promised, ''A new heart I will give you and a new Spirit I will put within you; and I will take out of your flesh the heart of stone and give you a heart of flesh'' (Ez. 36:26). Memories are healed when hearts are exchanged on Calvary.

The Eucharist has a built-in pattern for exchanging hearts on Calvary.

Penitential Rite	Work through denial by recognizing the hurt and my anger.
Liturgy of Word and Offertory	Work through anger by listening to Jesus' view and offering the gifts of my offender.

Eucharistic Prayer	Cancel my bargains to accept that person unconditionally as Christ does in the Eucharist
Our Father Communion	Recognize my depression over my sins and ask for forgiveness
After Communion	Thank Jesus for the gifts from the hurt and ask to be one in living out his reaction.

Often I do not go through all five stages but might spend the entire liturgy going through one stage. When in the depression stage, for example, I might spend much of the Mass telling the Lord about my sinfulness and see how he responds in each part of the liturgy. The important thing is not to make it through all five stages in a liturgy, but rather to keep telling the Lord how I feel and then absorb his response so I can "go in peace to love and serve the Lord."

"Go in peace to love and serve the Lord" has replaced the ending, "Go the Mass is ended" because the Mass and its healing continues as we bring Christ into our homes and community. Healing happens not just around an altar but in a community whenever people meet Christ's love in each other. In our work- shops, participants' painful memories get healed not only through prayer and Eucharist but also through meeting a loving person who frequently resembles a parent, teacher, or someone who has hurt them. Just as we have power to hurt a person, making it difficult for him to love people like us, so too we have Christ's power to love unconditionally a wounded person and free him from fearing people who resemble us. If we hear, "I wish my friend had been more like you," our friendship has usually healed some wounds from the other friend.

But to continually heal wounded people in this way, we need help in laying down our lives as totally as Jesus did on the cross and continues to do in the Eucharist. For instance, if a family came to us without food, clothing or education, and needed a home, health care, and a job, could we meet all their needs? No matter what a person needs, we need a community because none of us alone has all the resources to care for someone as lovingly as Christ cares. As we in a loving community take care of each other's needs, we begin to heal our painful memories and live out the Eucharist.

One loving community which seeks to live out the Eucharist by meeting the needs of each other is Our Lady of Mercy parish in Hicksville, N.Y. This small parish is flooded every First Friday with two thousand people hungry for the power of the Eucharist to heal their broken lives. They overflow even into the basement where they can only hear (not see), because the upstairs Mass is crammed with worshipers expecting the Eucharist to heal the barriers between a husband and wife seeking separation, a teenager and parent not speaking to each other, and the chasm between what one would like to be and what one is. Every First Friday the crowd grows because people finding the healing love of Christ in the Eucharist return next month with a friend. Even teenagers on drugs discover Christ's love and bring their disbelieving parents anxious to check out what has changed their son or daughter. Those who come take the power of the Eucharist out into the community through groups that weekly pray together, visit the elderly and sick, or minister to the jails near the parish. They know and experience that "Eucharist" means "to give thanks" for the healing body of Christ which makes them healers of the body of Christ.

Part Six:
Getting Started
on Healing a Memory

We limit healing of memories the same ways we limit our encountering of Christ. Many can find Christ in the Gospel events of two thousand years ago but they can't find Jesus in their present day. Others feel that they can meet Christ today in prayer but not while doing boring housework. For both groups Chapter 13 reveals how to find the healing Christ especially in the most difficult moments of the present day. If each day's hurts are healed, we do not pile up a cesspool of anger and guilt polluting the next day.

Still others can turn over to Christ their past painful memories and their present hurts but they cling to their fears of the future. They fatalistically believe that what will happen will happen. As if paralyzed, they fear the future's trials rather than by prayer and action healing the future to change what can be changed and to grow from what must be endured. Chapters 14 and 15 can get us in touch with how to heal the future's hurts rather than passively get crippled by them.

Some can find Christ only when praying privately alone while others always need another to pray with them. Chapter 16 is written to help find the healing Christ both when praying alone and when praying with another.

Chapter 17 is for you to write because there are as many ways of healing memories as ways you can meet Christ.

13
EVERYDAY PRAYER FOR HEALING
ONE MEMORY

Perhaps, after separately studying each stage, you are wondering how a prayer for healing one memory sounds when you put all five stages together. This evening as I began praying my usual end-of-the-day prayer for healing one memory, I found myself reluctant to pray. In the morning my prayer had been difficult: dry, without apparent consolation and riddled with distractions. I had found myself having a monologue because nothing seemed to sink into my heart. I had even quit ten minutes early to eat breakfast. Recalling how disappointed I felt that morning when I quit prayer ten minutes early, that evening I prayed the following prayer to heal my hurts in prayer.

Denial

"Lord Jesus Christ, you have been searching for me all day. Help me to search now for where you have been during my day. Let me take you within as I breathe in and out your Spirit saying your name—Jesus . . . Jesus . . . Jesus . . . Help me relax every muscle in your strength so that my body belongs totally to you. I give you my eyes; give me yours. Let me see the times I found you and grew. Help me also to see the times I was hurt and missed your call to grow more. How do you see my day?

"Help me to thank you for the times I was loved, loving, forgiven or forgiving. Thanks for the letters I finally wrote and for those that arrived telling of the way you work. Thanks too for the times I noticed your other gifts—time to research, the friendship of George, being able to accept a compliment from Bill, and the times I really enjoyed what I was doing. What were those times? Jesus, I'm full of thanks and out of touch with the day's struggles. Help me look too at the events today for which I can't yet give thanks.

Anger

"Even as I look at the way you have healed me and want to heal me more, I find deep resistance to even praying now. I find myself wanting to race through this prayer, to say 'thank you' with words but not with my heart. Everything seemed to go O.K. today except for my morning hour of prayer. Help me to get in touch with the way I feel about it so that I can give you my mind and heart and take on yours. I feel that I tried to do my part by giving you my best time for prayer, living my days as you would, taking the time to get centered, and praying in a quiet place. What more could I do? I guess I'm a bit angry that I do my part, but you don't seem to do your part to make my prayer better. I could have talked to my lamp and received more insight and light into that Scripture passage than you gave me. Why do you call me to heal memories through prayer and then not help me to pray? I can't write or give retreats about what I don't experience. I was hoping that this week I could really pray because I need your help in preparing for the weekend retreat. Your silence hurts not just me but those others who need to hear about you through me. Lord, I don't want to be a hypocrite telling people to speak with a silent, hiding God. It sounds as though I'm angry just at you today. What are you saying?

"I hear you saying to me, 'I don't like dry prayer any more than you. Your prayer this morning wasn't as dry as what I experienced in the garden when I got up and down three times trying desperately to get Peter, James or John to pray with me. It's the same loneliness that later made me scream "My God, my God, why have you forsaken me." '

"Jesus, I do feel forsaken like you. Just as you wanted someone to be with you in the garden during your desolate prayer, please come and be with me as I relive with you my desolate prayer this morning."

Bargaining

"Lord, let me pinpoint my bargains, the changes I want. What would make it easier? I could forgive you and take your silence in prayer if I knew why it was happening. Are you hiding as you did during years of dry prayer with John of the Cross so he would choose you and not your gifts? Unlike John of the Cross I don't find myself having continual trouble praying. Or am I hiding from you because I need to change some area? I'm not sure what I need to change besides my dry prayer. Or am I just too tired to face you? I don't think I'm too tired. I have energy for everything but prayer. I could forgive you if I knew why dry mornings like today happen.

"I have another bargain. I could take your silence in prayer if I could still write and give retreats. But I feel like a dried up, wrinkled raisin, and I can't write or talk about your closeness and care. Lord, did you ever feel as though you couldn't do what you had to do?

"I think you want to say, 'When I found myself in the garden with no followers and a Father who didn't seem to be hearing my prayers, I wrestled with the same bargains. Why did the Father put me through a desolation so dark that not even Peter, James, or John wanted to face it? I seemed powerless to convince even my sleepy apostles that the Father cared. I wept over Jerusalem and sweated blood because there was so much to do and so little that I had accomplished. I wanted things to change. That's why I said, "Father, if it be possible let this cup pass from me." '

"Now, Lord, help me to let go of my demands, my conditions just as you did by finally saying, 'Yet not my will but yours be done.' I too want to be able to face darkness even when it means I don't understand and can accomplish little."

Depression

"Lord Jesus Christ, your death spoke more eloquently than all your teaching. Forgive me for thinking that you need my words in books and retreats more than my surrender to the Father's way. Forgive me for being so attached to results that in desolation I abandon you and cut my prayer short. I tell others to love unconditionally, but I am a conditional lover turned off when you and others are silent. I want to be healed at any price, but in your way and at your pace. Whisper into my heart what you want to say so that I can be closer to you than ever.

"You seem to put your hand on my shoulder and say, 'I chose you and my apostles not because you had great talents but because you were weak and would be forced to rely more on me. You still feel that you must earn my love by success in retreats and writing. But I give you even the successful retreat when you listen to my Spirit. Don't fear the times you can't pray because then you can give me your emptiness to fill. Quit trying to love me and allow me to love you. Right now just relax and breathe in and out my healing love until it flows into every cell.'

"Lord, I feel your healing that relaxes my need to be in control rather than under your control. I also want to let go of past times that taught me to measure my worth by success rather than by your success in loving me first."

Anger

"Bring to mind the times I felt worthless because I didn't produce: the first year of teaching, the lost debates, the low marks in school, times when I didn't have the right answers, and, because of that, friends and teachers withdrew from me. Move into all those times draining out the hurt and pouring in your love. Heal also the times that I have been hurt by silent people when I was hungry for a response."

Depression

"Is there any time you especially want to heal? The most painful seems to be the debate in which I forgot all my debate cards and fell flat on my face, making the school lose the tournament. I felt after that a drive to always be prepared. Maybe that's why I feel that prayer has to fill me with insights and a warm glow so that I am prepared well to give retreats. Forgive me for carrying that hurt around all these years. Help me to relive the scene, give you all my feelings of despair, and watch what you would do and say to me. Heal me so that I have a gift of being prepared rather than a compulsion demanding success and making me rely more on myself than on you."

Acceptance

"Lord, I have asked you to heal the present and the past; now heal the future. You have promised that your power working in us can do infinitely more than we can ask or imagine (Eph. 3:20).

What gifts from difficult prayer should I ask you to increase and what new possibilities should I imagine?

"I can remember a year ago how my difficult, dry retreat was not what I wanted but what I needed to work with the Sioux. The agony of your silence sensitized me to how my silence hurt the Sioux when quietly ignoring social issues, being unable to speak or understand Lakota, failing to encourage the alcoholic struggling through a dry day, and saying little because I was only half listening. That difficult retreat made me learn Lakota, speak out to defend another, and be more patient with weakness in myself and others. Lord, let me listen to you tell me how my difficult prayer will be a gift."

Jesus seemed to answer: "When I left the garden after that desolate prayer, I felt very alone. I too became very sensitive to people feeling alone, just as you did with the Sioux. Silence in prayer sensitized me to the women who were weeping, to my mother and John, to the good thief, and to many others feeling alone. Your feeling of aloneness enables you to speak to struggling retreatants and to those who sense of aloneness will bring them to read your writing. My aloneness and desolate prayer also made me count on others like Simon, Veronica, and my apostles. I want your desolate prayer to make you count more on the prayer of others during retreats."

"Lord, thank you for letting my prayer make me needy of others and also sensitive to those feeling lonely and desolate. Thank you for every way that my difficult prayer will make me search to find ways of praying better. Thank you for strengthening me by your absence and a hunger for your presence."

Daily Healing One Memory —Effective and Easy

Does the above prayer sound familiar? This prayer for the daily healing of a memory parallels the traditional examination of conscience by which saints for centuries every night repaired their sinful response to the day's hurts.[1] Healing a memory through private prayer was for most saints the core of their prayer. If a busy man could only do one spiritual exercise in a given day, St. Ignatius put the highest priority on a fifteen-minute examination of conscience. He taught his followers to look at each day and discern the

Spirit's movements (faith, hope and love) that lead to God and the movements (unhealed anxiety, fear, anger, and guilt) that lead away from finding God in all things. For St. Ignatius, a wise man was not the man who studied many books, but the man who studied his day and reflected on his experiences.

When using the fifteen minute examination of conscience to heal memories, it is crucial to uncover *feelings and attitudes* throughout the day that lead to good or sinful actions. We look back on events and moments in our day which prompted peace, joy, and love in us, and we acknowledge those which produced anxiety, depression, anger, self-pity, or loss of hope. We become attuned to the movements of the Spirit in our lives as well as to the movements of the flesh (Gal. 5:16–24). In this discernment process we are not preoccupied with mechanically listing sinful actions during our day; rather we are more concerned to acknowledge and offer for healing the *feelings and attitudes* which produce in us sinful or loving responses.

In my own examination above, rather than focusing on the action of not praying, I focused on the denied cause, the hurt of God's silence and its angry feelings and attitudes (bargains such as that I will pray only if I can get results for my retreats and writing). If I can forgive the hurts (God's silence and the debate debacle) which I allow to make me insecure, I won't need my sinful response (too much concern for security through success). Rather, if I forgive the hurts, then a hurt like God's silence will not lead to sin but instead to gifts such as an awareness of my need to count on others or an awareness of how my silence hurts others.

In the above prayer I simply told the Lord in each stage how I felt and listened for him to tell me how he felt. Usually my prayer has fewer insights and more quiet moments, but when I exposed my anger at not being able to pray, my anger driving me to quit became instead a gift to pray by sharing my feelings. Sometimes, as in the depression stage of this prayer, Jesus would take me back to a root memory, a hurt like the debate loss that shaped the way I feel and act now. These deeper hurts can be found by asking the questions "When did I first begin feeling this way?" and "When do I most feel this way?" Sometimes Christ leads me to drop the hurt I started with and leads me through the five stages on a deeper hurt that came up or maybe just lets my anger and depression surface as happened in this prayer. Other stages such as the acceptance of gifts that came from forgetting my debate cards and losing can wait for later prayers.

Maybe I will spend tomorrow's prayer quietly, just thanking God for the gifts from losing the debate and not even touching the other stages. Many of my most healing prayers were only the first stage of simply giving thanks for the Lord's love toward me and through me during the day. Healing comes not from plowing through the stages systematically but from telling Jesus what is in my heart and discovering what is in his heart. I simply tell Jesus my feelings and then let him love me in his way and time. Deeper hurts such as a friend's devastating criticism may take many days to work through just one stage.

Time spent on daily healing of memories by sharing feelings with Jesus is never wasted. A busy Philadelphia psychiatrist quit seeing his clients for a full hour because he found more growth occurred when he spent only forty-five minutes with the client and the other fifteen minutes healing in himself the hurts that the interview surfaced. He simply told the Lord what he was feeling, especially toward his client or those who had hurt his client, and then listened to the Lord's healing response. This not only gave him insights for future therapy but a clean slate to really listen to and love the next client rather than react to him out of the past hour's hurts. He also teaches his clients how to look at the day's feelings and share these with him or with Jesus if they are open to prayer.

Some people need more help to tell Jesus their feelings and to hear his. In the Appendix the bare bones of this prayer are outlined in the Daily Healing of One Memory and enfleshed in the detailed outlines for each stage. Sometimes a hurt can be healed by just a simple prayer for peace, other times by fifteen minutes of Daily Healing of One Memory, or by extended prayer on one stage. If I sense a deeper faith, trust, love, surrender, joy, peace or patience even in the midst of trials, I have been listening to the Spirit (Gal. 5:22) and not just to myself. I will have the Spirit's new freedom to act rather than react.

14
HEALING THE FUTURE

"Healing of memories may work for others but I can't remember any painful past hurts. How can I pray for inner healing?" Variations of this question get repeated endlessly at workshops by those with short memories or happy childhoods. I simply ask, "What would be the worst thing that could happen to you?" Answers range from the death of their wife, a car accident bringing paralysis for life, or a son drifting away from God and into the drug scene. Then we imagine that scene, filling it with all the fears imaginable and give it to Christ as we watch him step into the scene and show us how to deal with it. When the person can tell me what Christ is saying and doing with what he fears most, his muscles relax, and he is no longer paralyzed to step into the future. He becomes free as Christ shows him how growth can come from a wife dying, a paralyzing car accident or a son drifting into the drug scene.

Whatever fear is faced in the imagination, especially with the support of a friend, becomes easier to face successfully when it really looms. Even basketball players know that if you imagine the ball arching to split the net, you make twice as many baskets as when you fear it might bounce off the rim. Success comes also to clients who in therapy imagine "future scenarios" of what they fear yet still must face, such as a job interview, speaking before a crowd, writing a difficult exam, or being forced into retirement. Fears that are delineated and prepared for tend to lose their paralyzing grip. Likewise, fears that are faced with Christ can not remain the same.

Christ wants our fears placed in his hands so that he first can show us what he and we can do to prevent the evil and then can show us how we can grow from what must be faced. No matter what must be faced, we can have a loving response opening us up to new growth and a deeper love of God, neighbors, and ourselves—if we cooperate with God (Rom. 8:28). Paul could teach "give thanks in all circumstances" (1 Thes. 5:18) because he knew the greatest future tragedies could not keep him from the deepest growth, growth closer to Jesus Christ.

> For I am sure that neither death, nor life, nor angels, nor principalities, nor things present, *nor things to come*, nor powers, nor height, nor depth, nor anything else in creation, will be able to separate us from the love of God in Christ Jesus our Lord (Rom. 8:38).

Unfortunately, Paul's doctrine of praising God in everything (1 Thes. 5:16–18) has become distorted in a series of books claiming that if we just praise God, all will work out the way we hope. If, for example, we lose our job, we praise God and that will guarantee that God will find us another one. First, we should not praise God for the evil he wants to stop—the violence of wars, the teens lost to drugs, devastating unemployment or the breakup of families. We work against these situations and praise him for the good he can even bring out of evil such as the way the rest of the family is called to come closer together when one teenager is on drugs. We praise him for the possible growth and take steps to seize it.

Second, praise should not be a subtle way of manipulating God to get our way. Rather, like Jesus in his agony, we should be ready to surrender to the Father even if we don't get our way. Jesus, Paul, and others called to come closer get not a tranquilized future but the cross leading to a deeper love and surrender. The ideal is not to use praise as a bargain manipulating the Father to accept our way but to praise him for whatever growth in loving Christ can come from his way. Paul praised God for his Roman imprisonment, but he found that it led not to his freedom but to his beheading.

Throughout the centuries saints have echoed Paul in facing all fears and finding Christ present in the midst of them. Religious with the vows of poverty, chastity, and obedience find growth in loving Christ when facing the great Old Testament fears of being destitute, childless, and a slave obedient to another. St. Ignatius wrote the *Spiritual Exercises* so that retreatants through prayer could shed fear and grow closer to Christ regardless of what happens to them, be it poverty or riches, sickness or health, honor or dishonor, a long life or a short life. Generations of martyrs have chosen Christ in the most feared tragedy, including torture and death. What do we have to fear that thousands haven't faced triumphantly?

Dealing with Future Fears

Christ during the agony in the garden gives us the model of how to face our fears. He faces his fear of the suffering ahead and imagines it even to the point of sweating blood. He tries to share his fear with his sleeping friends. Finally he shares it with his Father, praying two ways: "Father, if thou art willing, remove this cup from me; nevertheless not my will, but thine be done" (Lk. 22:42).

The steps of the agony are the same for healing anything we fear in the future:

1. Tell Christ what we fear until we really bodily feel that fear.
2. Watch Christ react to what we fear.

A. What does Christ or the Father want done to prevent this? (Remove this cup.)

B. How does Christ or the Father promise that growth can come if it is his will that I go through what I most fear? How would Christ go through it?

Healing comes to the degree we face the fear, put the whole thing in Christ's hands and then absorb his reactions to prevent the evil that can be prevented and to grow in walking through whatever still comes. Gradually our eyes shift from the fear to Christ and his promise, "I am with you always" (Mt. 28:20).

About two-thirds of our fears never happen or can be prevented from happening. We have power to change the future just as the citizens of Nineveh repented and averted the holocaust prophesized by Jonah. Another woman gets warnings in her dreams of events that actually occur. One night she dreamed of her husband having a construction accident and a week later it occurred in the same way. Then she realized that through prayer she had power to ask Christ, "Father, if it is possible, let this cup pass from me." Sometime later she dreamed of her son being hit by a black car speeding around the corner. During the next two weeks she gave her private fear to Christ and asked protection for her son.

The next day her son came home shaking with fright because he just missed being hit by a black car turning the corner. Just a coincidence? Maybe, but a more likely explanation is that much of our future can be shaped by prayer and action.

But even if we pray, friends die and accidents occur. Just as important as asking God to prevent the evil is stretching to say, "Not as I will but as you will." That's easy to say but the test is to imagine the worst happening until we feel that we could go through it as Christ would face it. When we aren't denying that an event could occur but instead asking how we can grow through it, then fear evaporates.

Soaking Prayer for Future Fears

Sometimes fears leave immediately but more often each time we soak ourselves in repeated prayer less fear is evident. When I was making a retreat at the College of Steubenville, I went out to pray on the cliffs which drop straight down five hundred feet into the Ohio river. I was carefully stepping along about twenty-five feet from the edge when a jogger ran by right on the cliff's edge! One misstep and he would never have to take a shower. Others too could step to the edge and look straight down while I shook just looking at them. Then I realized that I had an abnormal fear of heights and of death coming through a fall. I tried all the behavior modification tricks I knew to desensitize myself to heights (rewarding myself for each step closer I took) but the next day I had to start all over.

And so I sat down and shared my fears with Christ. I surveyed all the ways I could prevent myself from falling—the trees I could grab, crawling closer on all fours, etc. After resting in Christ's reaction, trusting in his Father to keep this hill from caving in suddenly and thanking him for my sure-footedness I stood up without feeling fear and took three steps toward the edge before panicking and sitting securely again on the firm earth. Just imagining that the fall would never happen wasn't enough to banish the fear.

The next day I went back to the cliff and made it within twenty feet of the yawning edge. The roar of traffic speeding below made me step back, so I sat down and gave Christ my fear of being smashed in a traffic accident. This fear was rooted in past accidents, so I prayed through the accident scenes until I was grateful for escaping with the gift of life. I then went and asked my brother priests to pray with me for healing my fear of death.

The next day still another fear began to surface. What if I approached too close to the edge and the hill caved in, sending me air mail into the Ohio? This was rather unlikely, since the jogger had stood on the edge and I was fifteen feet from it. Why did I fear falling? I focused on the feeling of falling, but no memories of bad falls came to mind. Therefore I dreamed up the catastrophe that best fit my fear of falling.

This fear seemed to be a future fear of death in a plunging airplane, an elevator cable snapping, or driving off a cliff on a slippery mountain road. Driving off a cliff on a slippery mountain road fit what I was now feeling above the Ohio. In my imagination I drove off the mountain and landed unhurt in a snow bank miles below.

That was easy, so I drove off again and ended up dead but welcomed into eternity by Christ's loving arms. I could face that too, so it was time to try the most feared mountain drive off the cliff. I drove off and ended up with a life racked with pain and paralysis. In my imagination with Christ I went through all five stages. Finally I could say, "I thank you that paralysis gives me a daily experience of my dependency on you and the depth of your love. I still want to be healed from this paralysis but in your time and your way."

On the last day I again gingerly stepped to about eight feet of the cliff's edge before feeling the familiar panic that made me want to jump back. Why did I still have such a fear of death? It wasn't a fear of a painful death because a fall of three hundred feet would bring instant, pain-free death. Deeper still was a clinging to those I loved and who would be left behind suffering because I was gone. I thanked the Lord for each of these people and tried to place each one in his hands and release my own selfish grip. I exposed my bargain, "Jesus, you can take anything in my life, but don't take my parents, Denny . . ." and canceled it. A new feeling of freedom flooded me and I could take another step to the edge. That brought me about four feet from the edge, which seemed just the right distance because I need some fear of death to keep me from taking unnecessary risks. To this day I do not have a fear of the cliff.

To see how healing the future works, just share with Christ any fear, whether it is of high places, a neighbor's tongue, what might happen to the children, the death of your best friend, or the scariest scene you can imagine. Preferably take something you can test out so that you can see progress, as I could with the cliff. Then sit back and watch Christ enter the scene you fear most and absorb his reactions until they feel comfortable and you can imagine yourself doing the same things. Then, leaning on his love and strength, face what you fear, and take another step closer to the cliff until you have another feeling of fear to give him again. Some deep phobias may need professional help too, but even professional insights can be better utilized if worked through with Christ. Professional insights can especially help you focus your prayer.

Many have found relief from deep fears simply by sharing them with Christ. A seventy-five-year-old woman had a deep fear of flying that kept her from ever seeing her sister across the nation. She simply exposed her fear and gave it to Jesus who could heal the fear. Then she stepped aboard the plane and imagined Jesus sitting next to her. Throughout the flight she kept focusing on his love rather than the deep fear of flying. Her flight was a deep prayer experience and she was healed of her fear of flying. Now she wants to fly everywhere.

It's never too late to heal a fear. Even if we are afraid to walk on water, we can find Jesus calmly extending his hand while saying, "Take heart, it is I; have no fear. . . . Come" (Mt. 14:27–29).

15
HEALING THE FUTURE THROUGH DREAMS

Have you ever prayed for seven straight hours? It's as easy as falling asleep. St. Ignatius would tell his retreatants to focus on a prayerful thought just before going to sleep and again on awakening. This programs the mind to keep praying at the subconscious level while sleeping. Many in our workshops find that key memories surface while they sleep—not necessarily when they fall asleep during our talks but when they fall asleep at night.

I usually go to bed saying, "Jesus, heal me and make me like a sponge soaking in your love while I sleep. Bring to mind a dream that will heal whatever way I cannot yet absorb your love." Then I relax every muscle in Jesus' strength until I feel like a floating sponge filling every pore with his living waters. In the morning I awaken refreshed and often with a dream in mind that unlocks another fear for healing.

Healing a dream is a safe way to heal the subconscious, because we dream what is struggling to become conscious and healed.[1] In the morning while still in bed and with my eyes still closed, I begin by writing my dream with as much detail as I can recall. Just "owning" a dream as a "friend" on paper often heals whatever had to hide from my waking consciousness. Writing today's dream also helps me understand tomorrow's dream, since dreams come in series and get repeated until healed.

I especially try to catch the dream's feelings and whatever images and ideas are associated with these feelings. Many of the dream's images simply reflect yesterday's activities that went to bed with me (e.g., the late movie I saw and reran all night). But often each person and object in the dream represents a part of me and is like a mirror exposing feelings and fears I have denied. Dreaming of a dog may only represent my pet dog but often represents my ferocious German shepherd side or my vain, prim, poodle side. I ask: What does this dream mean to me? Then I work with its meaning.

Though I write many dreams down, I find that I only work with a few. If in the dream I find myself in a crippling situation feeling fear, anxiety, anger or guilt, I will often go back to that dream in prayer and heal the dream just as I would heal any crippling memory. I am usually all the characters in a dream, so I simply ask what each was feeling. Next I ask when I most felt that way and stay with the feeling until I can share it with Jesus and then watch how Jesus reacts. Sometimes I imagine Jesus entering either the dream scene or the memory that the dream recalls and watch what he says and does to me. At other times I absorb a Scripture passage or make the stations of the cross (fourteen events of his passion) until I have interiorized his reaction.

Most of my dreams express what I fear to face when awake and must face with Jesus. First, I tell Jesus what I am feeling and then watch what Jesus would do to prevent the feared situation from happening or to help me grow from it happening. For example, right before giving a workshop, I dreamed that I was presenting a talk, forgot what I intended to say, but went on talking until hopelessly confused. Afterwards, I ran off to be alone because I feared that all the people would talk about my failure. This had never happened in a workshop, and I wasn't aware of any conscious fears over the coming workshop. I recorded the dream and wondered why I had such a dream?

Since I was at a retreat house in sunny California, I decided that the best way to heal my dream would be making the outdoor stations of the cross. I began by trying to remember the dreams, anxious, confused feeling. Was it like the confusion from being mocked, making mistakes, or going crazy like a babbling fool? I didn't mind making mistakes as much as being mocked by friends (this made me tense up). When did I experience that?

I prayed for insight but nothing came, so I just hung on to the feeling of being mocked. Suddenly into my mind flashed a scene I had never recalled to heal, and it intensified the dream's feeling of confusion and mockery. I saw myself in seventh grade studying about the Blessed Virgin so I could appear on Fr. Gales' TV program representing the school. I did well until I answered a question about the shrine of Lourdes, using all the material I had read about the shrine of Fatima. I remember Fr. Gales trying to sort out the difference between Lourdes and Fatima. Then I replied with a red face (grateful that color TV hadn't yet been invented), "That's what I meant to say." I crawled home humiliated and feeling that I had let down my family and school.

In this instance, the memory of a real event surfaced immediately to help me grasp a childhood source of the anxiety in my present dream. Sometimes, however, I pray for an insight into what hurt is behind the fearful dream, and no insight comes. I am not able to connect the dream with a real event such as the time I appeared on Fr. Gales' TV program. If I am not able to remember any real event, then I deal with the dream event much as I would with any other memory. Thus in the dream just described, I work through my feelings of guilt for giving a confused talk and through my feelings of anger toward others in the dream for mocking me until I can see the entire incident as gift. As I heal the event in the dream, I am also healing the hurts and fears that occurred through the forgotten Fr. Gales' TV program or whatever else the dream symbolizes.

To heal my present fear of again becoming hopelessly confused and mocked, I started by thanking the Lord for many times in the past he healed my confusion and fear of being mocked. I thanked him for several times when I was able to get rid of those feelings of confusion before an exam or before a homily and he had really answered my prayers. I asked him to save me again from whatever confusion and mockery I feared. I knew that the Lord would save me whenever mockery and confusion would be overwhelming and crippling. But I also felt that there might be some time when he would ask me to endure it. I took an hour to make the stations of the cross, slowly watching how Christ grew from the mockery and confusion I feared.

At the first station, I felt the weight of Herod's mockery as he threw a kingly cloak over the shoulder of Jesus. I felt our Lord's pain as soldiers jabbed at his wounded side and demanded that he "play the prophet" and "save himself." By the time I arrived at the eighth station, I felt that Jesus endured the depth of confusion and mockery that I had feared in my dream and had felt during that TV program.

At the eighth station where Jesus tries to comfort the women of Jerusalem weeping for him, the outdoor cross was missing. Suddenly it hit home that like the women of Jerusalem I had a choice to either focus on the mocking crowd and be filled with fear or to focus on Jesus and be filled with compassion. As the women focused compassionately on Jesus, I could hear the crowd mock both Jesus and the women in much the same way that I feared people in my dream would mock me.

I tried to listen to what Jesus was telling these women. He seemed to speak directly to their fear of being mocked: "Because I am mocked by Herod and the soldiers, I have extra compassion for those who feel dejected and abandoned. I will reach out and give my lonely mother to John, and I will welcome the abandoned thief into paradise. Because you women are mocked by this crowd right now, you have extra compassion for me and for those who are lonely and abandoned. Do not weep for me but for those without compassion who fear mockery."

Perhaps the outdoor eighth station was missing because Jesus wanted me to be the eighth station, to have the same opportunity that he offered the women: to let unearned insults gift me with compassion to reach out to the lonely and abandoned. I could imagine myself giving a talk, becoming hopelessly confused and people laughing at me. But that scene no longer made me fearful. I could see how, even if that did happen at a workshop, the Lord would use those feelings of being confused and rejected to help me to touch the people who would come to our workshops, especially those experiencing similar fears. I was ready to walk through insults with Jesus. Deep-down I felt freed, as if a rope around my head had snapped. I even gave my talks for the first time without using my notes, because I was no longer guarding against mistakes but ready to grow from them.

Because Jesus healed my dream, others do less dreaming in our workshops. This is somewhat unfortunate because many experienced healing while falling asleep and dreaming during my talks. One man who feared dogs dreamed of a puppy jumping into his baby carriage when six months old. He awoke, asked another to help him invite Christ's love into the traumatic scene, and left minus his phobia for dogs.

These events shouldn't surprise us since Scripture presents dreams as God's favored time of ministering. While Abraham was pretending Sarah was only his sister, King Abimelech married

Sarah (Gen. 20:1–18). In a dream Abimelech is told that he is guilty of taking Sarah from Abraham and that Abimelech will die unless he returns Sarah to Abraham who will pray for healing. When Abimelech returned Sarah, "then Abraham prayed to God and God healed Abimelech, and also healed his wife and female slaves so they bore children" (Gen. 20:17). Without his dream Abimelech would not have known that his improper marriage was causing his death and barrenness to his slaves.

In these times of his Spirit, God wishes again to speak his healing word frequently through dreams (Acts 2:17) so that our lives may be guided by his Spirit rather than by our fear, anxiety, anger and guilt buried in our subconscious. God wishes during a dream to expose and heal these feelings as he did with Abimilech's guilt or my guilt over my TV failure. We may have discovered how to listen to TV waves but with our jaded senses we are rapidly losing the delicate art of listening to God's healing word during our sleep. Job warns us:

Why do you contend against God saying, "He will answer none of my words?" For God speaks in one way, and in two, though man does not perceive it. In a dream, in a vision of the night, when deep sleep falls upon men, while they slumber on their beds, then he opens the ears of men, and terrifies them with warnings, that he may turn man aside from his deed, and cut off pride from man; he keeps back his soul from the pit, his life from perishing by the sword (Job 33:13–18).

16
GETTING STARTED: PRAYING ALONE AND WITH OTHERS

Have you ever watched a loved one die complaining, cursing God, or fearful of what lies beyond the last breath? Many never reach acceptance even with their last breath. Some even freeze their bodies with hope that a future technology will return them to life. Why do some die in the acceptance stage while others even die in denial or anger?

A chaplain, Mwalimu Imara, in research with Dr. Kubler-Ross, discovered that the dying patients who move more quickly to acceptance of death are those who can share their real experience and philosophy of life.

> It demonstrated that people who deny less and are more able to move through the five stages after they discover that they have a terminal illness are those people who (1) are willing to converse in death with significant others about what their present experience is like, (2) meet others on equal terms, that is, are able to enter into real dialogue with others where both can share what is "real" with the other, and (3) accept the good with the bad. They have a framework within which the tragic and the happy events of their present and past life take on meaning and give their life a sense of direction and fulfillment.[1]

He concludes that these same three conditions are necessary not just to reach acceptance in our final death, but to grow in the daily process of death and rebirth. We die whenever we are hurt or called to grow and throw off the old self.

Note how similar these three conditions are to the three steps for working through any stage of forgiveness. Discovering our experience, dialoguing with a significant other, and living to grow from the good and the bad are parallel to (1) telling Christ how I feel, (2) listening in order to put on the mind and heart of Christ, and (3) living out Christ's reaction.

Praying Alone

To the degree that Christ is a real person with whom I can share my true feelings and find love, I can heal a time of hurt in private prayer. Nearly every saint had some form of private prayer, such as the examination of conscience, for healing daily hurts as soon as they happen. But often I will also need some help from another either to get in touch with my feelings, with Christ's love and view or with the gift in a hurt so deep that even after prayer I feel no hope. If I can't immediately speak to another, writing my feelings and Christ's response can initiate deep healing. We must be able to find the healing mind and heart of Christ both alone and with another prayer partner.

Any prayer that gives the mind and heart of Christ can be a prayer for the inner healing of a hurt. I simply tell Christ how I feel and then ask him what he said and did when hurt that way. If he were in my shoes, how would he pray each phrase of the Our Father? At Mass how does each part of the Eucharist stretch me to react as Christ? During the stations of the cross when was Jesus hurt like me and how did he respond? What mystery of the rosary comes closest to what I am feeling? What Psalm or Scripture passage would Christ pray if he had been hurt as I was? What song would he sing? Inner healing comes with any prayer that fits what I am feeling and stretches me to take on what Christ is feeling.

Whether praying alone or with another, start with the easiest way to experience Christ's love. Much inner healing of a hurt occurs even through a simple prayer asking the Lord to remove evil and to give his help: "Lord, I am impatient with the kids. Take away my crippling impatience and give me your patience." If I have more time, I might imagine the kids screaming and then imagine Jesus entering the room amid the thrown toys. Then I watch what Jesus would say and do to me and respond to him. Next I watch what Jesus would do and say to the kids until I can imagine myself imitating his behavior. There are just three steps: (1) creating a scene, (2) having Jesus enter to heal myself and another, (3) do as Jesus did.

This simple prayer of "creative imagination" really works and has healed past traumas as deep as rape and even fears of what might happen.[2] One woman kept fearing that her husband would come home violently drunk. She spent several days simply imagining the worst and having Jesus enter the scene to see how he would react to her and her husband. Finally she saw how she could grow even from what she most feared and was no longer paralyzed by her fear. Christ can heal past, present and future hurts if we just have him enter the scene and watch him until we have his reactions.

But process of denial tempts us to put off dealing immediately in private prayer with the hurt we feel. We wait until we see a friend, attend a prayer meeting or go to confession. Yet seeking healing at a prayer meeting or at confession is shallow unless we come with a hunger to forgive and be forgiven that flows from working through anger and depression. Confession's healing comes not just from five minutes of praying with a priest, but through the preparation spent alone with Christ daily examining wounds, asking for contrition and thanking him for helping to build bridges. Likewise healing a memory depends not just on praying with another but upon the preparation and follow-up alone with Christ.

Praying with Another

God forgives and heals outside the confessional but confessing to another deepens the healing. Sharing my brokenness with a priest in confession forces me to grasp my vague experience of growth and failure that usually eludes me. The ring of my words tells me whether I really am sorry and want to change or am just in denial. By the confessor's words and prayer I grasp and am grasped by the most "significant other," Jesus with his healing power and love. Deep healing flows not only because of the sacrament but also because I have gathered with another in Jesus' name to share my mind and heart and enter the Lord's. Through another I have died and received Jesus' unconditional love and acceptance until I really believe that I am lovable and that I can offer that same acceptance in loving those who hurt me.

A friend's warm understanding can also help us to concretely experience Jesus loving us so that we can accept ourselves and extend the same acceptance to whoever hurts us. Sometimes our emotional blocks demand the gifts of another such as wise counsel, a doctor's medicine, a word of knowledge to pinpoint the deeper hurt, another's viewpoint revealing our gifts, or a prayer of deliverance to remove the evil so that God's love can then fill the emptiness.[3] The deeper the hurt, the more we need another's help to grow. Ideally we should live and pray in a Christian community known for its love.[4] Whether praying alone or with another, the goal is to experience God's love so that we know we are lovable and can return that love in the face of any fear.

Often I feel as though I am bothering another when asking him to listen to my experience or pray with me for healing a hurt. Yet by sharing with another I do him a favor just as others do when coming to me for confession. Hearing a confession ranks first among growthful experiences because the person sharing his struggle calls me as a priest to honestly face my own struggles and awakens my hunger to grow. Just being with another in his struggle brings growth to both. That's why Alcoholics Anonymous works. We should never hesitate to share our struggle with another for fear of bothering him. "I shouldn't bother him" often masks depressions: "I am embarrassed that I am an adult, yet got hurt and need help. What will he think of me?"

Sharing with another our struggle to forgive also has risks. We must find a friend who can keep our struggles confidential. Too many have been further wounded when they find that strangers know the secrets intended to be shared with only one friend. Our friend must not only respect our privacy but be reverently gentle. If he probes and surfaces what we need to deny because we are too weak to face a deep hurt, then we can be wounded more deeply. Even if he knows the real problem, he should not bludgeon with his insight but gently listen or drop an open question leading to discovering the insight at the Lord's pace. A word of knowledge such as "At the age of twelve you had incest with your father" is better given as "How did you get along with your father?"

Healing depends not as much on insight as on a deep experience of being compassionately loved by Jesus. A friend stimulates our growth not by weeding out our faults, but by finding our gifts and building them. The friend who can love the sinner in us that we can't love, and thus loves us as much as the Father loves us, heals us as the Father heals us.

We should be wary of the friend who freely gives advice that makes us feel guilty rather than loved. Some judgmental friends preach the gospel of "you shouldn't feel that way . . ." rather than help us to expose the way we really feel and accept us the way we are as Christ does. Others block healing with "I know just how you feel—it's like the time when I . . ." and rob us of the chance to have our unique feelings exposed and accepted. We need the friend who gently accepts yet stretches us to see how Christ would deal with our feelings.

What if another asks us to prayerfully help him through a hurt? Just as we don't have to be experts on dying to help a person face death, we don't have to be professional psychologists to help another face a hurt. (We should never hesitate to use professionals too.)[5] We help another to the degree that we love him and are at home with our own feelings, especially anger and guilt, so that he can face his feelings too. We don't need answers or fancy prayers but only two ears to silently listen and a warm heart that understands. The *heartfelt* prayer will save the sick man (Jas. 5:16).

By now this might sound complicated. I should simply pray in whatever way I can best experience God loving me. If I pray with another, I simply love him with all his feelings as Jesus would. I can pray alone or with another following the five stages or just silently resting with Jesus. The five stages are not a magical formula for healing but just a way of helping me to open my heart rather than hide it from Christ. Inner healing of a hurt comes when I can give Christ my mind and heart and take on his mind and heart. Use whatever gets to the mind and heart of Jesus. At Emmaus Christ didn't leave a special prayer like the Our Father for healing all hurts. He simply let a heart speak to a heart.

Getting Started

It may sound easy, but it's hard to begin. I knew about healing of memories several months before I ever tried it. I thought that maybe it was for someone else, but not for me. I was the kind of person who seldom got hurt or hurt others. I hardly ever felt angry—just more tense. I could forgive with a word rather than use a lengthy process. Maybe I wasn't a great saint but I was rather comfortable with myself.

Then the day came when I thought I would try it so that I could help those other sinners who really needed to heal their memories.

The more I healed my hurts, the more new memories surfaced to heal. I began to see the shallowness of my forgiveness in bargaining for another to change before I built a bridge. It was depressing to see that I was now hurting others who before had hurt me. What was happening?

The answer boomeranged when telling a retreatant what to expect after a retreat. She would be more sensitized to her and others' faults so that it would look as though she were going backward rather than forward. The honeymoon would be over because she loved God more and could see many more ways that she was loved, yet was indifferent to him. Previously she could ignore taking time to pray and meet Christ. Now she would see that as wrong because she had experienced his love in prayer. It wasn't that she would be living a worse life, but now she would be sensitized to her former lukewarm love. My friends told me that the same thing was happening to me. I was easier to live with, was taking more risks, and had found a new power to grow in life-choking crises. I was growing through healing memories but would never see my halo.

Deep progress in healing a memory usually remains hidden. Progress is not having fewer memories to heal (deeper ones can now surface), healing more quickly (deeper ones are often slower), or getting hurt less (when others are hurt, I now hurt more). I do hurt others less but never see this, since healing brings new sensitivity to my sin.

How can I measure my progress? Am I aware of my weakness (my denied anger, my bargains, my sin), and do I bounce back more quickly by bringing it to Christ who loves the sinner? Am I catching more quickly my feelings after being hurt? Am I more human and more my true self? Am I more aware of people who are hurting and of people I hurt? Do I keep discovering new ways of living out Christ's mind and heart? Today did I take new risks and build new bridges even if they failed? Am I more grateful for receiving love and compliments? Am I more grateful for the success of others, especially for those I have forgiven? And, finally, the easiest sign—am I becoming more grateful, especially for the difficult moments in the day? If I can answer "yes" to these, then I am growing in healing memories even if it doesn't feel like progress. A caterpillar in its straitjacket of a cocoon feels as though it's dying rather than progressing into a butterfly free to fly in a new flower world.

I find that memories are like an iceberg and that unconditional love is like the blazing sun. As the blazing sun shines and melts the surface of the iceberg, the submerged parts of the iceberg surface and expose themselves to the blazing sun. Doing healing of memories every day, either alone or with others, I find that deeper and deeper parts of the submerged unconscious get exposed to the Lord's warmth and tenderness. Just as the blazing sun soaks up part of the iceberg's surface every day, so too healing of memories through continual prayer becomes not a digging or probing expedition but a gradual giving over to the Lord what he gently brings to the surface in prayer. Under the Lord's warm sun our gray iceberg melts into a beautiful, sparkling jewel supplying fresh water for new life.

The Spirit and the Bride say, "Come!" Let him who hears answer, "Come!" Let him who is thirsty come forward; let all who desire it accept the gift of life-giving water (Rev. 22:17).

APPENDIX

I. Daily Healing of One Memory—Summary

Relax and breathe in the Spirit. Find God within.

A. DENIAL—Lord, let me see what you see in my day.
  Where did God love me or love through me?
  Give him thanks, especially for any growth.

B. ANGER—Lord, take away my hurt.
  What am I less thankful for?
  What do I wish happened differently?
  Where was I hurt?
  Whom am I blaming?

  What am I feeling?
  When did I most feel like that?
  Recreate in the imagination all the destructiveness of the situation and share with Christ how I feel.

C. BARGAINING—Lord, let me forgive like you—unconditionally.
  Do I want to be healed by thinking and feeling as differently as you?
    As Christ see—the pressures on the one who hurt you, his good side, the whole picture
        say—what Christ said to his closest friends, sinners
        do—what Christ would do to give the love needed by the one who hurts you
  Do this until all conditions for change drop and I can say and do all that Christ would like to do through my prayer.

D. DEPRESSION—Lord, forgive me.
  Ask forgiveness for being like that person and for contributing

to the problem by overreacting, closing up, and failing to build bridges.

> Ask forgiveness for past hurts like this that make it easy to close up.*
> Give thanks for Christ's forgiveness and unconditional love for both of us.

E. ACCEPTANCE — Lord, thank you.
Thank Christ for the growth and for the possible growth due to the healing. (New openness to God, others, my true self)
> *Perhaps some other time take this and other new memories through the above steps to heal further roots that close me up.

II. Detailed Steps for Healing One Memory:

A. DENIAL (This is not a rigid method. Use the steps that help you. Add what works for you.)

1. Relax in the presence of Christ who sees the past and wants to heal its effects.
   Ask Christ to see the past as he sees it and have it healed at his pace and in his way.

2. Thank God for the times you were loved, loving, forgiven, forgiving.
   Thank him for the time that involved the most healing through suffering.
   In the seed on page 220 list at least ten of your talents, strengths, and good points that Jesus uses. Thank him for so much growth potential.
   Thank the Creator for each part of your body.

3. Pinpoint the hurt.
   For *what* are you less grateful?
   What do you wish had happened differently?

What would it take to have everything feel perfect?
When have you suffered most?
What is the worst that could happen?

Whom do you blame for the above?
Whom do you fear, avoid, judge harshly, tune out, neglect giving thanks for?
If you could change anybody, who would it be?
For whose success is it hardest to thank God?
Write his name also inside your seed because much growth will come from this hurt.

4. Tell Christ how you feel hurt.
   When did you feel most that way?
   Ask Christ's help to reconstruct that scene until you relive the way you felt.
   Have Christ enter the scene. What does he do and say to you?

5. Ask Christ's help in living out his reaction.
   What one thing will you do to live out his reaction?
   Write this along the outside of the seed to remind yourself of what will release the seed's potential growth.

Pray Psalm 103 thanking the Father for the ways you are loved. Select a seed to plant. The seed represents the potential for growth in the hurt.

B. ANGER

1. Take a time when you were hurt (see Denial). When did you most feel like that? Whom are you blaming?
   Write his name in the seed.

2. Ask Christ to help you reconstruct in your imagination how your antagonist hurt you. Put in details until you can see his face, smell the room, hear his words and feel the original pain.

   Tell Christ how you feel. Be honest and expose all for healing.

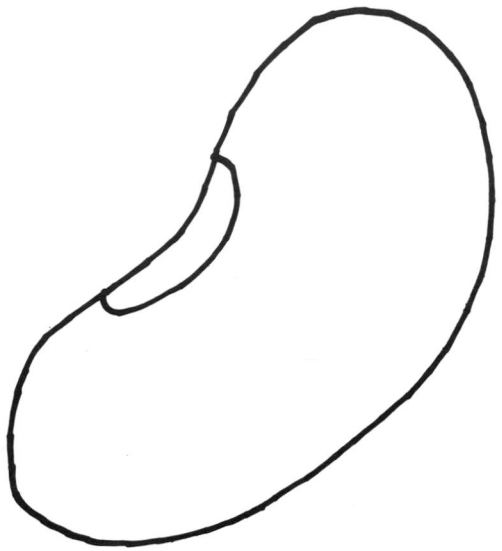

HEALING DENIAL—SELECTING THE SEED OF GROWTH

Do this until your angry words seem empty, exaggerated.

Tell Christ how your antagonist hurt you, himself and others, who in turn hurt others.

What healing, what changes do you want?

For him? List these in the soil below to the right of the seed.

For yourself? List these in the soil below to the left of the seed.

Pray for that healing.

3. When did Christ most feel like you or respond to someone like you?

Prayerfully read the Scripture passage until you can begin to think and feel like Christ.

4. Have Christ now enter the scene where you were hurt and watch him.

What does he do and say to you?

What does he do and say to your antagonist?

Now do and say to your antagonist what Christ did and said.

Write key words summarizing Christ's reaction below the seed.

5. What one thing does Christ want you to do to live out his reaction?

Do one positive thing.

Write above the seed a word or two summarizing this one positive thing you will do to give the seed new growth.

Pray all of Psalm 139. "O Lord, you have probed me and you know me. . . ."

Plant seed in soil.

C. BARGAINING

1. Recreate the scene with all its pain and tell Christ how you feel.

HEALING ANGER—Planting the Seed in Dark Soil

2. What changes would you like in your antagonist?
   Tell Christ all the ways you still want your antagonist to change, apologize, suffer, learn.
   List these along the sun's rays on the next page.

   Tell Christ why you want to be healed. What changes would you like in yourself.
   Ask Christ why he wants to heal you.
   Tell Christ one or two reasons why it will be hard to be healed (e.g. nice to look down on another and feel superior, feel sorry for yourself, not need to take new risks).
   Ask Christ why it will be hard to be healed.

   Pray that you will have as much desire to be healed as Christ desires to heal you.

3. When did Christ most feel like you or respond to someone like you?
   Prayerfully read the Scripture passage until you can begin to think and feel like Christ.

4. Have Christ now enter the scene where you were hurt and watch him.
   What does he say and do to you to heal you?
   What does he say and do to heal your antagonist?
   What good does Christ see? How does Christ pray that the good will grow?
   What pressures led to the persons hurting you? How is he responding to other hurts?
   How does Christ give your antagonist the power to change rather than ask for changes?
   How does Christ love your antagonist enough to let him make mistakes and grow from them?

5. Minister to your antagonist as Christ would until you feel that there is nothing more Christ would do or say.

   To see if you have reached this level, look at the ways you

wanted your antagonist to change. Can you cancel your bargains?

Ask Christ's help to no longer demand these changes. Pray until you feel that even if he never changes in ways you deserve, you still want to forgive and respond to his need to be loved.

As you can cancel these bargains, draw a line through each changing it into a life giving ray of the warming sun.

Pray that your antagonist's strengths will grow.
Next to each bargain you cancel, write down one of his good qualities after you have prayed to have it grow.

6. What one thing would Christ want you to do to live out his reaction?
Do a hidden favor for your antagonist.
After you do this, write in the seed a word or two describing this.

Pray the prayer of St. Francis found in Chapter 9. Expose the seed-plant in sunlight.

D. DEPRESSION

1. Recreate the scene and tell Christ how you feel.
Tell Christ how you wish you were different:
How you allowed yourself to get antagonized.
How you failed to think and act like Christ.
The destruction caused by you.

Tell Christ about the destruction caused by you.
How you could have reacted differently to your antagonist before the hurt.
How you could have reacted differently to your antagonist during the hurt.
(What you should have said and done.)

HEALING BARGAINING—Exposing Seed to Sun

How you could have reacted differently to your antagonist after the hurt.
(Built bridges instead of daily delaying forgiveness.)

How have you hurt others in the same ways for which you criticized your antagonist?

How do your bargains show you your own need to change? (You project your weaknesses and proud strengths at another.)
Along the raindrops on the following page, write the things you did for which you are sorry.
Speak to Christ on the cross and ask forgiveness for hurting him in yourself and others. How do you wish you could change to love him more?

2. When did Christ feel most like you or respond to someone like you?
   Prayerfully read the Scripture passage until you can begin to have Christ's mind and heart. Maybe make the stations of the cross or look at a crucifix.

3. Have Christ now enter the scene where you were hurt and watch him respond to you.

   What does Jesus say and do to heal you?
   What good does he see in you and pray that it will grow?
   What hurts and pressures led you to hurt another? How does he heal these times too?
   How does he smile in forgiving a debt of five hundred times rather than fifty?
   How does he tell you that he can be closer than ever?
   How does he embrace you just as you are, asking not for change but for a chance to love?

4. Let Christ minister to you until you feel that there is nothing more Christ would do or say to make you feel more loved.

When you feel that you have reached this level of loving yourself as much as Christ loves you, try looking at the ways you wanted to change.

Could you accept Christ's love and love yourself as much as he does even if these changes had never occurred?

Pray until you feel that even if you never change in the ways you want to change, Christ would die for you. (He loves you not because you change but in order to give you power to change.)

Pray that your strengths will grow.

Write in the seed three strengths that Christ shows you.

5. Continue absorbing Christ's forgiveness for yourself and your antagonist until you can offer as much forgiveness to yourself and your antagonist as Christ does.

Cross out each unloving action that you are sorry for, yet able to forgive in yourself as Christ does. Now you have rain ready to bring life to your seed.

6. What one thing would Christ want you to do to live out his reaction? Write this above your seed.

Pray Psalm 32 thanking God for his forgiveness.
Begin to water the seed.

E. ACCEPTANCE

1. Recreate the scene and tell Christ how you feel.

Thank him for the difference between the scene this time and how you felt when first reliving it. Any change is due to his healing in prayer.

2. Read the Beatitudes exercise on pp. 169–70. Prayerfully pray each beatitude, asking Christ to show in each how you have been healed or can be healed.

HEALING DEPRESSION—WATERING THE SEED

Thank Jesus for the healing that has happened.

Ask Jesus to walk into the future, showing you how a day will be different due to his healing.

Thank Jesus for the healing that has or will come and yet will never be seen.

In the petals of the flower on the next page, write the gifts that have come to you from the hurt.

3. Live out Christ's healing.

Ask Christ to gift your antagonist as he has gifted you.

What does Christ most want to give him through you? Write these in the leaves of the flower.

Ask Christ for help in building a bridge to him even if he never responds.

What would Christ do for him through the new you?

Write this along the stem of the flower between your gift-petals and his gift-leaves.

As you continue to discover new gifts that were hidden, write these on the hidden roots.

Pray Mary's Magnificat (Lk. 1:47–55) as your thanksgiving.

Thank God for the seed's growth representing the Spirit's growth within you.

Be sure to give thanks for the invisible growth beneath the soil.

III. Gifts and Struggles Exercise

1. Under "Hurts," list ten times you have been hurt (what are the times in your life you wish were different?).
2. Under "Gifts," list ten ways God uses you (what you enjoy doing, your skills, the best times, whom you can best understand, etc.).
3. Times of hurt often initiate or deepen gifts. Connect with a line

HEALING AND ACCEPTANCE—GIVING THANKS FOR SEED'S GROWTH

the hurts and gifts that are related (e.g., the loss of a child giving empathy with those losing a child or loved one).

Hurts	*Gifts*
1.	1.
2.	2.
3.	3.
4.	4.
5.	5.
6.	6.
7.	7.
8.	8.
9.	9.
10.	10.

The times that are connected to gifts are healed memories where you are able to focus not on the pain but on the growth in gifts. Take the time least connected with gifts and begin to heal that memory.

IV. The Seven Last Words—Measuring Stick of Forgiveness

To forgive as deeply as Christ forgives, you must be stretched by Christ's mind until you can speak as he did his seven last words, his final attempt to forgive. If a person has hurt you, Christ waits to say today through you the same words he spoke two thousand years ago at the cost of pain and life.

Steps:
A. Pick one person who has hurt you (one you are not grateful for and would like to change).
B. Recreate in your imagination the scene of the hurt until you can feel anger, fear and the reaction you had when first hurt. Share these feelings with Christ.
C. Take the first of Christ's seven last words and ask forgiveness for any way your forgiveness doesn't match Christ's forgiveness.

D. Looking at a crucifix, continue to say that last word until you can say it as Christ hurt within you says it. When you have the gift of being able to say that word as Christ does, fill in the cross (p. 236) for that word and take the next one, until the entire cross is filled in as a sign of gratitude for your life's cross being transformed into the redeeming cross of Christ.

1. Father, forgive them, for they know not what they do (Lk. 23:34).

> For the times I hated the sinner in another or myself rather than loved the sinner and prayed for the Father's care, Lord, have mercy.

> For being blind to the pressures and past hurts that make people unintentionally hurt me, Lord, have mercy.

> For being more concerned about how others hurt me rather than how they hurt the Father, Lord, have mercy.

> For not taking Christ's initiative to forgive but waiting until others had earned my forgiveness by changing, Lord, have mercy.

2. This day you will be with me in paradise (Lk. 23:43).

> For relying too much on my own efforts to achieve the paradise of acceptance rather than asking and depending on your power, Lord, have mercy.

> For allowing pain, criticism, or the projection of my own faults to blind me to the good in another, Lord, have mercy.

> For the times my forgiveness did not begin "this day" but days later, Lord, have mercy.

> For not wanting another with me, closer than ever before and sharing all I can give, Lord, have mercy.

3. Son, behold your mother. Mother, behold your son (Jn. 19:27).

For focusing on my own pain and loneliness rather than on my responsibility for the pain and loneliness that others feel, Lord, have mercy.

For treating others like strangers—judging, ignoring, hearing their words but ignoring their feelings, seldom asking for help—for being so slow in extending my family, Lord, have mercy.

For the times I ran from insults, humiliations and hurts rather than standing on Calvary grateful to suffer with Christ and offer his love in return for abuse, Lord, have mercy.

For failing to change structures and utilize the gifts of others so that love is given even when I am gone, Lord, have mercy.

4. My God, My God, why have you forsaken me? (Mt. 27:46)

For feeling sorry for myself and failing to make forsaken times an opportunity to trust more in God and know that I could be closer than ever, Lord, have mercy.

For failing to see my own limitations in overreacting to the hurt, failing to build bridges, and acting coldly due to a history of other hurts, Lord, have mercy.

For equating closeness to God with feeling close rather than finding closeness with him in my neighbor, Lord, have mercy.

For trying to hide from God feelings I didn't want to face— anger, fears, depression and choking off my cry, "My God, my God . . ." Lord, have mercy.

5. I thirst (Jn. 19:28).

For not being tortured by a thirst for Christ's view, Lord, have mercy.

For a thirst to escape pain rather than a thirst to love unto death and be hurt again and again in taking new risks to love, Lord, have mercy.

For failing to hunger and thirst for justice enough to prevent the hurts that happened to me, Lord, have mercy.

For adding to Christ's thirst to love because closing my heart has closed other hearts and spread distrust around the earth, Lord, have mercy.

6. It is finished (Jn. 19:30).

For feeling that forgiveness was accomplished if I felt comfortable rather than sensitized to others' suffering and driven to heal their hurts and repair my destruction, Lord, have mercy.

For thinking I was finished when I asked God to forgive the evil in others and failed to see the same evil in myself or failed to forgive as much as God has forgiven me, Lord, have mercy.

For finishing forgiveness without building bridges and creating a more loving environment, Lord, have mercy.

For finishing a day without healing it so that my life tomorrow has direction and power to love without a backlog of hurts, Lord, have mercy.

7. Father, into thy hands I commend my Spirit (Lk. 23:46).

For failing to trust your hands by praying to release the Spirit and heal to the degree that you alone can heal, Lord, have mercy.

For failing to see that Christ's passion continues in my life and that the Father's hands are always present drawing greater good from all suffering that I face with Christ's view, Lord, have mercy.

For failing to let my hands become your hands to change what should be changed and for not letting your hands take what cannot be changed, Lord, have mercy.

For not seeing your hands everywhere and not thanking you for the growth and possible growth in loving you, others and myself, Lord, have mercy.

V. Healing Memories with the Stations of the Cross

Healing Many Memories

Nearly every hurt possible is portrayed in the stations of the cross. If we have been hurt by hypocrisy, we will be sensitive to Pilate washing his hands when guilty and can heal that hurt by taking on Jesus' pain and reaction. Where we feel more pain, we should spend more time absorbing Jesus' reactions to heal hurts connected to that pain. Likewise there is probably need for healing the stations we want to pass quickly. If we had a poor relationship with our mother, the fourth station where Jesus meets Mary may be distasteful but very needed. Where there is attraction or repulsion, pause for healing. Three questions asked at each station may help.

1. How is Christ feeling hurt?

2. When did I feel the same way?

3. Can I forgive whoever made me suffer just as Christ forgives, and can I have the same reactions that Christ did?

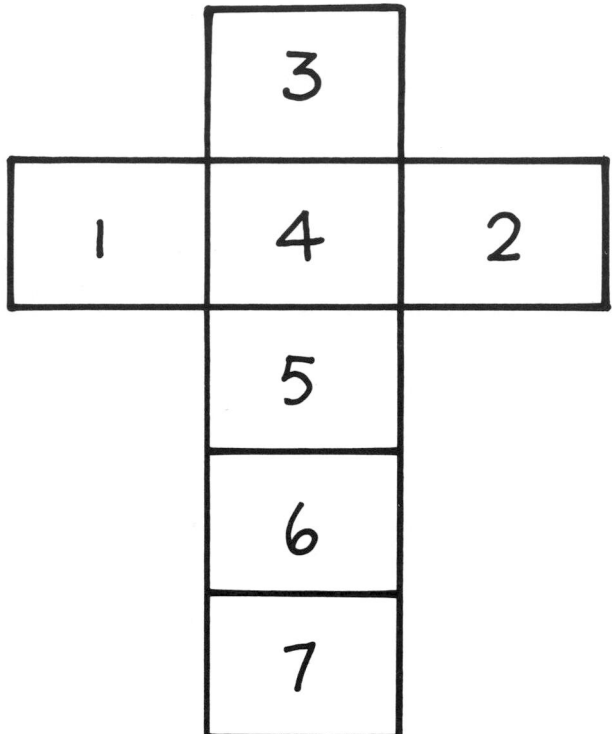

Healing One Memory

One memory of a hurt can be healed in greater depth by watching Christ in each station deal with what I felt when hurt. Thus the memory of being humiliated during seventh grade while giving a wrong answer on TV can be healed as I watch Christ dealing with humiliation in each station. The process is one of giving Christ my feelings and taking on his reactions.

1. When was I hurt? (What do I wish had happened differently?)

2. How do I feel as I relive that hurt in my memory?

3. Make the stations, asking at each station how Christ feels like me or responds to someone feeling the way I do.

4. After making the stations take a few minutes to relive that memory, watching how Christ would enter the scene and respond. Do what Christ would do and say.

5. Live out Christ's reaction.

VI. Healing the Future

1. Read Luke 22:39–46 (the agony in the garden).

2. Ask Christ to help you create in your imagination the scene of what you most fear or want to be able to face in the future.

3. Face the fear or hurt until you feel it bodily. Share how you feel with Christ.

4. Ask Christ to help you absorb how he would react—his thoughts and feelings.

   A. What does Christ want done to prevent this fear (Remove this cup . . .)?

B. How does Christ promise that growth can come if it is the Father's will to go through what I most fear to face?

    1. How would Christ go through it? What would he say, do, see, etc. In your imagination react like Christ.

    2. After doing this, what is still difficult to face? How does Christ find gift in this fear?

5. Live out Christ's reaction by taking one step to face this fear (e.g., take a step closer to the feared cliff; if you fear death make a will etc.).
Thank Christ for whatever has happened during the prayer and rest in his strength.

Epilogue: Fifteen Years Later

As you read the previous chapters, we hope you at times disagreed with us, because your world today is different from the world we (Dennis and Matt) faced when we started to write this book in 1975. Back then the Catholic Charismatic Renewal refused to sell our first book, *Healing of Memories* (1974), because it was "too psychological." Some leaders of the Charismatic Renewal criticized our book for suggesting that psychology and spirituality could work hand in hand in finding God by working through emotions. Yet our experience confirmed the possibility of such a partnership.

At that time we worked as therapists in a psychiatric clinic, and we also gave thirty-day retreats based on *The Spiritual Exercises of St. Ignatius*. We saw the same process of healing of memories over time take place in our therapy clients and in our retreatants. In those days we felt alone because we did not know of any therapists who prayed through hurts with their clients, as do many of our Christian therapist friends today. Nor did we know of healing prayer ministers who understood the process dimension of healing. We did know people who prayed for healing of memories, but only by naming each memory briefly as part of a long list. If negative feelings were stirred up, prayer ministers prayed for peace to replace anger, which was considered dangerous. If a particular painful memory surfaced, the minister usually prayed only once and then told the wounded person to forgive and get on with life.

There was little sense of how to help a person stuck in grieving a hurt and unable to forgive after one prayer. Grieving was for the weak who couldn't be like the stoic Jacqueline Kennedy refusing to shed a tear during her husband's funeral. Elisabeth Kubler-Ross had just revealed the natural grieving process of the dying, but no one had yet applied it to grieving the loss behind any hurt. Our chapter on the psychosomatic link between body, mind, and emotions was considered heresy by many doctors who now listen to Dr. Bernard Siegel speak of the need to grieve the losses that occurred before, during, and after cancer. So in a world that denied the connection between God, psychology, and medicine, we emphasized a psychological grieving process that in prayer brought life to the whole person. All this was new ground and not nuanced by more recent movements, especially 12 Step Recovery for abuse survivors and Christian feminism. In a world that allowed only a psychological process in therapy but not also a process in prayer for healing hurts, we stressed what could be done in a process with God alone and under-emphasized the healing that comes from sharing with a friend, support group, or therapist.

Christian Feminism

Christian feminism is bringing a balance to the skewed masculine western spirituality that originally influenced this book. As we already mentioned, this balance has come through the addition of Sheila in 1981 to our team of two males. Through this change we have become more sensitized not only to obvious issues, such as sexist language, but also to our whole way of perceiving the inner and outer world. Women speak "in a different voice."[1] We are learning to hear the feminine voice as well as the masculine one that we knew so well.

Over the past fifteen years, what I (Dennis) value most from Christian feminism is that it has helped me discover the healing that comes from changing our image of God. For me, the healing of many hurts happened when I changed my image of God, especially when I discovered and began relating to the feminine side of God.[2]

For you to understand why this was so healing, you'd have to understand that I come out of two families, a German one and a Jesuit one. Despite all their gifts, they both wounded me in a similar way. The German side was very self-righteous. Emotions were looked down on and judged harshly. From the Jesuit side I picked up lots of clericalism. (No doubt you caught the idealizing of celibacy and the vows in this book, as well as the implication that "vocation" refers only to religious and that sacramental confession is superior to other experiences of healing.) I lived my life with a masculine skew: great at getting things done, thinking for myself, and finding God "out there," but almost totally lacking in the feminine values of simply being, feeling deeply, and finding God within.

At first when I prayed through this hurt of being out of touch with my feminine side, using the five stages, very little changed. But a year later, when I prayed through the same five stages, I experienced profound change. I changed because during that year my image of God had changed. We not only mimic many of the traits of our families, but we also mimic the traits of our God. And unfortunately my God was a male, celibate, self-righteous German. No matter how hard we pray, we generally become only as healthy as the God we adore. Only when I became comfortable with not only praying to Jesus or God the Father but also to the feminine side of God, God the Mother, did my "male skew" hurts begin to heal as I prayed through the five stages.

Erik Erikson's essay, "Womanhood and Inner Space," broadened my understanding of what I had experienced.[3] Erikson describes how the masculine physiologically and psychologically emphasizes outer space, while the feminine focuses on inner space. He suggests that the masculine image of God is more transcendent—a mighty God who is "out there," always inviting us to change and grow. In contrast, the feminine image of God is more immanent—a God within who meets us in whatever we presently are experiencing.*

So how would I rewrite this book to include both dimensions? In each of the five stages, we asked the reader to share his or her reality with Jesus and then enter Jesus' reality. The implication is that we should move on and change to be more like the "ideal" Jesus. This is the masculine value of surrendering ourselves to a transcendent God who is inviting us to change and grow. While there is truth to this, today I would also encourage the feminine value or feminine side of God already loving us and present in whatever emotion we feel. I added to the male skew in our presentation of the five stages because I suggested that the

----

*Pope John Paul II, in speaking about the two Hebrew words for mercy, *hesed* and *rahamim,* also emphasizes this need for both dimensions of God.[4]

model for doing this process came from the story of the prodigal son, where God the Father throws a party and welcomes us home (Lk 15:11–32). Because I was so into my male skew, I completely skipped over the story immediately above, which describes how God the Mother also wants to throw a party and welcome us home (Lk 15:8–10). Removing sexist language and using this and other scripture stories of God as Mother (Num 11:12; Is 49:15; 63:15; Ps 131:2) would be for me symbols of my desire to perceive my inner and outer world in a new way in order that the five stages might heal hurts more deeply.

Abuse and Recovery

In addition to Christian feminism, the three of us have also learned from the 12 Step Recovery movement we explored in *Belonging: Bonds of Healing and Recovery* (1993). This movement has sensitized us to co-dependency, in which we orient ourselves around others' reality and care for their needs at the expense of our own. The recovery movement has also sensitized us to shame and the other effects of abuse.

When I (Sheila) first read *Healing Life's Hurts* in 1978, I was co-director of a training program in healing ministry. Like Dennis and Matt, I had observed that people who prayed usually didn't understand psychological process, and therapists who understood psychological process were often suspicious of prayer. I had two reactions to this book. I thought it was a brilliant integration of spirituality and psychology which would surely become a classic in healing literature (as it has), and exactly what I needed in my own ministry. At the same time, I sensed that some of it just wouldn't work for me. I felt the same vague lack of inner at-homeness that I had often experienced in theological school, where the spirituality was based upon a skewed male view of the world. Now I know that my second reaction to *Healing Life's Hurts* came not only from the male skew discussed above, but also from my own issues of abuse and internalized, toxic shame.

I experienced sexual abuse as a child. As is typical of abuse victims, I blamed myself. I believed that something in my very being had caused this awful thing to happen, and my belief became a core of shame. Shame is the belief that *I* am bad, while guilt is the belief that I *did* something bad. When I read this book as an adult in 1978, I hadn't yet learned that an abused child is never in any way at fault for the abuse and that neither shame nor guilt is appropriate. Yet, when I read the chapter on the depression stage, I somehow sensed that for me to follow its suggestions would be extremely unhealthy. The last thing I needed was to ask forgiveness for my part in the abuse. Like Linda (see the Introduction), I needed to know that Jesus honored my anger at the abuser.

Abuse and the chronic shame that resulted reinforced the denial of my feminine identity that I experienced growing up in this culture and in theological school. In a culture that encourages women to overlook their own legitimate needs in order to serve others (i.e. to be co-dependent), and that views male reality as normative and right, women often experience themselves as fundamentally wrong. In theological school I was taught that the fundamental human sin is pride, an exaggerated sense of self-importance. I felt anything but self-important, and I remember the shock of relief I felt when I read Ann Ulanov's comment, ". . . for a woman, sin is not pride, the exaltation of the self, but a refusal to claim the self God has given."[5] Often when this book speaks of sin, it presumes that sin is pride and that the remedy is to give up one's own way for the sake of another. For me, as a woman and as an abuse survivor, the remedy for sin has been reclaiming my lost self by honoring my anger and my needs. I believe the same applies to those men who have taken abuse too long and denied themselves too much.

Being with Feelings in the Five Stages

Becoming aware of the co-dependent way that not only women but I too as a man ignore my own needs has helped me (Matt) to heal hurts more deeply through the five stages. I was not aware of my co-dependency years ago when I went through the stages of forgiving Gus. The five stage process is still the primary way I work through hurts, but I go through each stage differently today.

In the first stage of denial, today I spend more time taking in love rather than pushing myself to face a painful hurt before I am ready. In other words, now I am more likely to honor my resistances. Fifteen years ago, I saw resistance as weakness to overcome rather than the very place to meet God. Today this meeting often takes place by listening to my body. For example, when I am feeling denial's vague anxiety, I focus on where my body carries it and am lovingly present to that feeling without trying to fix or change it. Then I sense what images, words, etc., fit the way my body feels. Right now I feel a vague, tight anxiety in my chest as if I don't have enough breath . . . life . . . energy . . . to finish writing at this late hour. When I just named my fear of running out of energy, my body let go of the anxiety, for it was no longer denied.

I also would handle my anger differently today. I notice that in the chapter on the anger stage, I wrote only two sentences about resting and receiving what I needed for my wounds. All the rest was about trying to change Gus and finally seeing his wounds. To be that concerned about the person who hurt me and neglect my own needs was co-dependence. Now I take time to see how Jesus is also angry on my behalf because Jesus loves me and hates the destruction done to me. Then I take time to get in touch with what I need and ask for it from Jesus and others. Today perhaps I would even go directly to Gus and express my anger to him.

In the bargaining stage I also wish I had been more attentive to my needs. I've learned that bargains are an expression of our sense of justice and integrity, and some bargains are to be spoken rather than discarded in the name of unconditional love. I wish I had told Gus how I needed him to change: "I am feeling unsure of myself this first year of teaching. So if I do something well, I need to hear that. If you ever have any problems with anything I do or say, I want to be the first to hear it from you. Too many here are saying things behind another's back." If I had said something like this, I would have been caring for my fear that maybe I am failing in ways I don't know and therefore can't correct. Bargains reveal needs, and the more I ask others and Jesus to meet them, the more my wounds get healed. Unconditional love means forgiving Gus even if he can't live up to my needs, but I must still honor my needs.

In the depression stage, I feel surprised by how readily I blamed myself with "I should have . . . (loved Gus more)." I never said, "I should have taken better care of myself." Some reactions that fifteen years ago I labeled as "sin," I now see as my own normal, human grieving reactions to how deeply Gus had hurt me. I waited too long to care for myself by confronting Gus, and so when I finally did, Gus conveniently said that he couldn't remember anything about my talk or his response. I also wince at the way I ran over my resistance by pushing myself to feel more contrition and forgive even if I didn't feel like it. It probably would have been more helpful to tell Jesus, "I don't feel much contrition or forgiveness toward Gus." When I can't feel, it is usually because I am burying a stronger feeling, in this case probably anger. I could then have taken time to listen to my anger rather than bury it under trying to be nicer to Gus. Resistance is valuable because, like pain, it tells me where the wound still needs healing and keeps my relationship with Jesus honest.

I am also surprised that in the depression stage and during the entire process, I didn't write more about how I needed and got support from the Jesuit community and other teachers. The teachers even voted me teacher of the year, and that, as much as anything else, helped pull me out of my depression. I needed love and affirmation from other human beings as well as from Jesus in prayer.[6] In summary, recognizing that God meets me in my needs and in my resistance has helped me to receive more life in each of the five stages.

SUMMARY

Fifteen years after this book was first published, the three of us are more aware than ever of the validity of this five stage process of grieving with another to forgive and heal hurts. Today we understand this process more deeply. Only when we honor our reality with all its emotions is forgiveness healing rather than a destructive short-cut burying anger and our needs under smiling denial. To the degree we share our hearts with Jesus (or with God the Mother) as a loving friend who embraces our pain and loves us in it, we experience healing love and the power to then become more like the God we adore. The other route of simply embracing Jesus' reality is co-dependence, stamping out our reality and his call to be co-creator. As co-creator we meet the creator everywhere—in prayer, with others, indwelling all creation, and especially in our deepest self.

Studies done since 1975 confirm that grieving hurts is the key to physical health. For example, Dr. James Pennebaker established that the bereaved who bear their pain alone have more physical ailments after a death, but those who work through their grief by confiding in another have no increase in health problems.[7] Grieving is also the key to emotional health. Dr. Erich Lindemann found that psychiatric patients had six times as many situations of loss requiring grieving in their lives as did the general population.[8] Another study, of aging seniors, asked why many grow more bitter while others grow more loving and mellow in advanced years. The study found that those who grieved well the losses of their lives aged well. They could grieve the diminishments of old age rather than get stuck in anger and depression.[9] So to the degree you have found life in these pages, you are likely to find life in old age too. To the degree we have healed hurts and grown from them, we can grow from future hurts too. Then with Dag Hammarskjöld we can say, "For all that has been, thanks. For all that will be, yes."

Notes

CHAPTER 1

1. Rollo May, *The Art of Counseling* (Nashville: Abingdon, 1967), 35.

2. For the healing of hurts that distort our image of God, cf. Matthew & Dennis Linn and Sheila Fabricant, *Healing the Eight Stages of Life* (Mahwah: Paulist, 1988).

CHAPTER 2

1. Elisabeth Kubler-Ross, *On Death and Dying* (New York: Macmillan, 1969).

2. Elisabeth Kubler-Ross, *Questions and Answers on Death and Dying* (New York: Macmillan, 1974), 31.

3. Mwalimu Imara, "Dying as the Last Stage of Growth," *Death: The Final Stage of Growth* (Englewood Cliffs: Prentice-Hall, 1975).

4. Walter Abbott, S.J. (ed.), *The Documents of Vatican II* (New York: America Press, 1966), 269.

5. Consult Chapter 3 for further explanation of "Our Father" and five stages. Consult Chapter 12 for further explanation of eucharist and five stages. Only when hurts are healed can the *Spiritual Exercises* retreatant be free to follow Christ in the third degree of humility because she or he knows from experience that Christ can bring life from insults and poverty. Cf. Ignatius Loyola, *The Spiritual Exercises,* tr. George Ganss (St. Louis: Institute of Jesuit Sources, 1992).

CHAPTER 3

1. The accounts of Phil and Annette are found in Chapter 7, 95.

2. James C. Coleman, *Abnormal Psychology and Modern Life* (Glenview: Scott, Foresman and Co., 1976) 58.

3. To these four are often added sadness (which we treat as grief) and shame (which says I am a mistake, in contrast to guilt which says I made a mistake). Shame is often labeled "unhealthy guilt," and guilt which focuses on behavior as "healthy guilt." Cf. Joan Borysenko, *Guilt Is the Teacher, Love Is the Lesson* (New York: Warner, 1990). Since we are using guilt in the broad sense as anger turned inward, it also includes shame. For an understanding of shame and how it is healed, cf. Gershen Kaufman, *Shame: The Power of Caring* (Rochester: Schenkman, 1980) and John Bradshaw, *Healing the Shame That Binds You* (Deerfield Beach: Health Communications, 1988).

4. For more on the interaction of fear and anger, cf. Harriet Lerner, *The Dance of Anger* (New York: Harper & Row, 1985).

5. For the healing of hurts and wounded emotions that underlie compulsive patterns, cf. Dennis Linn, Sheila Fabricant Linn and Mat-

thew Linn, *Belonging: Bonds of Healing and Recovery* (Mahwah: Paulist, 1993).

CHAPTER 4

1. Hippolytus, *Apostolic Constitution,* V:11, 27.

2. Morton Kelsey, *Healing and Christianity* (New York: Harper & Row, 1973), 177.

3. Irenaeus, *Contra Haereses* II:32, 4–5; Ephrem, *Sermo* 46; Caesar, *Sermo* 52, 5; Bede, *in Marci Evangelium Expositio* 2, 6.

4. Placid Murray, O.S.B., "The Liturgical History of Extreme Unction," in *The Furrow,* XI (1960), 573, citing Antoine Chavasse, Etude II (unpublished) 210.

5. Jean-Charles Didier, "Death and the Christian," *Twentieth Century Encyclopedia of Catholicism,* LV (New York: Hawthorn, 1961), 46.

6. Abbott, *op. cit.,* 161.

7. *Pastoral Care of the Sick: Rites of Anointing & Viaticum* (New York: Catholic Book, 1983).

8. W.B. Cannon, "The Emergency Functions of the Adrenal Medulla in Pain and Major Emotions," *American J. of Physiology,* 33 (1914), 356.

9. Physical changes can be so great they can cause death, as Cannon noted, and is evident today in those dying after forced retirement. Larry Dossey, M.D., *Meaning & Medicine* (New York: Bantam, 1991) 57–61.

10. Walter Cannon, *Digestion and Health* (New York: Norton, 1930).

11. Hans Selye, *The Stress of Life* (New York: McGraw-Hill, 1956).

12. Coleman, *op. cit.,* 273.

13. Meyer Friedman and Ray Rosenman, *Type A Behavior and Your Heart* (Greenwich: Fawcett, 1974). Although Friedman thought the primary factor of the Type A complex was simply pressuring oneself to hurry, later the work of Dr. Redford Williams (Duke University Medical Center) found the crucial factor may be the hostility, distrust, and anger harbored by the overly time-conscious person. Cf. Chris Raymond, "Distrust, Rage May Be 'Toxic Core' That Puts 'Type A' Person at Risk," *J. of Am. Medical Association,* 261:6 (1989), 813.

14. O. Carl Simonton, M.D., et al., *Getting Well Again* (New York: Bantam, 1980). For more on the healing of cancer through dealing with emotions, cf. Bernard Siegel, M.D., *Love, Medicine, and Miracles* (New York: Harper & Row, 1986).

15. Patrick Young, "Cancer and Personality: Can They Be Connected," *The National Observer,* 15:14 (April 3, 1976), 16–17. Young cites Dr. Silverman. For how stress is a trigger for all illness, cf. Blair Justice, *Who Gets Sick: Thinking and Health* (Houston: Peak, 1987). For a profound integration of the physical, emotional and spiritual factors in illness and healing, cf. Deepak Chopra, *Quantum Healing* (New York: Bantam, 1989).

16. For the interaction of emotional and other factors in illness, cf. Justice, *op. cit.*

17. Thomas Holmes and Richard Rahe, "The Social Readjustment Scale," *J. of Psychosomatic Research,* 11 (April, 1967), 213–18.

18. Coleman, *op. cit.,* 120.

19. Friedman & Rosenman, *op. cit.,* 80.

20. *Ibid.,* 9.

21. *Ibid.,* 102.

22. *Ibid.,* 103.

23. *Ibid.,* 80.

24. *Ibid.,* 218. Cardiologist Dean Ornish taught stress management over 24 days to Type A cardiac patients. Researchers noted significant results, including a 20% decrease in cholesterol levels and a 90% reduction in angina attacks associated with coronary artery disease. Dean Ornish, et al., "Effects of Stress Management Training & Dietary Changes in Treating Ischemic Heart Disease," *J. of Am. Medical Assn.,* 249:1, 54–59.

25. *Ibid.,* 219.

26. The most heart attacks cluster around 9:00 A.M. on Monday, when the new work week with its negative memories begins. This is also the time of most strokes and has twice the rate of sudden deaths as does 5:00 A.M., when the incidence is lowest. Cf. Dossey, *op. cit.,* 62–65.

27. First our artery walls are exposed to large amounts of cholesterol. This cholesterol does not depart easily and can cause plaque formation on artery walls. Then, in fight-flight situations, the nervous system triggers the hormones epinephrine and norepinephrine. These hormones precipitate clotting elements in the blood, which enlarge further the plaques on artery walls, and they also narrow the small capillaries nourishing the arteries and the plaques. The plaques can easily decay and become life-threatening. Cf. Friedman & Rosenman, *op. cit.,* 199–206.

28. Henry Russek and Linda Russek, "Is Emotional Stress an Etiologic Factor in Coronary Heart Disease?" *Psychosomatics,* XVII:2 (1976), 63. Another study found that the best predictor for heart disease was *not* any of the major *physical* risk factors (smoking, high blood pressure, elevated cholesterol and diabetes mellitus) but *job satisfaction.* Cf. Dossey, *op. cit.,* 63.

29. Russek, *op. cit.,* 66.

30. Simonton & Simonton, *op. cit.,* 30.

31. *Ibid.,* 31.

32. Jeanne Acterberg, Stephanie Matthews, and O. Carl Simonton, "Psychology of the Exceptional Cancer Patient: A Description of Patients Who Outlived Predicted Expectancies," *Psychotherapy: Theory and Research and Practice* (June 21, 1976), 13–14. This was verified also by Leonard Derogatis' tests indicating that breast cancer patients who felt and freely expressed much anger, fear, depression and guilt lived far longer than patients who showed little of these emotions. Cf. Siegel, *op. cit.,* 104. Likewise David Spiegel at Stanford U. Medical School followed 86 women with breast cancer for ten years and found that those dealing with their emotions through group therapy and lessons in self-hypnosis

lived twice as long as those given only traditional medical treatment. D. Spiegel, et al., "Effects of Psychosocial Treatment on Survival of Patients with Metastic Breast Cancer," *Lancet* (Oct. 15, 1989).

33. A film produced by the American Cancer Society, "The Embattled Cell," is filmed in lapsed time and magnified three thousand times.

34. For a summary of the work of Dr. Robert Good and Dr. George Solomon, cf. Kelsey, *op. cit.,* 216.

35. Acterberg, Matthews & Simonton, *op. cit.,* 14.

36. For a summary of the research of Dr. William Greene, Dr. David Kissen and Am. Psych. Assn., cf. Young, *op. cit.,* 16. For 200 articles in the medical literature, cf. Acterberg, Matthews, & Simonton, *op. cit.,* 15. For a summary of research on cancer and the mind, cf. Steven Locke, M.D., *The Healer Within: The New Medicine of Mind & Body* (New York: Mentor, 1987), 152–176.

37. For how the mind influences the body through the nervous, endocrine, and immunological systems, cf. Dossey, *op. cit.*

38. Acterberg, Matthews, Simonton, *op. cit.,* 7.

39. Dr. H. Becker studied 49 women with breast cancer and found that while the older women had normal emotional losses, close to three-fourths of the younger women had experienced a tragic loss in their lives and had had a more difficult childhood. Cf. Locke, *op. cit.,* 158.

40. The best books on physical healing are the following: Francis MacNutt, *Healing* (Notre Dame: Ave Maria, 1974); *idem, Power To Heal* (Notre Dame: Ave Maria, 1977), Dennis & Matthew Linn and Barbara Shlemon, *To Heal As Jesus Healed* (Notre Dame: Ave Maria, 1978).

41. Ignatius Loyola, *The Spiritual Exercises,* tr. Louis Puhl (New York: Newman, 1959), 142.

42. *Ibid.,* 143.

43. MacNutt, *Power To Heal, op. cit.*

44. Boone Porter, "The Origin of the Medieval Rite for Anointing the Sick or the Dying," *J. of Theol. Studies,* 7:2 (Oct. 1956), 214–17.

CHAPTER 5

1. Dr. Raymond Moody, *Life After Life* (Covington: Mockingbird, 1975).

2. In her foreword to Dr. Moody's *Life After Life,* Dr. Elisabeth Kubler-Ross supports his conclusions on the basis of her interviews with hundreds of patients who had life after life experiences. For more cf. Kenneth Ring, *Life at Death: A Scientific Investigation of Near Death Experience* (New York: Coward, McCann & Geoghegan, 1980).

3. For a readable survey of false images of God see the classic, J.B. Phillips, *Your God Is Too Small* (New York: Macmillan, 1969).

4. William Glasser, *Reality Therapy* (New York: Harper & Row, 1965).

5. Carl Jung, *Modern Man in Search of a Soul* (New York: Harcourt, Brace & Co., 1933), 235–36.

CHAPTER 6

1. Teresa of Avila, *The Autobiography of St. Teresa of Avila,* tr. E. Allison Peers (Garden City: Doubleday & Co., 1960), Bk. I, Ch. 8.

2. For a recent adaptation of Eugene Gendlin's focusing process for listening to the body, cf. Edwin McMahon and Peter Campbell, *The Focusing Steps* (Kansas City: Sheed & Ward, 1991).

3. John Powell, *Reason To Live, Reason To Die* (Niles: Argus, 1975), 145.

CHAPTER 7

1. We have a self-protective mechanism that keeps us from uncovering a memory we are not strong enough to face without undue anxiety. When praying with another it is important to respect this self-protective mechanism and not probe or push. Listening that is loving, compassionate, non-judgmental, and reverent heals. For the process of praying with another, cf. Dennis & Matthew Linn and Sheila Fabricant, *Praying with Another for Healing* (Mahwah: Paulist, 1984).

2. Paul Tillich, *The Eternal Now* (New York: Scribner, 1963).

3. Teresa of Avila, *The Interior Castle,* Sixth Mansion, Ch. 7 in *The Complete Works of St. Teresa of Jesus,* tr. & ed. by E. Allison Peers (New York: Sheed & Ward, 1950), Vol II, 305.

4. Teresa of Avila, *The Life of the Holy Mother Teresa of Jesus,* Ch. 22, *ibid.,* I, 139.

5. Teresa of Avila, *The Way of Perfection,* Ch. 36, *ibid.,* II, 159–60.

6. Thomas Verny, *The Secret Life of the Unborn Child* (New York: Summit, 1981).

7. For a practical introduction to the Jesus prayer, cf. George Maloney, S.J., *The Jesus Prayer* (Pecos: Dove, 1975).

8. For help with prayer of the imagination and two hundred other ways to pray, cf. Matthew & Dennis Linn and Sheila Fabricant, *Prayer Course for Healing Life's Hurts* (Mahwah: Paulist, 1983).

9. For a basic treatment of healing through active imagination cf. Ruth Stapleton, *The Gift of Inner Healing* (Waco: Word, 1976) and *The Experience of Inner Healing* (Waco: Word, 1977).

10. For the classical spirituality of living out Christ's reaction by finding God in the present moment, cf. Jean Pierre de Caussade, *Abandonment to Divine Providence,* tr. John Beevers (Garden City: Doubleday, 1975) and Thérèse of Lisieux, *Story of a Soul,* tr. John Clarke (Washington: Institute of Carmelite Studies, 1975).

CHAPTER 8

1. Drs. Meyer Friedman and Ray Rosenman, *op. cit.,* describe this "hurry sickness."

2. John H. McKenzie, *Dictionary of Biblical Theology* (Milwaukee: Bruce, 1965), 32.

3. Viktor Frankl, *The Doctor and the Soul* (New York: Bantam, 1967).

4. Dr. Floyd Ring, in "Testing the Validity of Personality Profiles in Psychosomatic Illnesses," *Am. J. of Psychiatry,* 113 (1957), 1075–1080.

5. For a popular introduction to the psychological dimensions of anger and how to deal with it, cf. Lerner, *op. cit.*

6. Many forgive too soon and cut off the anger that allows us to own the depth of the hurt and to feel the wounds that need healing. For example, the abuse victim must often rage and be loved in that rage by an enlightened witness who believes in the victim's story and underlying goodness and validates his or her feelings. Cf. Alice Miller, *Banished Knowledge* (New York: Doubleday, 1990). After the depth of the anger is expressed and the victim's wounds are healed, the victim often automatically is drawn to see his or her aggressor as likewise a wounded person needing healing and forgiveness. Saying an angry "no" to forgiving too soon is an important part of the forgiveness process. For an example of this, cf. Linns & Fabricant, *Healing the Eight Stages of Life, op. cit.,* 10–19. For a discussion of the related need to make amends to oneself as part of Steps 8 and 9 of the 12 Steps (of Alcoholics Anonymous and now applied to a wide variety of addictions), cf. Dennis Linn, Sheila Fabricant Linn and Matthew Linn, *Belonging: Bonds of Healing and Recovery, op. cit.,* Chapter 7.

7. This method of conversing with Christ was popularized by St. Teresa of Avila. For helps on how to pray this way, cf. Peter Thomas Rohrback, *Conversations with Christ* (Chicago: Publishers Assn., 1956).

8. These are similar to the steps outlined for dealing with anger in L. Madow, *Anger* (New York: Scribner, 1974). Anger is a key time to heal our wounds with the love of Jesus and others. We can ask: What losses did I experience and how can these be restored?

CHAPTER 9

1. Abraham Maslow in *Toward a Psychology of Being* (New York: Van Nostrand Reinhold, 1968) distinguishes between B-love (being love—a gift love motivated by the value perceived in the other) and D-love (deficiency love—a need love given in order to receive and motivated by the need in the lover). In Maslow's terms, bargaining is the stage when D-love starts to evolve into B-love finally reached in the acceptance stage characterized by Maslow's self-actualizer. In terms of transactional analysis, cf. Thomas Harris, *I'm OK, You're OK* (New York: Harper, 1967). Bargaining can be the "I'm not OK, you're not OK" that frequently is the transition between anger's "I'm OK, you're not OK" and depression's "I'm not OK, you're OK" on the way to acceptance's "I'm OK, you're OK." On the other hand, bargaining can also be an "I'm OK, you're OK" stance, in that I respect myself and the one who hurt me enough to set limits on how much injustice I will take, and to ask the other for what I need. See the Epilogue.

2. Joachim Jeremias, *New Testament Theology* (New York: Scribner, 1971), 122ff. Jeremias sees Christ's message of forgiveness as *ipsissima vox Jesus.*

3. For a refutation of Anselm's theology of Christ paying the Father's price, cf. Don Gelpi, *Charism and Sacrament* (New York: Paulist, 1976), 234–238. Gelpi also relates healing to the sacraments. For how Anselmian theology represents only one of three dominant New Testament theologies cf. Dick Westley, *Redemptive Intimacy* (Mystic: Twenty-Third, 1981), 110–112.

4. For the fathers of the church and their view of heaven as an eternal growth in love, cf. George Maloney, *Inward Stillness* (Denville: Dimension, 1976) and *The Everlasting Now* (Notre Dame: Ave Maria, 1980).

5. For the story of Mother Teresa, cf. Malcolm Muggeridge, *Something Beautiful for God* (London: William Collins, 1971).

6. Jean Vanier, *Be Not Afraid* (New York: Paulist, 1975).

7. For an inside experience in the Haitian community, cf. William Clarke, "Comfort for the Afflicted," in *The Way,* XVI:3 (July, 1976), 199–207.

8. Jean Vanier, *op. cit.,* viii.

9. *Ibid.,* 95.

10. For the *agapao vs. phileo* argument in John 21, cf. John Marsh, *Saint John* (Baltimore: Penguin, 1968), 668.

11. Corrie Ten Boom, *The Hiding Place* (Old Tappan: Spire, 1971), 238.

CHAPTER 10

1. For the classical treatment of projection and other ego defense mechanisms, cf. Anna Freud, *The Ego and the Mechanisms of Defense* (New York: International Universities Press, 1946).

2. Karl Menninger, M.D., *Whatever Became of Sin?* (New York: Hawthorn, 1973).

3. John McKenzie, *op. cit.,* 817–821.

4. Albert Ellis and Robert Harper, *A New Guide to Rational Living* (N. Hollywood: Wilshire, 1975). For a popularization of the spiritual dimensions of Ellis, cf. John Powell, S.J., *Fully Human, Fully Alive* (Niles: Argus, 1976).

5. Ellis & Harper, *op. cit.,* 203.

6. Dr. Carl Jung continually stressed coming to wholeness by loving the shadow, the disowned side of our personality that we hide. Although we would not want to act out this shadow side in destructive ways, it is important that we love and integrate it, since whatever part of ourselves we deny will dominate us.

7. For how we can heal through our wounds, cf. Henri Nouwen, *The Wounded Healer* (Garden City: Doubleday, 1972). Another of his books, *Reaching Out* (Garden City: Doubleday, 1975), describes the spiritual life in three essential stages: from loneliness to solitude (accepting ourselves), from hostility to hospitality (accepting others), and from illusion to prayer (accepting God). All three movements are essential to healing a deep hurt and all three occur in the depression stage if it is genuine.

8. Loring Swaim, M.D., *Arthritis, Medicine and the Spiritual Laws* (New York: Chilton, 1962). Guilt may also increase the risk of death. In one well-known study, in which death during sexual activity accounted for 0.6 percent of sudden deaths from internal causes, most of these occurred in the setting of extramarital intercourse. Cf. Dossey, *op. cit.*, 38.

9. For how Christ is the self within me or another, cf. Clarence Enzler, *My Other Self* (Denville: Dimension, 1958). This book is a reflection on the traditional Christian belief in the mystical body of Christ in 1 Corinthians 12.

10. For a simple treatment of how much God loves us, cf. Peter van Breemen, *As Bread That Is Broken* (Denville: Dimension Books, 1974).

11. For how to heal the hurts of children and our own inner child, cf. Linns & Fabricant, *Healing the Eight Stages of Life, op. cit.*

12. Dennis and Matthew Linn, *Healing of Memories: Prayer and Confession—Steps to Inner Healing* (New York: Paulist, 1974). The psychological dynamics of the deprivation neurosis which makes us unable to love and forgive ourselves are discussed in Dr. Conrad Baars, *Born Only Once* (Chicago: Franciscan Herald Press, 1975) and also in Dr. Anna Terruwe and Dr. Conrad Baars, *Healing the Unaffirmed* (New York: Alba House, 1976). For healing depression that has its roots in the loss of a loved one, cf. Matthew & Dennis Linn and Sheila Fabricant, *Healing the Greatest Hurt* (Mahwah: Paulist, 1985).

13. For healing through the 12 Steps of Alcoholics Anonymous, cf. Linns, *Belonging: Bonds of Healing and Recovery, op. cit.*

CHAPTER 11

1. This is the theme of John Powell's excellent book, *Fully Human, Fully Alive, op. cit.*

2. *Ibid.,* 169.

3. David Stanley sees the essence of Paul's prayer as joyful thanksgiving in *Boasting in the Lord* (New York: Paulist, 1975), Ch. 4.

4. A. Adler, *Practice and Theory of Individual Psychology* (New York: Harcourt, Brace and World, 1927); G.W. Allport, *The Individual and His Religion* (New York: Macmillan, 1950); A. Maslow, *op. cit.;* Rollo May, *Love and Will* (New York: Norton, 1969); C.R. Rogers, *Client-Centered Therapy* (Boston: Houghton Mifflin, 1951); Viktor Frankl, *The Doctor and the Soul, op. cit.,* 72. For the healing power of authentic love in the process of recovery from addiction, cf. Pat Carnes, *Don't Call It Love* (New York: Bantam, 1991).

5. Viktor Frankl, *Man's Search for Meaning* (New York: Washington Square, 1963), relates his prison experiences.

6. Every hurt has a gift, and under every addiction is a genius. Cf. Linns, *Belonging: Bonds of Healing and Recovery, op. cit.*

CHAPTER 12

1. Luke uses "took, blessed, broke, gave" to speak eucharistically even if Christ didn't consecrate the bread. Cf. Carroll Stuhlmueller, "The

Gospel According to Luke" in *Jerome Biblical Commentary* (Englewood Cliffs: Prentice-Hall, 1968), 163.

2. The translators of the *New American Bible* (New York: Thomas Nelson, 1971), p. 1203, indicate in a footnote that the meal in John 21 may have had eucharistic significance for early Christians since John 21:13 recalls John 6:11 which uses the vocabulary of Jesus' action at the last supper. Even if Jesus didn't consecrate the bread, the author of John 21 seems to be speaking eucharistically.

3. To see how healing happens every day, try the delightful autobiography of Agnes Sanford, *Sealed Orders* (Plainfield: Logos, 1972).

4. For a survey of how church fathers such as Gregory of Nazianzus, Ambrose and Augustine experienced the healing power of the eucharist, cf. Kelsey, *Healing and Christianity, op. cit.,* 167–191.

CHAPTER 13

1. For a parallel approach to the examination of conscience, cf. George Aschenbrenner, S.J., "Consciousness Examen," in *Review for Religious*, XXXI:1 (January, 1972).

CHAPTER 15

1. For a secular interpretation of dreams, cf. Carl Jung, *Memories, Dreams, Reflections,* recorded and edited by Aniela Jaffe (New York: Pantheon, 1963); *idem, Dreams,* tr. R. Hull (Princeton: Princeton U., 1974). For a Christian interpretation of dreams, cf. Morton Kelsey, *Dreams and Revelation* (Minneapolis: Augsburg, 1974); Louis Savary and Patricia Berne, *Dreams and Spiritual Growth* (Mahwah: Paulist, 1984).

CHAPTER 16

1. Mwalimu Imara, *op. cit.,* 160.

2. This simple but powerful prayer is presented in Ruth Stapleton, *The Gift of Inner Healing, op. cit.*

3. Prayer for deliverance should be used only after prayer for inner healing. For its uses and cautions cf. Matthew & Dennis Linn, *Deliverance Prayer* (Ramsey: Paulist, 1981).

4. Ideally, prayer for inner healing needs support and follow-up from a prayer community and perhaps a 12-Step group committed to spiritual growth.

5. For professionals who join prayer with therapy, contact the Association of Christian Therapists, 14440 Cherry Ln., #215, Laurel, MD 20707.

EPILOGUE

1. For a groundbreaking discussion of the difference between men's and women's reality, cf. Carol Gilligan, *In a Different Voice* (Cambridge: Harvard University Press, 1982).

2. For a discussion of the healing that comes from changing our image of God, cf. Linns, *Belonging: Bonds of Healing and Recovery, op. cit.*

3. Erik Erikson, "Womanhood and the Inner Space," in *Identity, Youth and Crisis* (New York: W.W. Norton, 1968), 293–94. See also James B. Nelson, "Male Sexuality and Masculine Spirituality," *SIECUS Report,* 13:4 (March, 1985), 2.

4. John Paul II, "Rich in Mercy," footnote #52. For a discussion of God as Mother as well as Father, and the importance of inclusive language for God, see Sandra Schneiders, *Women and the Word* (Mahwah: Paulist, 1986), and Elizabeth Johnson, "The Incomprehensibility of God and the Image of God Male and Female," in Joann Wolski Conn (ed.), *Women's Spirituality* (Mahwah: Paulist, 1986), 243–260 (originally published in *Theological Studies,* 45 [1984], 441–465).

5. Ann Belford Ulanov, *Receiving Woman* (Philadelphia: Westminster Press, 1981), 134. Based upon an essay by Valerie Saiving Goldstein, "The Human Situation: A Feminine Viewpoint," in Simon Doniger (ed.), *The Nature of Man in Theological and Psychological Perspective* (New York: Harper & Row, 1962), 151, 153, 165.

6. The male bias discussed in this chapter tends to overemphasize autonomy (including getting our needs met by God alone) and to discount our need for human love and affirmation. "As sensitive women and men are recently pointing out, the result of this bias has been that differentiation (the stereotypically male overemphasis in this human ambivalence) is favored with the language of growth and development, while attachment (the stereotypically female overemphasis) gets referred to in terms of dependency and immaturity . . . if women are more vulnerable to fusion . . . it is also possible that they are more capable of intimacy. . . . And if men find it easier to reach psychological autonomy—not to be confused with human maturity—it is also possible that they find it harder to evolve to more mature mutuality and relational inter-dependence . . ."—Joann Wolski Conn, "Spirituality and Personal Maturity," in Robert J. Wicks, *et al.* (eds.), *Clinical Handbook of Pastoral Counseling* (New York: Paulist, 1985), 37–57. See also Robert Kegan, *The Evolving Self* (Cambridge: Harvard University Press, 1982).

7. James W. Pennebaker and Robin C. O'Heeron, "Confiding in Others and Illness Rate Among Spouses of Suicide and Accidental-Death Victims," *J. of Abnormal Psychology,* 93:4 (November, 1984), 473–476.

8. Erich Lindemann, "Grief and Grief Management: Some Reflections," *J. of Pastoral Care,* 30:3 (September, 1976), 198.

9. Scott Sullender, *Grief & Growth: Pastoral Resources for Emotional & Spiritual Growth* (Mahwah: Paulist), 1985.

About the Authors

Matthew Linn, S.J. and Dennis Linn, M.Div. wrote their first book, *Healing of Memories,* in 1974. That book records the healing process they witnessed as hospital chaplains, therapists at Wohl Psychiatric Clinic, and retreat directors. Because of the book's impact, Matt's and Dennis' Jesuit provincial asked them to spend the next ten to fifteen years working full-time in the healing ministry. Dennis then left his work as superior of a community of Jesuit seminarians who were working in various inner city pastoral ministries, and Matt left his work with the Sioux people as director of the religious education program. Since then they have tested the material in this book at hundreds of "Healing Life's Hurts" conferences in over forty foreign countries as well as with a broad audience in the United States: hospital and nursing personnel, psychiatrists and psychotherapists, religious communities, prayer groups, 12-Step recovery groups, and those reached through their university course on healing at Marquette University and Edgewood College. In writing *Healing Life's Hurts,* they consulted with a surgeon and professors in scripture and psychiatry so as to combine the best insights from medicine, spirituality and psychiatry. This book prays through Elisabeth Kubler-Ross' five stages of dying so that the crippling hurts of life become opportunities for emotional, physical and spiritual healing.

Since *Healing Life's Hurts* was published, Dennis and Matt have completed nine more books, the last five co-authored with Sheila Fabricant Linn, M.Div., who joined their team in 1981. Dennis and Sheila were married in 1989. As a team of three the Linns have continued to integrate spirituality with what the medical and human sciences can teach us about human growth and healing. Thus, for example, their book *Healing the Eight Stages of Life* (Paulist, 1988) integrates Erik Erikson's system of human development with contemporary spirituality, with a special emphasis on how our image of God is formed or deformed at each stage of development. The most recent book by Dennis, Sheila and Matt is *Belonging: Bonds of Healing and Recovery* (Paulist, 1993).

Resources for Further Growth

Prayer Course for Healing Life's Hurts, by Matthew & Dennis Linn and Sheila Fabricant (Mahwah, NJ: Paulist Press, 1983). Ways to pray for personal healing that integrate physical, emotional, spiritual and social dimensions and that develop the five stage process discussed in this book. The book can be used by itself or in conjunction with twenty-four thirty-minute sessions available on audio or videotape. The course may be taken alone, with a friend or with a group.

Healing of Memories, by Dennis & Matthew Linn (Mahwah, NJ: Paulist Press, 1974). A simple guide to inviting Jesus into our painful memories to help us forgive ourselves and others.

Healing the Eight Stages of Life, by Matthew Linn, Sheila Fabricant and Dennis Linn (Mahwah, NJ: Paulist Press, 1988). Based on Erik Erikson's developmental system, this book helps to heal hurts and develop gifts at each stage of life, from conception through old age, and is especially helpful for inner child work. Includes healing ways our image of God has been formed and deformed at each stage. Audio or videotapes and a course guide are available for use with the book as a course in healing the life cycle. The course may be taken alone, with a friend or with a group.

Belonging: Bonds of Healing and Recovery, by Dennis Linn, Sheila Fabricant Linn and Matthew Linn (Mahwah, NJ: Paulist Press, 1993). 12-Step recovery from any compulsive pattern is integrated with contemporary spirituality and psychology. Defines addiction as our best attempt to belong to ourselves, others, God and the universe, and helps the reader discover the genius underneath every addiction. Audio or videotapes and a course guide are available for use with the book as a program of recovery. The course may be used alone, with a friend or with a support group.

Healing the Greatest Hurt, by Matthew & Dennis Linn and Sheila Fabricant (Mahwah, NJ: Paulist Press, 1985). Healing the deepest hurt most people experience, the loss of a loved one, through learning to give and receive love with the deceased through the communion of saints. May be accompanied by the audio tape series *Healing Our Image of God* (St. Louis: Christian Video Library).

Praying with Another for Healing, by Dennis & Matthew Linn and Sheila Fabricant (Mahwah, NJ: Paulist Press, 1984). Guide to praying with another to heal hurts such as sexual abuse, depression, loss of a loved one, abortion, etc. Book includes course guide, and tapes are available in audio and video versions. *Healing the Greatest Hurt* (see above) may be used as supplementary reading for the last five of these sessions, which focus on healing of grief.

Healing the Dying, by Mary Jane, Matthew & Dennis Linn (Mahwah, NJ: Paulist Press, 1979). The dying need to go through the same seven last words and deeds as Jesus. This book may be used to accompany the audio- or videotape series, *Dying to Live: Healing through Jesus' Seven Last Words,* by Bill & Jean Carr and Dennis & Matthew Linn. This series explores how the same seven words and deeds for dying well are also needed by all of us for living well.

Books are available from Paulist Press, 997 Macarthur Boulevard, Mahwah, NJ 07430, (201) 825-7300.

Audiotapes for *Belonging* are available from Credence Cassettes, 115 E. Armour Blvd., Kansas City, MO 64111, (800) 444-8910. Audio tapes on *Healing Our Image of God* are available from Christian Video Library, 3914-A Michigan Ave., St. Louis, MO 63118, (314) 865-0729. All other audiotapes are available from Paulist Press at the above address.

Videotapes for all courses (except *Belonging*) are available from Paulist Press at the above address. For information on

Belonging videotapes, contact Christian Video Library at the above address.

VIDEOTAPES ON A DONATION BASIS

To borrow any of the above videotapes, contact Christian Video Library at the above address.

SPANISH BOOKS AND TAPES

Several of the above books and tapes (including this one) are available in Spanish. For information, contact Christian Video Library.

RETREATS AND CONFERENCES

For retreats and conferences by the authors on the material in this book and other topics, contact Dennis, Sheila & Matthew Linn, c/o Re-Member Ministries, 3914-A Michigan Ave., St. Louis, MO 63118, (314) 865-0729 or (303) 476-9235.